Information Feudalism

For Frank and Vlasta Drahos

Information Feudalism

Who Owns the
Knowledge Economy?

Peter Drahos

with

John Braithwaite

THE NEW PRESS

NEW YORK
LONDON

Originally published in the United Kingdom by
Earthscan Publications Ltd, London, 2002
Published in the United States by The New Press, New York, 2003
This paperback edition published by The New Press, New York, 2007
Distributed by W. W. Norton & Company, Inc., New York

ISBN-13: 978-1-56584-804-7 (hc) 978-1-59558-122-8 (pbk)
ISBN-10: 1-56584-804-7 (hc) 1-59558-122-7 (pbk)
CIP data available

The New Press was established in 1990 as a not-for-profit alternative to the large,
commercial publishing houses currently dominating the book publishing industry.
The New Press operates in the public interest rather than for private gain, and is
committed to publishing, in innovative ways, works of educational, cultural, and
community value that are often deemed insufficiently profitable.

www.thenewpress.com

Printed in the United States of America

10 9 8 7 6 5 4 3 2 1

Contents

Preface

The idea for this book occurred at a bus stop in Geneva in 1993. Drahos and Braithwaite were on their way to conduct some interviews at UNCTAD for a project on global business regulation. The bus was a natural choice for two impecunious academics not wishing to be profligate with their funders' money (the National Science Foundation, the American Bar Association and the Australian Research Council). Drahos was going on about the importance of the changes in intellectual property regulation. Braithwaite, after some patient listening, interrupted, suggesting that they write two books together, one on the globalization of business regulation and another on the globalization of intellectual property. Drahos agreed. The bus arrived taking the duo to the first of their interviews at UNCTAD that morning.

The book on the globalization of regulation was published in 2000 under the title *Global Business Regulation*. The writing of it drew on more than five years' work in the field, during which time more than 500 key informants were interviewed, all of them by the authors, most by both together. This current book also draws on that data, in addition to which some further interviews were conducted, some as late as 2001. A discussion of the methodology underlying this fieldwork, as well as a list of those interviewed, is to be found in *Global Business Regulation*. Many of the regulatory standards that have a global reach in our world are shaped by informal negotiations of which no written record is made. Our purpose in conducting so many interviews has been to reveal what the formal language of international intellectual property agreements does not: the informal dynamic of power that determines the choice of words, their meaning and subsequent utilization. Aside from the fieldwork data, this book overlaps with *Global Business Regulation* in other ways. In that book one of our conclusions was that big business sovereignty over the regulatory standard-setting process often results in the regulation of markets, whereas citizens would benefit more from deregulated, competitive markets. When governments set intellectual property rules, they interfere in markets in information. This is justifiable if the costs of deregulated information markets outweigh the benefits. Our work suggests that governments rarely take a cost-benefit approach to intellectual property. The intellectual property standards we have today are largely the product of the global strategies of a relatively small number of companies and business organizations that realized the value of intellectual property sooner than anyone else. It is only now that these standards affect basic goods such as seeds, services and information flows in a global trading economy that their full costs to citizens and business in general are coming to be appreciated.

During the course of this project we have received help from a number of sources and people. The fieldwork foundations of this book were laid in 1994 when Drahos spent a year at the Research School of Social Sciences (RSSS) at the Australian National University as a Visiting Fellow under the Reshaping Australian Institutions Project. Our thanks go to Geoffrey Brennan, the director of the RSSS at that time, as well as to the many scholars there who helped to shape our thinking on the issues in question. In September 1998 Drahos took up an appointment as the Herchel Smith Senior Research Fellow in Intellectual Property, at the Intellectual Property Unit of the Centre for Commercial Law Studies at Queen Mary College, University of London. The Intellectual Property Unit has long had a reputation for excellence in research and teaching. It proved to be a wonderfully collegial place in which to carry out research on intellectual property. Professor Michael Blakeney, the head of the Intellectual Property Unit and director of the Queen Mary Intellectual Property Research Institute, supported this project. No one could have done more. We take this opportunity to thank him for his intellectual input and the practical assistance he rendered. Our thanks also go to other colleagues at the Unit. Ellen Gredley, responsible for, among other things, the Unit's excellent specialist library, tracked down references for us and drew our attention to other valuable material and lines of inquiry. Upon Ellen's retirement in 2000 her successor Malcolm Langley dealt with all requests with calm efficiency. Alison Firth, Gary Lea and Noel Byrne through conversation and suggestion steered us down fruitful paths. Special thanks go to our families, especially Julie Ayling and Valerie Braithwaite who helped in very many different ways.

Finally, a note of explanation concerning the authorship of this book. Right at the end of writing, and just as Drahos was in the middle of shifting countries, Braithwaite announced that it should be credited as "Drahos *with* Braithwaite" rather than "Drahos *and* Braithwaite." It would be tedious to recount the many conversations that this particular Braithwaitean initiative inspired, but in the end and under considerable pressure Drahos relented. Drahos now, however, invites the reader to read the "with" as an "and," since the "with" does not reflect Braithwaite's wonderful contribution to this book and the way in which he inspired the greater intellectual project of which this book is a part. No doubt if Braithwaite were given the opportunity to reply he would insist on the "with" in his customary self-effacing and generous style. But as Drahos pens this last sentence on a beautiful summer's day in Canberra he has decided not to give Braithwaite that opportunity.

Peter Drahos *and* John Braithwaite
Research School of Social Sciences
Australian National University
December 2001

Chronology of Key Events

1972	Edmund Pratt becomes CEO and chairman of Pfizer.
1974	US Trade Act passed. It includes the Jackson–Vanik Amendment linking trade to intellectual property.
1979	Edmund Pratt appointed to the Advisory Committee on Trade Negotiations (ACTN).
1979	The Tokyo Trade Round, which had begun in 1973, ends. The attempt by the US to include a code on trade in counterfeit goods fails.
February 1980	Member states of the Paris Convention for the Protection of Industrial Property meet in a Diplomatic Conference for the Revision of the Convention.
1981	Edmund Pratt becomes chairman of ACTN.
1981	William Brock, the US trade representative, forms the Quad.
1981	Nairobi Revision Conference of the Paris Convention. No agreement and strong North–South divide apparent.
1982	Geneva Revision Conference of the Paris Convention. No agreement and strong North–South divide remains.
29 November 1982	General Agreement on Tariffs and Trade (GATT) Ministerial Declaration contains a decision authorizing GATT Council to examine the question of counterfeit goods.
1983	Caribbean Basin Economic Recovery Act (US) links trade and intellectual property.
1984	International Intellectual Property Alliance is formed to represent US copyright-based industries. Made up of eight trade associations, it represents approximately 1,500 US companies.
1984	US Trade Act amended to include intellectual property in the 301 process and the Generalized System of Preferences program.

1985	The Group of Experts on Trade in Counterfeit Goods, which was formed in 1984 pursuant to the GATT Ministerial decision of 1982, holds meetings. The report of the Group tabled in October 1985 does not recommend a concrete course of action.
June 1985	Meeting to resume Revision of Paris Convention ends in deadlock. Further revision conferences are not held.
1 September 1985	"A Trade-Based Approach for the International Copyright Protection for Computer Software," unpublished, authored by Jacques Gorlin.
November 1985	United States Trade Representative (USTR) self-initiates the 301 process against South Korea on the basis of its lack of protection for US intellectual property rights.
c 1985	Summary of the Recommendations of the Advisory Committee on Trade Negotiations Task Force on Intellectual Property.
March 1986	Recommendations covering Phase II made by the Task Force on Intellectual Property to ACTN.
March 1986	Intellectual Property Committee (IPC) is cofounded by Pfizer and IBM.
March–May 1986	"Friends of Intellectual Property" is formed. Consists of a group of states that support the creation of some kind of multilateral agreement on intellectual property in the context of the Uruguay Round. Key members are US, Europe, Japan, Canada, Sweden, Switzerland and Australia.
June 1986	IPC delegations visit Europe to explain to European business the advantages of a trade-based approach to intellectual property.
1 July 1986	The manufacturing clause of the US Copyright Act 1976 (Section 601) is allowed to lapse.
21 July 1986	White House announces an agreement between US and Korea on the protection of US intellectual property rights. The agreement becomes an influential model for other trade negotiations on intellectual property including the Agreement on Trade-Related Aspects of Intellectual Property Rights (TRIPS) and the North American Free Trade Agreement (NAFTA).
August 1986	IPC delegations visit Japan to explain to Japanese business the advantage of a trade-based approach to intellectual property.
September 1986	The Uruguay Round of Trade Negotiations launched in Punta del Este. The Ministerial Declaration of 20 September includes

a brief reference to "trade-related aspects" of intellectual property, stating that "the negotiations shall aim to clarify GATT provisions and elaborate as appropriate new rules and disciplines."

November 1986   IPC meets in Brussels with business representatives from the European business community to discuss the form and content of the agreement on intellectual property that the international private sector would like to see come out of the Uruguay Round.

March 1987   Weeklong meeting of "Friends of Intellectual Property" in Washington, DC. Paper by IPC on standards of intellectual property protection is discussed by members of the group.

March 1987   IPC meets in New York with business representatives from European and Japanese business communities to discuss the form and content of the agreement on intellectual property that the international private sector would like to see come out of the Uruguay Round.

May 1987   IPC delegation travels to Europe to meet with members of European private sector, European Commission (EC) officials and GATT officials to discuss forthcoming negotiations on intellectual property.

12 May 1987   Union of Industrial and Employers' Confederations of Europe (UNICE) releases a position paper on "GATT and Intellectual Property" arguing that the EC's approach to the negotiations has to be broadened to include the full range of intellectual property rights.

October 1987   US tables its proposal on intellectual property before the GATT TRIPS working group.

1988   The Omnibus Trade and Competitiveness Act of 1988 creates the Special 301 mechanism and makes improved intellectual property a priority in US trade policy.

January 1988   IPC delegation visits Hong Kong, Korea and Singapore to begin a campaign of winning support for a multilateral agreement on intellectual property.

IPC meets in Tokyo with business representatives from European and Japanese business communities to discuss the form and content of the agreement on intellectual property that the international private sector would like to see come out of the Uruguay Round.

March 1988   IPC hosts a dinner for trade officials who attend the weeklong meeting of "Friends of Intellectual Property" group in Washington.

7–11 March 1988	Delegations from 23 industrialized countries and the EC ("Friends of Intellectual Property") meet in Washington to discuss a US paper outlining proposals on substantive standards of intellectual property and enforcement. A document outlining the proposals and the reaction of delegations to them is circulated after the meeting.
May 1988	IPC meets in Brussels with business representatives from European and Japanese business communities to discuss the form and content of the agreement on intellectual property that the international private sector would like to see come out of the Uruguay Round.
14 June 1988	A Statement of Views of the European, Japanese and United States Business Communities entitled "Basic Framework of GATT Provisions on Intellectual Property," representing the collective efforts of the Intellectual Property Committee (US), the Keidandren (Japan) and UNICE (Europe) is released.
17 October 1988	A communication to the GATT dated 13 October 1988 is received from the USTR entitled "Suggestion by the United States for Achieving the Negotiating Objective—Revision," (GATT-Doc.MTN.GNG/NG11/W/14Rev.1 [17 October 1988]). The document draws heavily on the views contained in the "Basic Framework of GATT Provisions on Intellectual Property."
20 October 1988	The US president authorizes, under Section 301 of the Trade Act, the imposition of duties on paper products, non-benzenoid drugs and consumer electronics from Brazil.
1989	The USTR, on the recommendation of the Motion Picture Association of America (MPAA) and the International Intellectual Property Alliance (IIPA), uses Special 301 to target problem countries including Brazil, India, Mexico, China, Egypt, Korea, Saudi Arabia, Taiwan and Thailand.
February 1989	Developing country negotiators meet in the resort Talloires in France to develop a unified position on TRIPS for the Mid-term Review meeting in April. Essentially the last chance to stop the US and EC agenda on TRIPS.
1 March 1989	The US joins the Berne Convention for the Protection of Literary and Artistic Works.
April 1989	Mid-term Review of the Uruguay Round produces a text that gives the go-ahead to a full-blown agreement on TRIPS, thereby fulfilling a US goal for that meeting.
March 1990	The European Community tables "Draft Agreement on Trade-Related Aspects of Intellectual Property" during the Uruguay Round negotiations.

May 1990	The US tables "Draft Agreement on Trade-Related Aspects of Intellectual Property" during the Uruguay Round negotiations. US draft is similar to the European Community draft.
May 1990	Fourteen developing countries submit a draft text that is general in nature because of internal disagreements. It has only qualified support or no support from other developing countries.
12 June 1990	Chairman of the TRIPS Negotiating Group, Lars Anell, distributes a Chairman's Draft that represents a composite of the key proposals being put forward by the countries in the negotiating group.
December 1990	Draft text of TRIPS submitted to ministerial meeting in Brussels.
December 1991	Complete text of TRIPS (all options removed) included in Director General Dunkel's "Draft Final Act Embodying the Results of the Uruguay Round of Multilateral Trade Negotiations."
1993	NAFTA, which contains comprehensive provisions on intellectual property, is signed by the parties to it. The provisions of NAFTA on intellectual property offer the same or better protection than the provisions of TRIPS.
15 December 1993	The Uruguay Round comes to an end.
15 April 1994	TRIPS signed as part of Final Act of Uruguay Round.
1 January 1995	TRIPS enters into force.

Acronyms and Abbreviations

ACTN	Advisory Committee on Trade Negotiations
BIRPI	Bureaux internationaux réunis pour la protection de la propriété intellectuelle
Berne Convention	Berne Convention for the Protection of Literary and Artistic Works 1886, as revised
BSA	Business Software Alliance
CAFC	Court of Appeals for the Federal Circuit (US)
DAT	Digital Audio Tape
DMCA	Digital Millennium Copyright Act 1998 (US)
EC	European Commission
ECIS	European Committee for Interoperable Systems
EPO	European Patent Office
GATT	General Agreement on Tariffs and Trade
GNG	Group of Negotiations on Goods
GSP	Generalized System of Preferences
ICJ	International Court of Justice
IFPI	International Federation of the Phonographic Industry
IIPA	International Intellectual Property Alliance
IMF	International Monetary Fund
IP	Intellectual Property
IPC	Intellectual Property Committee
IPIC	Treaty on Intellectual Property in Respect of Integrated Circuits 1989
ITO	International Trade Organization
MAI	Multilateral Agreement on Investment
MITI	Ministry of International Trade and Industry (Japan)
MPA	Motion Picture Association
MPEA	Motion Picture Export Association
MPPC	Motion Picture Patents Company
MPPDA	Motion Picture Producers and Distributors of America
MSF	Médecins Sans Frontières
NAFTA	North American Free Trade Agreement
NEC	National Economic Council
NGO	Nongovernmental Organization
NIH	National Institutes of Health (US)
OECD	Organisation for Economic Co-operation and Development
Paris Convention	Paris Convention for the Protection of Industrial Property 1883, as revised
PTO	Patent and Trademark Office (US)

Rome Convention	International Convention for the Protection of Performers, Producers of Phonograms and Broadcasting Organizations of 1961
SAGE	Software Action Group for Europe
SCMS	Serial Copy Management System
SIA	Semiconductor Industry Association
TNC	Trade Negotiations Committee
TRIPS	Agreement on Trade-Related Aspects of Intellectual Property Rights
UCC	Universal Copyright Convention
UNCTAD	United Nations Conference on Trade and Development
UNESCO	United Nations Educational, Scientific and Cultural Organization
UNICE	Union of Industrial and Employers' Confederations of Europe
UPOV	International Convention for the Protection of New Varieties of Plants 1961, as revised
USTR	United States Trade Representative
WCT	WIPO Copyright Treaty 1996
WIPO	World Intellectual Property Organization
WPPT	WIPO Performances and Phonograms Treaty 1996
WTO	World Trade Organization

CHAPTER 1

Introduction

WHY "INFORMATION FEUDALISM"?

A child is using a swing in a public park. Instead of swinging backward and forward she swings from side to side by pulling on one chain first and then the other. A few days later her parents receive a letter from the Intellectual Property Enforcement Agency, an arm of the police force. The letter states that their daughter was caught by a surveillance camera using a method of swinging that is the subject of a patent. The method has been claimed in a patent belonging to PlayPay Inc. Her parents are given the choice of paying a license fee or facing prosecution for patent infringement.

In Phoenix, Arizona, a group of Americans get on a bus. They are going to Mexico to buy drugs for use in the US. They expect to make a killing. The prices of prescription drugs under patent in the US have hit astronomical heights. By buying generic equivalents in Mexico for their treatment needs they will save themselves thousands of dollars.

The first scenario is, of course, far-fetched, except for a couple of things. A patent *has* been granted on a method of swinging a swing in the US, and intellectual property owners increasingly look to technology to police their intellectual property rights.[1] The need to register a computer program or face lock out and the fact that some DVD players are restricted to playing DVDs from some geographical zones are two examples of this. The second scenario is true. US citizens are traveling to Mexico on special bus tours to buy generic medication they find increasingly difficult to afford in the US.[2] Spending on brand-name drugs in the US tripled between 1990 and 2000, going from US$40.3 billion in 1990 to US$121.8 billion in 2000.[3] Rising prescription prices, underpinned by the strongest patent laws anywhere in the world, are turning more and more retired US citizens into medical refugees.

"Information feudalism," the title of our book, seems too harsh and inaccurate a description of the modern knowledge economies in which intellectual property rights play a central role. Even if we can make the case that current standards of intellectual property protection are excessive, can we really say this will propel us into feudalism? Medieval feudalism was a response to the insecurity and dangers of the Dark Ages, the period from the 5th to the 10th centuries after the Roman Empire declined and fell. As established patterns of order and security broke down, small landholders began to look elsewhere for protection. Many looked to more powerful neighbors capable of shielding them against the attacks of brigands or barbaric tribes, offering in exchange their land and services. Land and liberty were in effect swapped for physical security. For many in the generations that followed, the swap did not work out. Feudalism became a system of government. The lords in the system gained the social subordination and services of the majority along with enormous economic power and wealth. The majority, the peasant serfs who had to work the land, had to live with the arbitrariness that absolute power brings. Dostoyevsky captures the pitiless brutality of the Russian version when, in *The Brothers Karamazov*, he tells the story of a peasant mother made to watch her young son being torn apart by a pack of hunting hounds because her boy had accidentally injured the paw of the master's favorite hound.

We do not mean to signal by our choice of title that the contemporary global redefinition of intellectual property standards being undertaken in international fora, such as the World Trade Organization (WTO) and the World Intellectual Property Organization (WIPO), will cast us back to the abject subordination of a medieval feudalism. In Chapter 13 we describe information feudalism as an incomplete project. The visionaries and entrepreneurs who work the international corridors of power on behalf of this project, many of whom we interviewed, want ever stronger and more rigorously policed international standards of intellectual property. They push a simple message—that the creation of more and more intellectual property rights will bring more investment and innovation. Like many simple messages, this obscures much. Copying and imitation are central to our process of learning and the acquisition of skills. As children we copy the artwork of others and imitate our sporting heroes. Copying and imitation never leave us, and without it a lot of socially valuable information would never be transmitted or learned. The creator of innovation is also always the borrower of ideas and information from others. Intellectual property rights put a price on information, thereby raising the cost of borrowing. Raising the costs of borrowing through the imposition of very high standards of intellectual property will progressively choke innovation, not increase it. Most businesses, we argue, will be losers, not winners.

There are connections between the project of information feudalism that we describe in these pages and medieval feudalism, as both involve a redistribution of property rights. In the case of medieval feudalism, the relationship of the lord to the land and vassals was a relationship of great inequality. The majority of humble folk were subject to the private power that lords exercised by virtue of their ownership of the land. This private power became, in effect, governmental power as lords set up private manorial systems of taxes, courts and prisons. The redistribution of property rights in the case of information feudalism involves a transfer of knowledge assets from the intellectual commons into private hands. These hands belong to media conglomerates and integrated life sciences corporations rather than individual scientists and authors. The effect of this, we argue, is to raise levels of private monopolistic power to dangerous global heights, at a time when states, which have been weakened by the forces of globalization, have less capacity to protect their citizens from the consequences of the exercise of this power. It was the loss of Rome's capacity to protect its citizens that provided an important condition for the feudalization of its social relationships.

THE RISKS

The grant of power that comes with intellectual property rights carries with it two great dangers. First, depending on the resource in question it may place the holder of the right, or a small group of holders, in a position of central command in a market. Competition suffers as a result. So, for example, if a fundamental method of doing business over the Internet falls under patent, this creates costs for other businesses in terms of license fees, inventing around the patent or using less efficient methods. Essentially the patent functions as a barrier to entry to the market, the height of the barrier varying according to the nature of the patent and market structure. Intellectual property rights are, in essence, government tools for regulating markets in information. The problems of government capture that we describe in this book have led us to the view that there should be a presumption against the use of these rights to regulate markets rather than a presumption in their favor.

The second and greater danger of intellectual property lies in the threat to liberty. When a group of scientists stop working on a protein molecule because there are too many intellectual property rights that surround the use of the molecule, a basic freedom, the freedom to research, has been interfered with. The liberty cost of intellectual property rights may seem remote because most of us do not carry out research on proteins. But we all have an interest in seeing public research programs into diseases and health being carried out. We want, for example, public researchers to continue working on the genes for breast and ovarian cancer and helping to develop cheaper, more effective clinical tests. We do not want them deterred by announcements like the following: "This important patent solidifies Myriad's dominant proprietary position on the BRCA1 and BRCA2 genes" (the genes linked to breast and ovarian cancer).[4] Companies are entitled to protect their treatments for disease but not, through use of their patents, to deter or prevent others from access to genes that are linked to the origins of disease.

Public research programs make concrete basic human rights such as the right to health and the right to food. When scientists abandon such programs because of the atmosphere of threat generated by companies wielding large patent portfolios, it diminishes the liberty of us all. Similarly, when copyright owners use copyright to threaten manufacturers of recording technologies, such as the tape recorder or the VCR, to raise the price of educational material to libraries and universities, to keep material out of the public domain with long copyright terms (many of which now run at a minimum of the life of the author plus 70 years), our interests in being able to exchange, access and discuss information are subject to interference. The exchange, circulation and communication of information among people is fundamental to the way a democracy works. The more power over the price of information a society places in the hands of intellectual property owners, the more it checks its citizenry from informing itself.

The danger to basic rights posed by intellectual property regulation is not an obviously visible danger. Rather it is a danger based on the quiet accretion of restrictions—an accretion hardly visible because it is hidden behind technical rule-making, mystifying legal doctrine and complex bureaucracies, all papered over by seemingly plausible appeals to the rights of inventors and authors and the need to encourage innovation. We experience these restrictions not as a mass of individuals living in a totalitarian society, but as members of smaller communities who find strands of intellectual property law settling on and changing the customary ways in which we have accessed and exchanged information. Farmers who follow ancient practices of saving, swapping, bartering or selling seeds to each other find that these practices have to take place in the shadow of patent claims over those seeds. Just what a farmer may or may not do with plants containing patented genes becomes a lawyers' game. Researchers from different institutions begin their conversations by swapping confidentiality agreements or not starting those conversations until the intellectual property lawyers have spoken. University librarians find themselves having to take down student material from a website because a copyright collecting society has threatened legal action if they do not. Interpreting copyright rules, especially on the complex issues raised by digital technologies, is hardly their field, so more often than not they comply. Academic institutions discover that they are paying huge license fees to publishers for articles in journals that their academic employees have researched, written and edited. All too often these fees are passed on to students. The local choirs, drama clubs and schools that bring culture to their community areas find themselves caught up in a mire of copyright rules that bring increased cost, uncertainty and anxiety. Computer programmers wishing to modify a program come across copyright or patent restrictions that block their way. Different Internet communities stumble into a worldwide web of intellectual property restrictions about what may be downloaded, what the rules are on redistribution, and the rules on the posting and linking of materials. Individuals everywhere increasingly find that every time they use information in some way they trigger an obligation to pay a fee to an intellectual property owner.

Not every individual intellectual property right leads to the two dangers we have mentioned. The market power that intellectual property rights confer depends on demand for the product and the degree of substitutability for it. A patent over a life-saving drug or an essential algorithm may confer great market power; copyright over a book may confer little—many ordinary citizens own copyright in poems or novels that no one wants to publish. In any case, thinking about the dangers of intellectual property at the level of individual intellectual property rights is a mistake. The dangers of central command and loss of liberty flow from the relentless global expansion of intellectual property *systems* rather than the individual possession of an intellectual property right. It is these expanding systems of intellectual property that have enabled a relatively small number of corporate players to amass huge intellectual property portfolios. We do not claim that intellectual property rights necessarily lead to excessive levels of private power. It is just that in our world they have. One place where the threats posed by information feudalism did briefly attract the attention of Western mass publics was South Africa

HEALTH-HELL IN AFRICA

Marrakech is the scene of one of George Orwell's essays. Writing of poverty, death and colonial empires he observes:[5]

> They rise out of the earth, they sweat and starve for a few years, and then they sink back into the nameless mounds of the graveyard and nobody notices that they are gone.

His description of the invisibility to Western eyes of death in Africa in 1939 could just as easily be applied to the AIDS-related deaths in Africa in the last decade. In sub-Saharan Africa alone more than 17 million people have died. The UNAIDS website carries statistic after statistic about AIDS in Africa.[6] They tell the story of people dying—dying on a scale that is not really comprehensible. If we live in a country with a comparatively medium-sized population, we can try to visualize it in terms of that entire population getting sick and then dying. There are also UNAIDS statistics that attempt to describe the way in which the scythe of AIDS will shape Africa's future.[7] They describe a future in which a third of 15-year-old boys in some countries will die, in which there are millions of orphans, and where education systems crumble as the teachers die. In this landscape, hope hides from view.

Hope in the case of a treatment for HIV/AIDS arrived in the West at the end of the 1980s in the form of anti-retroviral therapy. At first the treatments involved the daily consumption of a combination of drugs involving as many as 20 tablets to be taken at specific times of the day. During the 1990s the treatment progressively improved. Current anti-retroviral therapy can take the form of a triple drug combination taken as one tablet a couple of times a day. The shift to a one-tablet-a-day treatment is not far off. Anti-retroviral therapy is aimed at halting the replication of HIV in the individual and allowing the immune system to recover. The treatments have proven to be highly effective. They do not remove HIV infection, but with proper management they may allow a person to achieve a normal life span.[8]

When anti-retroviral therapies made their first appearance, they were expensive (in the range of US$10,000 to $15,000 per person per year). This had everything to do with the intellectual property protection used by the large pharmaceutical companies involved in their development. Generally speaking, when a large pharmaceutical company develops a therapeutic compound, it surrounds that compound with a wall of intellectual property protection. Patents are taken out on all aspects of the compound, including the compound itself, dosage methods and processes of making it. Some knowledge is held back and protected under trade-secret law, brand-name identity is protected through trademark law and a lot of written information is protected by copyright. The whole point of building this wall is to ensure that protection lasts well beyond the term of any single patent and keeps cheaper generic manufacturers out of the market for as long as possible.

For people in developing countries living on one or two dollars a day, the price of anti-retroviral therapies represented a king's ransom.[9] In some countries such as South Africa, some treatments were in fact more expensive. As an aside we might note that the phenomenon of patented medicines being more expensive in developing countries is not unusual.[10] The logic of patent monopoly is to have a safe and secure distribution system aimed at selling smaller numbers of expensive medicines to a wealthy class, rather than trying to distribute large numbers of cheap medicines at a few cents a day to the many poor. When large pharmaceutical companies speak about "growing the market" in developing countries, it is the wealthy segment of the market they have in mind.

South Africa has the biggest HIV-infected population in Africa.[11] In 1997 the South African government introduced a bill that gave the health minister some discretion in setting conditions to ensure the supply of affordable medicines. The bill was signed by President Mandela on 12 December 1997. It specifically allowed the importation into South Africa of patented medicines that had been put onto another market with the consent of the patent owner. The idea was to encourage the importation of patented medicines from the cheapest market (parallel importation), a form of importation that was allowed within the European Union (EU), among other places. The response of the US officials was to turn the passage of the South African bill into a trade matter. Agencies of the US government such as the Office of the United States Trade Representative (USTR), the Department of Commerce and the State Department, with the assistance of officials from the European Commission (EC), began to pressure South Africa to change the bill. One of their arguments was that the South African government in passing the Medicines Act would be in breach of its obligations under the Agreement on Trade-Related Aspects of Intellectual Property Rights (TRIPS), an agreement that the South African government was a party to by virtue of its membership in the WTO. TRIPS contains provisions on patents.

In 1998 the pressure on South Africa intensified. The USTR listed South Africa under its trade law for possible trade sanctions if it did not comply with the demands of the US pharmaceutical industry and, in February 1998, 41 pharmaceutical companies began proceedings in South African courts against the South African government, naming Nelson Mandela as first defendant. The trade dispute continued to climb up the totem pole of political importance. Senior officials from the US and the EU continued to draw attention to South Africa's obligations under TRIPS. Sir Leon Brittan, the then vice president of the EC, wrote to Thabo Mebki, at that time the deputy president of South Africa, drawing his attention to South Africa's obligations under TRIPS.[12] At the August 1998 US–South Africa Binational Commission meetings in Washington, Vice President Gore made the protection of US pharmaceutical patents the central issue.[13] European leaders quietly joined this backroom push to make South Africa fall into line. French President Chirac raised the matter during his July 1998 state visit to South Africa and the Swiss and German presidents also raised the issue privately with Deputy President Mbeki.

In March 2001, 39 pharmaceutical companies came to the Pretoria High Court armed with most of South Africa's intellectual property barristers and a barrage of arguments against the Medicines Act. TRIPS surfaced again, the line of argument being that TRIPS required that patents be "enjoyable without discrimination" as to the field of technology.[14] The South African Medicines Act was said to discriminate against pharmaceutical patents. In April 2001 the pharmaceutical companies withdrew from the litigation and the case settled.

What had happened? The answer lies in the power of publicity. For almost a decade a few activists, the most prominent being James Love, had been doing work on the links between intellectual property rights and the price of pharmaceutical drugs.[15] In essence they had been asking whether, as a matter of public policy, consumers would benefit from the sole reliance on stronger and stronger intellectual property rights or whether there were more efficient alternatives (for example, mandatory contributions to research and development [R&D] funds directed at important diseases). When intellectual property standards became part of the WTO trade regime, James Love was among the first to draw attention to the likely adverse impacts on the capacity of developing countries to get access to cheap medicines for their populations. Out of a meeting in 1996 in Bielefeld, Germany, organized by Health Action International (a network of public health workers, with members in more than 70 countries) there grew a coalition of health activists and organizations who began to mount a global campaign against the impact of patents and trade rules on access to medicines. The campaign grew and was joined by other prominent nongovernmental organizations (NGOs) like Médecins Sans Frontières (MSF) and Oxfam.[16] The international publicity this coalition of NGOs gave to the plight of South Africa was also accompanied by good public policy analysis that, at its core, raised a fundamental issue—could the world community continue to rely on a patent-based R&D system that contributes heavily to a situation in which only 10 percent of global health research investigates the causes of 90 percent of the world's disease burden?[17] For the first time, mass publics in the West learned that their governments had, in the 1980s, participated in trade negotiations that globally strengthened patent monopolies, that obliged developing countries to recognize product patents on pharmaceuticals and that reduced their sovereignty over health regulation.

In the face of growing international moral outrage, trade ministers and officials in the US and EC and the large pharmaceutical companies began to recalculate. The companies withdrew from the litigation. The real worry for the large pharmaceuticals was no longer the South African law, but the fact that the access to medicines campaign had triggered a much broader discussion about the links between patents, the price of drugs, the price of research and the risks that the companies took. People were beginning to question the assumptions the industry used to come up with the cost of researching and developing a new drug. Questions were being asked about just how much actual risk the companies took when so much drug research was in fact done in the public sector.[18] Activists like James Love had been raising these issues for a long time, but now others were raising them and, worse still, expressing skepticism about the industry's claims.[19]

The worst of all possible worlds was one in which the debate over the price of patented drugs for the poor in developing countries spilt over into the price of patented drugs in the US. If the price of prescription drugs in the US had tripled in the last decade, might they not triple again in the next? How many more US citizens, unable to afford patented drugs, would make that trip to Mexico? The bureaucrats that had been supporting the pharmaceutical establishment went into damage-control mode. The EC began to talk about the differential pricing of drugs for poor countries.[20] At a special meeting of the TRIPS Council in June 2001, developing states pushed for the recognition of a reading of TRIPS that permitted them to deal with health crises. Ultimately this produced the Declaration on TRIPS and Public Health at a WTO Ministerial Conference in November 2001, a declaration that affirms the right of developing countries to protect the health of their populations.

The campaign was instrumental in bringing down further the price of anti-retroviral treatments. It provided support for generic manufacturers in two key developing countries—Brazil and India—to make offers to other developing countries looking for anti-retroviral drugs that their populations could afford. In most cases these drugs were not under patent protection in Brazil or India, this having much to do with the fact that, prior to TRIPS, these countries did not recognize patents on pharmaceutical products.

Brazil especially was a key player in showing the world what a government could do if it was serious about combating HIV. Despite enormous trade and political pressure from the US and the large pharmaceutical companies, Brazil during the first part of the1990s had played a stalling game. In 1996 it did introduce a patent law that included protection for pharmaceutical products, but that law, especially the provisions on compulsory licensing, was shaped with the price of AIDS drugs in mind. With the encouragement of civil society, Brazil went down the path of providing free anti-retroviral therapy. In those cases where the drugs it needed were under patent, it threatened the use of compulsory licensing in order to bring the price down. The anti-retroviral Nevirapine, for example, which is of great importance in the prevention of mother-to-child transmission of HIV, is available from the Brazilian generic manufacturer FarManguinhos at US$0.59 per day. The results speak for themselves. Brazil does not face the HIV/AIDS crisis that many African countries do.

The Indian generic firm Cipla was also important in triggering price reductions for anti-retrovirals for the poor. At an international meeting in Brussels in September 2000 the CEO of Cipla, Yusuf Hamied, publicly stated the prices at which he could provide anti-retrovirals to developing countries, prices that at that time worked out to around a couple dollars a day. The pharmaceutical executives of major companies "listened agog to Hamied's matter-of-fact price list for chemical equivalents of Glaxo's Epivir, Boehringer's Nevirapine and Bristol-Myers's Zerit."[21] The crucial thing though was the very public nature of the offer—at an international meeting with the media in attendance.

The large pharmaceutical companies had also been making offers to developing countries, but only to some countries on some drugs and in secret, with lots of conditions attached. Once the generics went public with their price, developing countries knew whether the secret price discounts that they were being offered by the large pharmaceutical companies were good deals or not. Today the price of anti-retroviral therapy that generic companies are able to offer comes in at well under a dollar a day.

Behind the success of the access to medicines campaign there remains a structural reality that has everything to do with the redistribution of property rights that we spoke of earlier. It is a reality whose shadow extends beyond patents and medicines. Large companies own more intellectual property than at any point in human history, in areas such as agriculture, plants and food, financial methods of doing business and on the algorithms that drive the digital revolution. In the case of medicines, there are only six developing countries that have any serious generic manufacturing capabilities (Brazil, Argentina, China, India, Korea and Mexico). All are obliged to comply with TRIPS and therefore have to recognize patents on pharmaceutical products and processes, as well as the stronger protection for trademarks that TRIPS mandates. The generic manufacturers in these developing countries will eventually have to survive in a world of much greater intellectual property protection for pharmaceutical products and processes, a world in which large pharmaceutical companies own all the key patents in all the markets where they perceive the threat of competition from generic manufacturers. Nothing to date in the access to medicines campaign has changed this structural reality.

This raises a question: Why had states agreed to TRIPS? The dangers of imposing one set of patent standards, standards that best suited large pharmaceutical companies, were pretty clear. The poor are at a point on the demand curve that is of no interest to a large pharmaceutical monopolist in the absence of bad publicity and reputational losses.

WHY SIGN TRIPS?

During the course of an interview in 1994 with a senior US trade negotiator he remarked to us that "probably less than 50 people were responsible for TRIPS." TRIPS is the most important agreement on intellectual property of the 20th century. More than a hundred ministers signed it on behalf of their nations in the splendid Salle Royale of the Palais des Congrès in Marrakech on 15 April 1994.

TRIPS is one of 28 agreements that make up the Final Act of the Uruguay Round of Multilateral Trade Negotiations, the negotiations that had begun in Punta del Este in 1986. Another of those agreements established the WTO, and it is the WTO that administers TRIPS. In the US, high-technology multinationals greeted the signing of TRIPS with considerable satisfaction. TRIPS was the first stage in the global recognition of an investment morality that sees knowledge as a private, rather than public, good. The intellectual property standards contained in TRIPS, obligatory on all members of the WTO, would help them to enforce that morality around the world. In India, after the signing of TRIPS, hundreds of thousands of farmers gathered to protest the intrusion of patents on the seeds of their agricultural futures. The Indian generics industry warned of dramatic price increases in essential medicines that would follow from the obligation in TRIPS to grant 20-year patents on pharmaceutical products. In Africa there was little discussion of TRIPS.

TRIPS is about more than patents. It sets minimum standards in copyright, trademarks, geographical indications, industrial designs and layout-designs of integrated circuits. TRIPS effectively globalizes the set of intellectual property principles it contains, because most states of the world are members of, or are seeking membership in, the WTO. It also has a crucial harmonizing impact on intellectual property regulation because it sets, in some cases, quite detailed standards of intellectual property law. Every member, for example, has to have a copyright law that protects computer programs as a literary work, as well as a patent law that does not exclude microorganisms and microbiological processes from patentability. The standards in TRIPS will profoundly affect the ownership of the 21st century's two great technologies—digital technology and biotechnology. Copyright, patents and protection for layout designs are all used to protect digital technology, whereas patents and trade secrets are the principal means by which biotechnological knowledge is being enclosed. TRIPS also obliges states to provide effective enforcement procedures against the infringement of intellectual property rights.

One of the puzzles this book sets out to solve is why states should give up sovereignty over something as fundamental as the property laws that determine the ownership of information and the technologies that so profoundly affect the basic rights of their citizens. The puzzle deepens when it is realized that in immediate trade terms the globalization of intellectual property really only benefited the US and to a lesser extent the European Community.[22] No one disagrees that TRIPS has conferred massive benefits on the US economy, the world's biggest net intellectual property exporter, or that it has strengthened the hand of those corporations with large intellectual property portfolios. It was the US and the European Community that between them had the world's dominant software, pharmaceutical, chemical and entertainment industries, as well as the world's most important trademarks. The rest of the developed countries and all developing countries were in the position of being importers with nothing really to gain by agreeing to terms of trade for intellectual property that would offer so much protection to the comparative advantage the US enjoyed in intellectual property–related goods. An Australian study of copyright royalty flows during the 1990s showed that Australia paid out to overseas copyright owners around Aus$1.2 billion more than it received.[23] Another Australian study showed that the cost to Australia of the TRIPS provision, which extended the patent term of 20 years to patents *already in existence,* could be as high as Aus$3.8 billion.[24] In Australia, as is the case in all small- to medium-sized developed country economies and developing country economies, the vast bulk of patents is in foreign ownership.

One standard reply we received in our interviews when we put this puzzle to policy makers was that "TRIPS was part of a package in which we got agriculture." The WTO Agreement on Agriculture, however, does not confer anything like the benefits on developing countries that TRIPS does on the US and the European Community. There is also another irony here. Increasingly, agricultural goods are the subject of intellectual property rights as patents are extended to seeds and plants. Agricultural countries will find that they have to pay more for the patented agricultural inputs they purchase from the world's agrochemical companies. In addition they will have to compete with the cost-advantages that biotechnology brings to US farmers (not to mention the subsidies that US and EU farmers continue to receive). By signing TRIPS, agricultural exporters have signed away at least some of their comparative advantage in agriculture.

Sometimes we were told that "we will be eventual winners from intellectual property." While it is good to be optimistic about one's distant destiny, it does not explain why normally hard-nosed trade negotiators would take the highly dangerous route of agreeing to the globalization of property rules over knowledge that had brought their countries so few gains in the past. Of the 3.5 million patents in existence in the 1970s, the decade before the TRIPS negotiations, nationals of developing countries held about 1 percent.[25] Developing countries such as South Korea, Singapore, Brazil and India, which were industrializing, were doing so in the absence of a globalized intellectual property regime.

More disturbing for developing countries is the development cost of an intellectual property regime. The basis of competition lies in the development of skills. The acquisition of skills by newcomers disturbs roles and hierarchies. After India built a national drug industry, it began exporting bulk drugs and formulations to places such as Canada. A developing country that had acquired skills threatened those at the top of an international hierarchy of pharmaceutical production—the US, Japan, Germany and the UK. Australia has shown in the field of wine making that the acquisition of skills can upset a European-led hierarchy of wine quality and production. The French have responded, in part, by insisting on protection for geographical indications, a form of intellectual property protection allowing them to claim, for example, exclusive use of the "Burgundy" and "Champagne" labels. Underneath the development ideology of intellectual property there lies an agenda of underdevelopment. It is all about protecting the knowledge and skills of the leaders of the pack.

The answer to our question about why developing countries signed TRIPS has much to do with democracy—or, rather, its failure. We give a full answer in Chapters 12 and 13. Put starkly, the intellectual property rights regime we have today largely represents the failure of democratic processes, both nationally and internationally. A small number of US companies, which were established players in the knowledge game (see Chapter 3), captured the US trade-agenda-setting process and then, in partnership with European and Japanese multinationals, drafted intellectual property principles that became the blueprint for TRIPS (see Chapters 8 and 9). The resistance of developing countries was crushed through trade power (see Chapter 6).

One retort to this might be that corporations are entitled to lobby, and, in any case, developing countries agreed to TRIPS through a process of bargaining among sovereigns. It is indeed true that corporations are entitled to lobby. It is important that big business makes its views and policy preferences known to government since around the globe it represents hundreds of millions of jobs and investors. However, that lobbying in relation to property rights should take place under conditions of democratic bargaining. Democratic bargaining matters crucially to the definition of property rights because of the consequences of property rules for all individuals within a society. Property rights confer authority over resources. When authority is granted to the few over resources on which the many depend, the few gain power over the goals of the many. This has consequences for both political and economic freedom within a society.

The stakes are high in the case of intellectual property rights. Intellectual property rights are a source of authority and power over informational resources on which the many depend—information in the form of chemical formulae, the DNA in plants and animals, the algorithms that underpin digital technologies and the knowledge in books and electronic databases. These resources matter to communities, to regions and to the development of states. In the next section we outline the way in which efficiency, basic freedoms, democracy and intellectual property rights are connected.

EFFICIENCY, FREEDOM, DEMOCRACY AND INTELLECTUAL PROPERTY

The long-run performance of economies has much to do with efficiently defined property rights. Designed in the right way, property rights will reduce negative externalities (for example, the dumping of pollutants), allow for bargaining and avoid tragedies of the commons (for example, overfishing of a fishery held in common). Naturally, this gives rise to the question of how a society arrives at a set of efficient property rights. The economist Douglass North suggests that it probably has something to do with democratic institutions.[26]

Efficiency in the case of intellectual property rights is generally thought to involve a balance between rules of appropriation and rules of diffusion. Overly strong intellectual property protection leads to the problem of excessive monopoly costs of intellectual property rights, whereas weak protection leads to the problem of excessive free-riding and therefore under-investment in innovation. The difficult trick for any legislature is to find a balance between the rules of appropriation and the rules of diffusion.

Are there reasons to think that in democracies this balance is likely to be struck in ways that produce efficiency? Here we will focus on the economic theory of democratic bargaining and efficiency, but of course there are other reasons to do with deliberation and open discussion of ideas, which give democracy a better chance of discovering good solutions to problems. Economic theory suggests that bargaining among self-interested and rational actors can produce efficient outcomes by allowing resources to go to those actors who value them most.[27] The link between bargaining and democracy probably lies in the fact that democracies are better at supplying those networks of institutions that allow for all kinds of bargaining among citizens to take place. These institutions include contract, property and the rule of law. Even more important though is the fact that a rights-based democratic culture allows for the formation of interest groups from business and civil society sectors that bargain over resources that matter to them. This is one explanation for why democracies have proven to be better than communist societies at moving toward environmental regimes that to some extent reflect the true costs of using environmental resources.

One can imagine an interest-group model of democracy in which bargaining takes place among equally well-resourced and informed groups. In a democracy where producer and consumer interests in the production of information were equally well represented and where those interests had roughly equal powers of influence, one might expect an efficient set of intellectual property rules to develop. Consumers would concede that some level of intellectual property was necessary in order to secure dynamic efficiency, but would not agree to rules that unduly restricted the diffusion of information or competition in markets.

There are also reasons why democracies might fail to arrive at efficient definitions of intellectual property rights. For example, Mancur Olson's theory, that diffuse public interests will go unrepresented because the costs to individuals of organizing large groups will be outweighed by the small gains to each individual, might lead to the prediction that small numbers of intellectual property producers are more likely to organize than large numbers of consumers of intellectual property.[28] And then, even if producer and consumer interest groups are equally well represented, inequalities of power might destroy the efficient balance of intellectual property rules that bargaining might otherwise deliver. Both health-care consumers and pharmaceutical companies lobby in the US Congress, but it is only the pharmaceutical industry that has 297 lobbyists working for it—one for every two congressional representatives.[29]

The same tensions that exist between producers and consumers of intellectual property at the national level also exist at the international level among the community of states. Most states are in the position of being net importers of intellectual property rights. Certainly all developing countries are in this category. For countries that are importers of intellectual property the temptation is not to recognize the intellectual property rights of foreigners, thereby allowing for the possibility that their nationals will be able to free-ride on the research and development activities of foreigners. For exporters of intellectual property rights, the aim is to extend the length and breadth of intellectual property rights in order to gain the maximum return from the trade in intellectual property–related goods.

At least some of the tensions between intellectual property exporters and importers may be resolved through a process of negotiation. A state that had industries engaged in free-riding on the R&D of another state's industries might agree not to export copied products to the latter state's markets in exchange for that state doing nothing about the free-riding. In order for cooperative solutions to emerge among states, conditions of democratic bargaining have to exist. Domination by either producer or consumer states is less likely to produce international standards of intellectual property that promote efficiency gains.

In order for democratic bargaining to take place among sovereign states, at least three conditions need to obtain. First, all relevant interests have to be represented in the negotiating process (*the condition of representation*). (This condition, however, does not entail the participation of all at every stage or of equality of outcome for all interests.) Second, all those involved in the negotiation must have full information about the consequences of various possible outcomes (*the condition of full information*). Third, one party must not coerce the others (*the condition of nondomination*). The use of coercion to overcome the will of another is the very antithesis of negotiation. If our money is taken by a gunman, most of us would say that we had been the victims of robbery, not negotiation. It will be seen from this book that international intellectual property regimes including TRIPS have not met the three conditions that characterize democratic bargaining.

In the final chapter of this book we suggest ways in which we can move toward democratic property rights. Ours is not an anti-intellectual property tract. It is an argument against the domination of the intellectual property standard-setting process by a corporate elite that, for close to a century, has played the knowledge game with great social costs. The costs have been borne by citizens of all countries, with the heaviest burden falling upon citizens in developing countries in the form of a lack of access to medicines, technology and textbooks. These costs, ironically, include costs to innovation. Copyright, for example, is becoming an anti-innovation regime, used by establishment players like the music industry to suppress the threat of change that Napster-like innovations bring. A company like Intel expresses cautious support for Napster because it depends on that kind of innovation to fuel the demand for its chips. The truth is that current intellectual property regimes do a very poor job of channeling rewards (and therefore creating incentives) to creators. The bulk of intellectual property rights are owned not by their initial creators but by corporations that acquire intellectual property portfolios through a process of buying and selling, merger and acquisition. The justifications for intellectual property, which depend so heavily on the personal link between creator and creative output, do not in any way describe the commerce of intellectual property in which creators are routinely parted from their created products with little reward.

The corporate owners of intellectual property depend heavily on the public sector and the public domain, a dependence that suggests that society should be thinking about weaker and not stronger intellectual property rights. Much of the research that really matters to the biotechnology industry and pharmaceutical industry goes on at taxpayer expense in public universities (see Chapters 10 and 14). Through various legal mechanisms it ends up in patent portfolios where citizens pay for the same knowledge again. If governments do a bad job of encouraging competition in the post-patent period, the monopoly costs continue. Another example of the same pervasive phenomenon of recycling public knowledge for private reward occurs in the educational sector where copyright owners uplift university-generated, publicly funded research into journals or databases and then charge universities and students for the use of them. The costs of this have become so great to university budgets and students that it has triggered litigation between universities and the copyright collecting societies that represent the owners.

Intellectual property rights are justified using different kinds of theories such as utilitarianism, natural rights theory or theories of justice.[30] Current intellectual property rights regimes stack up badly against all of these.

A patent system that does not recognize the utility preferences of much of the world's population when it comes to disease can hardly look to utilitarianism (i.e., the greatest happiness of the greatest number) for comfort. Claims that intellectual property rights are natural rights akin to the right of liberty look implausible in a world where these rights are traded by corporate owners. A situation in which intellectual property rights are used to achieve massive wealth transfers to a small group of developed nations at the expense of other nations squares with no theory of justice we know of, except the one that Thrasymachus gives to Socrates in Plato's *Republic*: "I define justice or right as what is in the interest of the stronger party."[31]

Attempts by corporate owners to give legitimacy to their intellectual property empires through appeals to romantic notions of individual authorship and inventorship look less and less morally persuasive in a world where intellectual property rights, and TRIPS especially, are being linked to bigger themes and issues—widening income inequalities such as those between developed and developing countries, excessive profits, the power and influence of big business on government, the loss of national sovereignty, globalization, moral issues about the use and direction of biotechnology, food security, biodiversity (the last three all linked to patenting of plants, seeds and genes), sustainable development, the self-determination of indigenous people, access to health services and the rights of citizens to cultural goods.

The decline of moral respectability of intellectual property rights has been accompanied by increasing levels of transnational activism against the use and extension of intellectual property regimes. The US academic community, especially in the field of copyright, has become one of the principal defenders of the public domain. Through their writing, pro bono litigation, amicus curiae briefs, lobbying and the formation of the Digital Future Coalition, US academics in alliance with other groups such as librarians have fought the expansionist agendas of corporate intellectual property owners. Richard Stallman, the founder of the Free Software Foundation, has been a vital force in showing how a society can meet its needs for software without incurring the predatory costs of a Microsoft, which relies on copyright and patents to lock up software development. In the health field, as we saw at the beginning of this introduction, it has been activists like James Love and NGOs like Oxfam and MSF that have forced governments to begin a process of reconsidering the impact of patents and TRIPS on access to medicines. NGOs like the Rural Advancement Foundation and GRAIN have been important in drawing attention to bio-piracy. It has also been NGOs that have led the fight against the privatization of genetic resources through intellectual property rights. It is they who have forced states negotiating the International Undertaking on Plant Genetic Resources for Food and Agriculture (the international agreement that sets out governing principles on access and exchange of plant genetic resources for food and agriculture) to confront the creep of intellectual property into agriculture and food. Their argument has been that the International Undertaking should not defer to intellectual property protection in ways that threaten agricultural biodiversity, public genebanks and publicly funded agricultural research.

For the time being, many of the NGOs, businesses, individuals and professional organizations fighting for the preservation of the intellectual commons do so in isolation from each other. The groups that attempt to hold back the encroachment of intellectual property on the Internet and in our public libraries have not forged alliances with those groups defending the rights of farmers to seeds and indigenous groups to control the use of their knowledge. If the inequalities of information feudalism are to be successfully resisted, then broader global coalitions will have to be forged.[32] TRIPS, as we will see, was only possible because an elite of knowledge-based companies in the US, Japan and Europe set aside their differences and united on the need for global intellectual property protection. Resisting this new paradigm of information feudalism requires diverse groups and communities fighting in their area of the public domain and knowledge to unite around a global politics of intellectual property that forces governments to design intellectual property rights to serve the welfare and basic freedoms of citizens. Property rules have always entrenched inequalities—the property rules of Roman slavery and the property rules that made chattels of women and children are but two examples of this historical truth. TRIPS and the "investors-only" morality it serves will also perpetuate inequality. The alternative we argue for in Chapter 12 is democratic property rights that serve human rights values.

OVERVIEW

We have seen that lying at the heart of the knowledge economy are intangible assets—for example, algorithms that drive computers and formulae that underpin chemical processes of production. The intellectual property rules governing the ownership of these assets have been globally and profoundly changed in the last 20 years. These rules impact on who can and cannot be an entrepreneur in the knowledge economy. *Information Feudalism* will now tell the story of how these rules have been quietly redrawn, of a small number who were involved in the deals, a small number who resisted them and of the populations that have lost and will continue to do so.

Chapter 2 describes a rhetorical tool of persuasion that was used to change perceptions and thinking—the label of piracy. The knowledge game, a profitable cartelist game that has been played by a corporate elite for almost a century, is described in Chapter 3. Chapter 4 tells of the lead role played by Pfizer Corporation in changing international standards of intellectual property. Chapter 5 discusses how developing countries became part of the knowledge game and how they tried to change its rules. The linkage between the rules of intellectual property and the rules of trade is discussed in Chapter 6. Chapters 7, 8 and 9 trace the deal making at the General Agreement on Tariffs and Trade (GATT) that led to intellectual property becoming a part of the WTO. Chapter 10 looks at the impact of patents on biological knowledge and Chapter 11 looks at the impact of copyright on the Internet, movies, software and records. Democratic property rights are argued for in Chapter 12. Chapter 13 has some suggestions for how democratic property rights might be implemented, while Chapter 14 shows how the publicness of knowledge matters to competition and public goods.

CHAPTER 2

Piracy

CULTURAL TRESPASSERS

"That guy had to go to jail." We were in the offices of Eric Smith, executive director of the International Intellectual Property Alliance. It was October 1993. Six months later in Marrakech, 108 states would sign the Final Act of the Uruguay Round of Trade Negotiations, bringing to an end the trade negotiations they had started in Punta del Este in 1986. That Final Act, as we were to discover, was shaped in profound ways by Smith and a handful of other key individuals. Included in it was a deal on intellectual property known as the Agreement on Trade-Related Aspects of Intellectual Property Rights (TRIPS). This agreement would have important implications, not just for corporate America but for citizens of countries everywhere.

TRIPS was the beginning of a quiet revolution in the way that property rights in information would be defined and enforced in the emerging global information economy. Intellectual property rights are not like property rights in land. Lawyers refer to them as property rights in intangibles in order to distinguish them from the ownership of physical objects. Their reach extends to the building blocks of life and computing science. Through them, corporations have made things like DNA, algorithms and musical sounds targets of private ownership. What was once part of the intellectual commons has fallen into private hands. And, as we shall see, citizens have been turned into trespassers in their own cultures. Yet outside the professional elite that congregates around trade negotiations, few knew about TRIPS and even fewer understood its implications.

Smith was talking about a successful and highly respected Korean businessman who ran a publishing business called Tower Publications. Tower published textbooks for the South Korean market. This market had grown dramatically because South Korea had made the education and training of its population a priority. The presses at Tower reproduced tens of thousands of American textbooks, but American publishers and authors did not see any license fees or royalty payments. It was a familiar enough story throughout most of Asia. The price of Western textbooks as well as software was beyond the reach of most Asian students. A market in copying had sprung up. Businesses like Tower could take advantage of technologies that had made copying easier and, not having to pay license fees to Western publishers, could produce texts at prices that Asian students could afford to buy. As Smith observed: "American textbooks were being killed."

Korea had put a Copyright Act on its statute books in 1987, but that was where it had stayed. Copyright was not part of Korean legal practice, let alone general culture or consciousness. There were almost no copyright lawyers in Korea. Those with some knowledge of copyright had usually been trained in the US. Copyright law was for them the distant memory of lecture theaters. So far as Korean culture was concerned copyright was the most foreign of foreign transplants. Copying was regarded as a sincere form of flattery, something that should gladden authors rather than anger them.

US trade negotiators were wearily familiar with the cultural defense from Korean trade negotiators. They had been listening to it for years. They said unprintable things about it. Eventually they also crushed it. The Koreans were presented with a very simple choice: improve protection of US intellectual property or kiss their export markets in the US good-bye. There was nothing unlawful about the threat. In the early 1980s, the US had reformed its trade law to allow the US executive to impose trade sanctions on those countries that did not respect US intellectual property.

The head of Tower Publications spent eight or so weeks in jail. He was, as Smith pointed out, a businessman of enormous status in Korean society. Later, a Korean informant also involved in the US–South Korean negotiations over intellectual property confirmed for us that the jailing of this respected figure had sent "shock waves" throughout South Korean business and social circles. The bureaucratic elite that ran the South Korean economy had been sent a message.

These days when one goes to the Korean Patent Office in Seoul there is a sign in English that identifies the building as the "Korean Patent and Anti-Piracy Office." It is a polite, public indication of compliance with Western ideas of property. Western patent offices refer to themselves as patent offices. The enforcement of intellectual property is not their concern. That is a matter for the owner of the patent. Within the walls of the South Korean Patent Office work many young South Koreans, often American educated. One does not hear the cultural defense from their lips. They see intellectual property for what it is: a tool of business power and strategy. South Korea's experience with the US impressed that upon them. They all know of the Tower Publications episode and the problems over patent rights that South Korean companies had with Texas Instruments. They understand that intellectual property regimes are key to a new global business reality in which the acquisition and defense of intangible assets matter more to a company's valuation than its physical stock.

Piracy has not, however, vanished from South Korea. US business and US negotiators complain about the fraudulent use of copyright licenses in South Korea, and the piracy of South Korean corporations. As one of us left the South Korean office he asked whether it was still possible to buy cheap watches and CDs in Seoul. "Sure," they laughed, "you should go here," pointing to the spot on the map. Culture runs deep.

"A PYRATE AND A ROVER ON THE SEA"[1]

Piracy, of course, did not begin with the South Koreans. It is one of the world's oldest professions. Its practitioners have sometimes been well regarded. When Sir Francis Drake was sending Spanish galleons to the bottom of the ocean along with their crews, but minus their treasure, he was a national hero in England. Despite requests from the Spanish that "El Draque" be hanged, Queen Elizabeth I knighted Drake on the deck of his ship the *Golden Hind*.[2]

Under Elizabeth's reign, piracy became a large-scale business involving old aristocratic families and high-ranking navy officers. England was poor compared with Spain. The richly laden Spanish ships coming back from the Americas, the East and the West Indies provided easy pickings for English pirates. Behind the sailors that did the boarding and murdering there lay a complex infrastructure. The booty had to be landed in England. The coasts of Cornwall and Devon became favorite entry points. Port officials had to be bribed, the booty distributed and sold, the pirate crews paid, any damage to the ships repaired and so on. Piracy was, in effect, organized crime. The crime families that ran the piracy business, such as the Killigrews of Cornwall, had close connections to the Royal Court. These families were responsible for creating and maintaining the administration needed for the success of any major criminal enterprise.

Occasionally these families overreached themselves, as did Lady Killigrew on 7 January 1582.[3] On that night the lady and her retainers boarded a ship moored in Falmouth that was owned by two Spaniards. The ship had taken refuge in this Cornish harbor from a storm. The crew was murdered and the ship itself ended up in Ireland where the booty was disposed of. The Spanish owners brought a complaint before the Commissioners of Piracy in Cornwall, but perhaps because Lady Killigrew's son was the president of the commission she escaped conviction. Taking their case to London the owners received more satisfaction. Lady Killigrew and two of her servants received death sentences, although it was only the two servants who went to their deaths. Lady Killigrew's connections saw her escape execution. The death of the two servants was no doubt required by way of symbolism, to show the Spanish that Elizabeth was serious about tackling piracy, at least in Falmouth harbor. Piracy of intellectual property has also had its symbolic messages sent by way of the deaths of pirates. Probably in an effort to impress the US, the Chinese government was reported in 1994 to have executed some trademark pirates.[4] Copyright piracy also has its hazards in China. In December 1997 a Chinese People's Court gave life sentences to three men for attempting to smuggle pirated compact discs into Hong Kong.

Aside from the fact that large-scale piracy made an important contribution to England's economy, it aided Elizabeth in another way. It helped to form the fighting men and ships of the British navy that were eventually to strip the Spanish of their supremacy of the oceans. Boarding boats and hewing their occupants into small pieces was excellent practice for naval warfare. Piracy proved useful to Elizabeth both economically and militarily. Of course, in the 19th century, when England complained about the piracy of authors like Dickens by US publishers, the virtues of piracy had been forgotten.

North America, just like England, has its rich history of institutionalized piracy. The English helped to create it with their Navigation Act of 1697. Under that act, goods from the East had to be imported by North American colonies via England. As a result, the price of the goods went up. So did the incentive for piracy, for now pirates had a ready-made market in which they could engage in effective price competition. Fostering piracy through pricing is a bit of history that tends to repeat itself. US software corporations helped to create the piracy of their software products. In the early days they priced their software at such high levels that many individuals simply could not afford it. Moreover these corporations often simply dumped their products on customers. One Singaporean informant told us that you tended to get much better after-sales service from some software pirates. They understood the bugs in the programs, spoke the same language and were generally more helpful than a distant voice on a helpline somewhere in the US.

The colony of New England served as the base of a regular pirate round in the closing years of the 17th century. From Boston, New York and the other ports of New England, well-equipped ships with crews drawn from the toughest of the unemployed would set sail to the Red Sea, Persian Gulf or the coast of Malabar, where they fell upon the defenseless coastal shipping that ferried the silks and artistic crafts of the East. It was on this pirate round that Captain John Avery and William Kidd made their names. The slaughter that accompanied this round bothered few in the West for it was "universal pirate opinion that it was no sin for Christians to rob heathens."[5] The markets of New England and the other American colonies became crucial outlets for this plunder from the East. Just as piracy helped Elizabeth's England to prosper, so did it help the colonies of North America to grow.

One of the interesting things about the history of piracy is working out who were the real pirates. Schoolboy history and Hollywood have combined to tell us what pirates looked like and what they did. They were ugly (unless played by Errol Flynn), fierce-looking, cutthroat types who plundered and murdered without pity under the flag of the Jolly Roger. Henry Morgan, the famous 17th-century buccaneer, certainly had the bloodthirsty profile. When he attacked the city fort of Porto Bello, he forced nuns and priests to carry the scaling ladders, leaving the Spanish defenders with little option but to shoot them. The torture that accompanied the sacking of Porto Bello helped to establish Morgan's reputation as one of the most ruthless of all pirates. But was he a pirate? Morgan operated out of Port Royal in Jamaica. The governor of Jamaica, Sir Thomas Modyford, gave Morgan various commissions to move against Spanish shipping and towns. From time to time Morgan was ticked off about exceeding the terms of his commissions. But then he always came back laden with booty and all was forgiven. The next commission was issued. When he sacked Panama, he was taken back to England to be tried for piracy. The English and the Spanish had concluded a treaty and some evidence was needed that the English were serious about stopping the attacks on Spanish shipping. But things worked out better for Morgan than for Lady Killigrew's servants. He ended up being knighted and was sent back as the deputy governor of Jamaica.

The Spanish had little doubt that Morgan, like Drake, was a pirate. But Morgan no doubt took the view that he had a commission from the Crown and that he was therefore a privateer. Here we find that real history, unlike schoolboy history, is much murkier when it comes to the question of identifying the real pirates. Throughout history the word "pirate" has been used to describe the work of groups of men who very often operated with the authority, either express or tacit, of a sovereign. Occasionally those who have been described as pirates become so successful that others recognize them as having authority. The Barbary pirates are an example. Piracy in the Mediterranean increased in the 16th and 17th centuries as shipping increased and the expelled Moors of Spain had reason to organize against the Spanish. The early successes of the two brothers Barbarossa, Arouji and Kheyr-ed-in, against the Spanish led them to acquire many followers. The Barbary pirates became the Barbary communities of Tunis, Tripoli, Algiers and Salee. They were, in effect, recognized as states, for Western powers like France concluded alliances with them. These Barbary states exercised considerable power over shipping in the Mediterranean. Most European states paid tribute to them, as did the US at the end of the 18th century so that its ships would not be attacked.

The Barbary pirates were not the only ones raiding ships in the Mediterranean. In the 16th and 17th centuries the nationals of one country routinely preyed upon the shipping of others. Thus the English preyed on the Spanish, the Dutch on the English, the French on the Spanish, the English on the French, and the Barbary states on everyone, except those who happened to be their temporary allies. Everyone accused everyone else of piracy.

Piracy took a long time to acquire a legal technical meaning. The first scholar of note to provide some legal principle and argument for the category of piracy was the Italian-born scholar Albertico Gentili, who settled in England in 1580. Gentili linked the meaning of piracy to the lack of authority for the taking of goods, thus sharpening the distinction between piracy and privateering. This proved to be only the beginning of the legal debates over the meaning of piracy. These debates carried on well into the 20th century. As Rubin, in his masterful study of piracy, shows, there are at least six different meanings that can be attributed to it, including a nonlegal vernacular meaning, international law meanings and meanings based on national law.[6] Following the history of the legal intricacies of the term is not important for present purposes. In fact, as Rubin's work seems to suggest, the term has rarely been used with much legal precision. Because piracy is associated in the popular mind with a history of desperate outlawry and savagery, it has proved to be a particularly effective rhetorical tool. This popular folk image of pirates remains free of legal niceties concerning difficult questions such as the nature of property rights, the reach of national law, the content of international law and so on. A vague but powerful term, it has proved useful to many, allowing actors to achieve political ends that were otherwise out of reach. During the 19th century the British authorities in Southeast Asia regularly referred to problems of piracy among the Malays and others in the region, thereby creating a pretext on which to intervene militarily in their affairs.

Piracy was eventually stamped out by brutal means. The British Empire's hegemony came to depend on shipping lanes, and so an offensive was begun against pirates:

> Corpses dangled in chains in British ports around the world 'as a Spectacle for the Warning of others'. No fewer than 400, and probably 500–600 Anglo-American pirates were executed between 1716 and 1726.[7]

The same brutality that saw piracy largely eliminated had also played a significant part in its beginnings. Merchant seamen served aboard ships in the 18th century in conditions that were nothing short of horrific. Punishments such as the "whip and pickle" were common: offenders were whipped with a cat-o'-nine-tails and their flayed parts washed from a tub of brine or salt, the process then being repeated. It was ordered by captains that reveled in the absolute power they had over the lives of ordinary seamen. Little wonder that so many seamen joined the ranks of pirates when their ships were captured. They had only their degradation to lose. Piracy was in part a response to a system of official power that was based on systematic cruelty and gross inequality. Pirates formed codes of conduct in which their captains were given no great special privileges, important decisions were made by pirate councils involving all and booty was distributed according to a set of fair rules that recognized the contribution of all. Despised as vermin by authorities, they created for themselves a society that gave them the social and economic dignity that had been denied to them as merchant seamen.

The use of piracy in conjunction with intellectual property is another example of its rhetorical use for political and economic gain. As we shall see, during the 1970s, 1980s and 1990s most Asian countries were accused by US corporations of containing centers of intellectual property piracy. This was part of a domestic strategy to garner support for the global economic agenda of these key US multinationals. It proved very effective because it drew on prejudices and anxieties within the US about the future economic security of the US in a world where successful Asian "tiger" economies were on the prowl. More recently, and somewhat ironically, some of these same US corporations have been on the receiving end of this strategy, as indigenous people have accused them of bio-piracy: the theft of traditional medicines and knowledge. Just as in the 16th-century Mediterranean, everyone, it seems, is engaged in some kind of piracy.

The current US preoccupation with intellectual property pirates has much in common with the attitude of another empire toward piracy, the Roman Empire. Along the eastern Mediterranean there lived in the 1st century BC communities that accepted economic raids as part of a set pattern of life. These communities were, in the words of Plutarch, "a disgrace to Roman supremacy."[8] Piracy was used by the Romans to describe a customary way of life that was foreign to Rome. It was the refusal of these communities to accept the Roman imperium and the commercial order that went with it that brought about their destruction by Pompey the Great acting under a law of the Roman Senate of 68 BC.[9] The US, like Rome, has a deeply held belief about the proper ordering of global commerce. Key individuals within US policy circles routinely proclaim the arrival of the global information economy, the information society. They believe, with an almost messianic intensity, that new property rights based on the ownership of ideas and information have to be created, globalized and enforced.

INTELLECTUAL PROPERTY PIRACY

Each time you load a video you receive a little sermon about the evils of video piracy. Most people fast-forward their way through this bit of the show. This is not the only reminder we receive about the evils of intellectual property piracy. The US organization the Business Software Alliance (BSA) has been running an anti-software piracy campaign for over a decade. Microsoft software comes riddled with little indicators showing the potential buyer that it is the genuine article. Certificates of authenticity on special high-security paper, holograms on the hub of the CD, a heat-sensitive strip that, when rubbed, reveals the word "genuine" and a watermark are all part of the tips that Microsoft provides to its customers to let them know that they have a legal product.

Perhaps a less pleasing security measure, especially for those concerned about privacy, and not nearly so well advertised, is the unique serial number that Microsoft's Windows 98 program plants in every electronic document, thereby allowing the author of the document to be traced. This number tags the hardware of the user and, along with a product number for the Windows program, is part of the information that is transmitted back to Microsoft when a purchaser registers his or her copy of Windows. As the programmer who discovered the "globally unique identifier" pointed out, if Microsoft comes across the same product number relating to two or more different hardware numbers, it would conclude that there was piracy.[10] But it may not be piracy. Perhaps the first machine has broken down and Windows has been transferred across to a replacement. For privacy activists, one of the issues is what information is going back to Microsoft's internal databases and what is being done with it?

The corporate-sponsored literature on piracy makes dramatic reading. It has to. The truth of the matter is that most of us do not put intellectual property piracy in the category of serious crime. To begin with, many of us at some stage in our lives will have taped a CD or TV program, photocopied a book or made use of copied software. For most of us, there is a world of difference between this kind of activity and crimes like rape, murder or the supply of illicit drugs. Intellectual property piracy is just not an issue in the way that safe streets and better policing are issues in the public mind.

Companies like Microsoft are not naive enough to think that the money they spend on publicizing the problem of intellectual property piracy will cause a reordering in the public mind of criminal law enforcement priorities. They know full well that many will just shrug their shoulders and feel very little sympathy for a company like Microsoft. Bill Gates remains one of the richest men of all time despite the piracy problem. The BSA knows that it will get this kind of moral reaction. When it sends its smoothly suited teams of two on missions into the Asia-Pacific region to deliver the anti-piracy gospel, those teams come prepared to defend Bill Gates. In 1998 one of us attended a BSA presentation in Canberra. Before a somewhat jaded Australian audience, a member of the BSA, toward the end of his presentation on Internet piracy, raised the Bill Gates issue himself.

We're sometimes told that Bill Gates has made enough profit and that downloading a bit of software isn't going to hurt. What's wrong with that? [pause] [silence] Well it's still theft. You wouldn't think of stealing a Cadillac just because it belonged to someone wealthy. Software is no different [silence].

The meeting broke up soon afterward.

The analogy between software and the Cadillac is nice and simple, always important in presentations. It also doesn't work. Information isn't like a Cadillac. I can read your newspaper, acquire the information, but I haven't deprived you of it in the way that I do when I drive off with your Cadillac. Then what if I learn that your Cadillac is made up of bits and pieces that you have taken from others? I might not feel so kindly toward you anymore. Software programs are made up of lots of file routines borrowed from previous programs written by a previous generation of programmers. Bill Gates did not write DOS. Here we come to a fundamental problem in intellectual property law. Because intellectual property relates to information and knowledge, and because information and knowledge is built up over time by many people, it is hard to work out just what any given individual is truly responsible for. Ideas are triggered by related ones. All ideas have fuzzy boundaries. Working out where the fences of intellectual property ownership should go is very difficult. In the world of commerce it is legal muscle more than moral entitlement that determines the fence line.

The public anti-piracy campaigns are a part of a long-term game in which consumers are being "reeducated" about the seriousness of intellectual property piracy. The video you hire for a night's entertainment is doing its job because it provides you with a ready-made category of thought about the problem. But the education campaign is only part of a much more complex strategy that corporate intellectual property owners have for strengthening their hold over the ownership of ideas and information.

There are really two important frontline strategies. First, corporate intellectual property owners lobby policy makers intensively, arguing that more public money should be put into dealing with high-technology crime, by which they mean the copying of their products. There is in fact a worldwide campaign by corporate intellectual property owners aimed at getting governments to commit much more in the way of resources to the fight against piracy. So, for example, in Australia we were told by an official working on strategic crime policy that there was a lot of pressure coming from multinationals to make the fight against intellectual property piracy a major priority within the Australian criminal justice system. This was something that the individual in question had a hard time understanding given the resources available and other priorities like domestic violence. A second and more recent strategy by corporate owners of intellectual property is the attempt to link intellectual property piracy with organized crime, with crimes that the public are really scared of. It is easier to justify spending public money on the war against the illegal downloading of software, or the illegal taping of Michael Jackson's latest album, if those people doing the illegal copying are also members of neo-Nazi organizations or terrorist groups. Microsoft's response to the EC's Green Paper on Counterfeiting and Piracy reveals the kind of connections about which we can expect to hear a lot more, whether these connections exist or not. Here it is said that software counterfeiting operations are "financed and controlled by Asian crime syndicates," that there are "direct links between European counterfeiting operations and the narcotics trade" and that counterfeiting operations are tied to neo-Nazi and other paramilitary groups "who use counterfeiting proceeds to fund terrorist activities in Western Europe."[11]

There is a connection between organized crime and intellectual property that corporate owners of intellectual property do not like to advertise. During the course of our fieldwork we were told that some companies would deal with organized crime groups in Eastern Europe in order to solve the piracy problem. The problem for companies is that, in places like Russia where getting a job is hard and one that pays even harder, intellectual property piracy is a way of earning a living. Russian courts are not in a position to stop piracy. The search for a solution has seen some companies negotiating deals with organized crime groups like the Georgian Mafia. It is difficult to do business in Russia without the help of organized crime in any case. For a sum of money, a known pirate group can be shut down. It is a part of the protection service that the Russian Mafia runs more generally. There are plenty of ex-KGB and military personnel in Russia who have the necessary skills to eliminate the problem of piracy. It is quick and efficient in a way the Russian courts are not. It probably also has much more deterrence value than a fine handed down by a Russian judge.

So far we have been talking as if the meaning of piracy in intellectual property is perfectly clear. But intellectual property piracy, just like piracy on the high seas, is something that is hard to pin down legally. Most jurisdictions in the world do not use the term "piracy" in connection with intellectual property as a term of legal art. There is no legal definition of it that is universally accepted.[12] Within English-speaking jurisdictions piracy is a way of referring to copyright infringement (the copying of a CD or a play) while counterfeiting refers to the misappropriation of trademarks (using the Nike swoop on clothes without Nike's permission, for example). Piracy remains a powerful evaluative word. To be called an intellectual property pirate is to be condemned. In a world where attention spans are divided by the media into ten-second sound bites it is the perfect word to use on TV, videocassettes, newspaper headlines and the radio. The received folk memory of "pyrates and rovers" on the sea does the rest.

There is an important legal principle that goes right to the heart of the existence of intellectual property rights and that has an important bearing on whether piracy of any kind has taken place. Known as the principle of territoriality, it simply says that intellectual property rights operate in the territory of the sovereign that created them in the first place. US copyright law applies in the US, UK copyright law in the UK, and French copyright law in France. Similarly, trademarks that are registered in the US only have validity in the US. If US owners want trademark protection in a foreign jurisdiction they have to register the mark in that jurisdiction.

The principle gives rise to a problem. If I am a French author my work is not protected in Albania because French copyright law does not operate there. These days there are international treaties that take care of these kinds of problems. But in the days before international agreements on intellectual property, the intellectual property owner only got a right in a particular territory. Many states simply did not have copyright or patent law. Even if the state in question had intellectual property law, most courts took the view that foreign breaches of intellectual property could not be tried in domestic courts. UK courts decided that an act committed outside the UK that affected a UK copyright owner could not be heard as a copyright infringement action by a UK court. There was no legal obligation on states to recognize the intellectual property systems of other states. Moreover this was a principle accepted by all states. The principle of territoriality remained dominant in intellectual property law for centuries and still remains a central principle today. It is easy enough to see why states would support the principle. Why would states agree to US intellectual property law standards applying in their jurisdiction? These laws relate to the control of information and ideas. No state would want to cede sovereignty over something so important to the economic and social life of its citizens. Yet, as we shall see in subsequent chapters, a small group of men within the US were able to globalize a set of standards that primarily serve the interests of those US corporations with large intellectual property portfolios. When the history of 20th-century business regulation is written this will come to be seen as one the century's most remarkable achievements.

One reaction to the preceding discussion is to say that even if one state was not obliged to recognize the intellectual property law of another state, it was morally wrong not to do so. It was still piracy to take a foreign author's work even if the state in which the copying took place was not under an obligation to protect foreign intellectual property. Here we enter tricky waters, for, as we shall see in the next section, all states designed their intellectual property laws (or failed to by not having them) in a way that suited their economic interests. In the hurly-burly of international commerce all states at some point in their history were happy for their citizens or firms to copy the intellectual property of others without permission. Piracy was a customary practice in which all participated.

In any case it was far from clear that it was piracy, since intellectual property rights were for most of their history not seen as property rights, but rather as monopoly privileges. These monopolies were created by states for their own purposes and how they ran them remained their affair. The rules of international commercial morality were not like the moral rules we think about in relation to the possession of our car or jewelry. International commerce had created a very different kind of moral world for itself. In order to make all this clearer we need to understand some history.

A LITTLE INTELLECTUAL PROPERTY HISTORY

Intellectual property rights began life as tools of censorship and monopoly privileges doled out by the king to fund wars and other pursuits. In some respects not much has changed. Modern governments still rely on copyright in their documents to prevent their publication by newspapers. When artists like Andy Warhol place a corporate insignia like the Campbell's soup can label in an artistic context they change the message of that insignia. That is why corporations bring actions for intellectual property infringement against postmodern artists.

Copyright, like so much of European history, is bound up with Martin Luther's words and Johannes Gutenberg's invention of a printing press with movable type in 1450.[13] The Church at first supported the use of printing presses. It was a means by which to spread Church doctrine. It changed its mind about this in a few years. Printing presses began to print the heretical thoughts of humanist scholars, thoughts that questioned papal infallibility and the Church's authority. The Church began to move to put printers under ecclesiastical supervision. It also began to take the view that lay people should not be permitted to read the scriptures and that instead they should rely on interpretations put forward by Church officials.

Gutenberg's invention was completed in the free city of Mainz, one of the most important commercial centers in the Rhine district. After Gutenberg's invention, Mainz developed a strong printing industry. During a religious power struggle known as the "War of Bishops," the city was sacked by Archbishop Adolf's army in 1462. The printers of the city fled, scattering throughout Europe, taking their knowledge of printing with them. With the diffusion of printing technology throughout Europe, Martin Luther's heretical words were spread even more quickly.

Copyright begins life in England in the form of printing privileges granted by Queen Mary in 1557 to a craft guild known as the Stationers. Like all craft guilds, the Stationers had a serious interest in monopoly profits and a commensurate fear of competition. In particular this London-based guild did not want competition from regional printers or from across the border in Scotland. Queen Mary, like all monarchs, feared ideas that questioned her legitimacy. There could hardly be a greater questioning of a monarch who was bent on deepening the country's links with Rome than those posed by the ideas of the Protestant Reformation. During Mary's reign Protestants went to the stake or to prison. Mary also struck a deal with the Stationers: in exchange for a charter granting them a monopoly over printing, the Stationers would ensure that no "seditious and heretical books, rhymes and treatises" would see the light of day. After the charter, a person wishing to print books had to be a member of the Stationers' Company.

Over time the Stationers' Company became an executive arm of the state.[14] The company had its own court for matters of internal governance. As the company's powers increased so did those of its court. The Stationers were given powers of search and seizure. They were not shy about using these powers to put printers who were not part of their company out of business. Many "pirate" printers ended up in prison, their printing presses destroyed by the Stationers.

The Stationers' Company spent a good deal of its time fighting "piracy," which by all accounts flourished in the second half of the 16th century. But this was a piracy that the Stationers created through their ruthless administration of the monopoly. Printing outside London, with the exception of Cambridge and Oxford, was not allowed. All the bestsellers of the day, including the Bible, were tied up in company hands. The result was high prices for books and high unemployment in the printing trade. The circulation of books was much lower than it might otherwise have been. Only the well-off could afford the Stationers' prices. Those printers who were not members of the Stationers' Company continued to print books in order to survive. Nor did they meekly submit to the idea that they were doing something illegal. Men such as John Wolfe argued that as freemen of London they had the right to print books without the need of a privilege and, in any case, the queen did not have the right to grant privileges in a way that pauperized the majority of the printing trade.[15] Two other pirates, Bourne and Jefferson, argued in 1586 that the privilege system kept prices high, deprived the public of choice and was contrary to the common law.[16] This argument would be accepted by the common law courts in relation to monopolies generally in the 17th century, but in the Stationers' Court it had the impact of a snowflake on a hot summer's day. So effective did John Wolfe prove as a "pirate" that he was eventually bought off with company membership. Robert Waldegrave also defied the Stationers' Company. With the Stationers in hot pursuit he decided to take refuge in Scotland. There he was appointed the king's printer by King James. Waldegrave continued to print books in defiance of the Stationers' privileges, eventually returning to England in 1603 when James I acceded to the throne.

From this beginning evolved copyright law as we know it. These days, corporate copyright owners, unlike the Stationers, do not have permission to arrest, torture and imprison their business rivals. But they do hire private investigators to track down copyright infringers. These investigators gather information and present it to police authorities, pressuring those authorities to act. BSA members will accompany police on raids making sure that the war against the makers of counterfeit Microsoft mice gets the publicity it deserves. Photographs of thousands of hapless "pirate" mice being crushed by steamrollers occasionally make it into our newspapers. Sting operations in which orders for pirated goods are placed with suspected pirates are another private enforcement tactic.

Raids, sting operations and the use of stool pigeons were also part of the techniques used by the French "book police" in the 18th century, as they worked to prevent the circulation of "bad books" right up until the French Revolution.[17] The book trade in France, as in England, was organized around privileges issued by the state. In France these were held by a clique of printers based in Paris. In 1699 the Office of the Book Trade was established to carry out the censorship. The office became a special branch of the Paris police. Books had to be registered before they could be published. This Parisian model for controlling the book trade spread throughout the rest of France. The French book police infiltrated the book trade to an extraordinary extent. They kept detailed records of the location of printing presses, carried out regular inspections of printing shops and restricted the entry of books into France to certain designated points such as Paris, Lyon and Bordeaux. People receiving packages of books had to report to local authorities. The system for the control of the book trade grew into a monolith of surveillance that permeated French social and commercial life on a daily basis.

Despite this, "piracy" went on undeterred. Large numbers of people connected with the book trade went to jail. The statistics seem incredible to the modern eye, but during the 1750s 40 percent of those in the Bastille were there because of offenses related to the book trade.[18] The system reached its Kafkaesque apogee in a law of 1757 sentencing to death anyone involved in writings that, among other things, injured royal authority and troubled the "tranquillity of the state."[19] The French Revolution was 32 years away. The illegal imports of books continued, pirate editions continued to be printed and forbidden books (both political and pornographic) continued to be read.

The French Revolution brought with it freedom of the printing presses. The freedom of communication and of the press that the Declaration of the Rights of Man proclaimed was made concrete once printers no longer had to obtain the privilege of printing from the king. Members of the Paris Book Guild that for so long had controlled the production of literature in France saw their monopolies destroyed. From their world of privilege, power and status many of them sank into a netherworld of bankruptcy and anonymity.

Philippe-Denis Pierres, printer to the king, died in Dijon in 1808, a postal employee.[20] He was luckier than some of his fellow guild members who went to the guillotine. With the passing of the Paris Book Guild, publishing went through an extraordinary period of popular participation. A public dialogue and exchange of ideas spread through the medium of journals, newspapers, pamphlets and other ephemeral forms of publishing. In this deregulated market, the commercial production of the large printed book, a symbol of the absolutist past, went into decline. In this relatively short period before copyright law came back to restore "order" to publishing markets there was "an unprecedented democratization of the printed word."[21]

National copyright systems gradually spread throughout Europe in the 18th and 19th centuries. Authors slowly won more protection under these systems. Internationally, however, it was a very different picture. The pirating of foreign works was, for all intents and purposes, a customary norm of the international commerce in books. The same actors that preyed on each other's ships in the Mediterranean also helped themselves to each other's foreign works. The French and the Dutch reprinted English editions. The Dutch and the Spanish reprinted French works. Literary piracy was in many respects a much more egalitarian enterprise than piracy on the high seas. One did not have to be a great maritime power to engage in the reproduction of foreign works. Germany and Belgium were large centers for this activity. The Irish were a constant thorn in the side of English publishers. German authors suffered at the hands of the Austrians.

For a long time those engaged in the reproduction of foreign works did not see themselves as being in the piracy business. Rather it was an "honorable business" involving honorable men.[22] In the early 19th century, King William of Holland subsidized the reprinting of foreign works. In Belgium, ministers and magistrates sat on the boards of the large companies that reproduced foreign works. Many took the view that they were performing a public service by disseminating the knowledge in books more cheaply. That in part was what made it honorable. It is an argument with economic merit. Economic efficiencies are gained if information, once in existence, is distributed at zero cost. Once one farmer works out how best to grow a particular crop, everyone is better off if that information is made available to all farmers.

During the course of the 19th century, European states took to making bilateral deals with each other on the issue of protection abroad for the works of their nationals. Toward the end of the century a multilateral agreement in the form of the Berne Convention for the Protection of Literary and Artistic Works 1886 (Berne Convention) was agreed in Europe. There was a lot of rhetoric, especially from the French, about the immutable rights of authors, the need to protect works of genius and so on, but essentially trade agendas drove this process.

One state, the US, remained conspicuously absent from participation in these bilateral and multilateral deals, preferring to offer foreign authors little or no protection. American publishing was built on the piracy of European works. The linguistic diversity of America meant that there was a market in the US for English, German and French books. The extent of the piracy by US publishers drove European states to distraction, especially the English. Charles Dickens, one of the most heavily copied authors in the US, campaigned in the US in 1837 for the recognition of the rights of foreign authors. He left the US a disappointed man. Attempts by the American literati to change US policy always failed in Congress in the 19th century because of the opposition of American publishers. There was also a view that foreign copyright amounted to a tax in favor of foreign authors.[23] American publishers were nothing if not enterprising. In one incident, which eerily anticipates the Internet and copyright, American agents cabled from London to the US the entire contents of a book published by the queen within 24 hours of its release.[24] The American public had access to hard copies within 12 hours of the end of the transmission.

Within Europe, committees of authors and commissions of policy makers would meet in renaissance capitals to decry the piratical practices of the New World. Victor Hugo became one of the key organizers of an authors' movement for international copyright protection. Retaliation was a word to be heard on the lips of gentlemen. Suspend the recognition of the copyright of American authors in the UK was the suggested form of retaliation. In an 1876 report of the English Copyright Commission, retaliation was ruled out. The commission preferred to see British copyright law stick to "correct principles, irrespective of the opinions or the policy of other nations."[25] Actually, noble adherence to principle was about the only option available to the UK. It could hardly invade the US over book piracy (in any case, it might have lost), the market for books by US authors in the UK was not that great and jeopardizing foreign relations over books seemed too high a cost to pay. English publishers did exact some revenge. Longfellow was widely copied by many publishers in the UK, and Harriet Beecher Stowe never received any royalties from British publishers, despite the fact that her *Uncle Tom's Cabin* became a bestseller in the UK.

The US did make some token efforts in the direction of protection for foreign works in the 19th century. Under an 1891 act, foreign works could gain protection in the US if they were published in the US simultaneously with the country of origin and the book was also printed in the US. The London *Times* saw this as an attempt to make New York the center of world publishing.[26] No one in America much disagreed.

As we shall see, the US did become serious about copyright protection. It did so when it realized that its giant software industry made it the biggest exporter of copyright in the world. Unlike the UK in the 19th century, however, the US did not choose noble adherence to principle as a means of combating copyright piracy. It had other options.

If the Americans were able to survey foreign copyright protection in the 19th century with equanimity, they became much more excitable on the question of foreign protection of American inventions. When the Americans heard that an International Exposition was being planned for Vienna in 1873 they hinted that they might not go. The reason lay with Austrian patent law. The Austrians required that a foreign invention be manufactured in Austria in order to gain patent protection. Obviously setting up a manufacturing plant in a country in order to gain patent protection there represents an investment outlay. This "preposterous requirement," it was said by the US, amounted to a virtual prohibition on the protection of foreign inventions.[27]

As with copyright the source of patents lay in the right of monarchs to grant exclusive trade privileges to chosen subjects. At first this power was used with some restraint and most probably with the public good in mind. In England "Letters of Protection" were issued in the 14th century to foreign tradesmen. The idea was to persuade skilled craftsmen to come to England to help develop English industry. Protection against imports was part of the incentive that was being offered. Letters of protection became "letters patent" (the term simply means open letters). Over the next few centuries the issue of letters patent proliferated, so much so that hardly any part of English commercial life remained unaffected by them.

English patent history shows that perhaps it is really men that tend to corrupt the exercise of power. In principle it seems like a good idea to give a wise and loving monarch the power to foster the growth of industry by means of the grant of patents. The actual historical experience of the English with patents turned out to be rather different.

Where there are monarchs there are courtiers seeking favors or payoffs for services rendered. Over time the practice developed of using patents to reward courtiers. Aside from patents for inventions, there were patents giving individuals the sole right to practice a particular trade, patents that gave the holder the right to supervise an industry like inns and alehouses, and patents that allowed the holder to avoid certain import or export restrictions. The monarch Elizabeth I took the granting of these patents to new heights. In a parliamentary speech in 1601 it was revealed that currants, iron, powder, ashes, vinegar, brushes, pots and oil, along with many other everyday items, were the subject of patents. After the list had been read out one Mr. Hackwell inquired whether bread was on the list. "'Bread,' cried everyone in astonishment, 'this voice seems strange.' 'No,' said Mr. Hackwell, 'but if order be not taken for these, bread will be there before the next parliament.'"[28]

Oddly enough, issuing patents on staples has parallels in our own times. As we shall see, much of modern agricultural production is bound up with the ownership of genes and plant varieties used in the growth of crops.

Elizabethan England offers us a model of what happens when patents are easy to get and apply to anything and everything. Prices go up. The monopolist is rarely an altruist. Trying to get into business and doing business becomes very difficult. Market opportunities that might be available to potential entrants in a free market are foreclosed or onerous conditions of entry imposed. Over time the ownership of patents becomes more concentrated as they are traded and bought up by the wealthy. In Elizabeth's time "almost all commodities were in the hands of a favoured few."[29] What seemed to grate more than anything on those in commerce were the powers of supervision and enforcement that were granted to patent holders. Being surveiled and inspected by the agents of patent holders (who one guesses were not always polite and pleasant) became a part of daily commercial life.

The discontented murmuring of traders, merchants and manufacturers concerning the use of patents became the loud voice of criticism of monopolies by Parliament. The use of the royal prerogative to interfere in matters of trade came to represent a deep intrusion on fundamental common law liberties. Patent monopolies were linked to a greater constitutional struggle between Parliament and the Crown. Monopolies, except for those in invention, were swept away by the Statute of Monopolies of 1624. But little changed. The statute swept away the monopolies of individuals, but not those of corporations. Thus in 1640 Sir John Culpeper in a speech in the Long Parliament observed that monopolies "like the frogs of Egypt, have gotten possession of our dwellings, and we have scarce a room free of them."[30] He was referring to monopolies on wine, coal, soap, salt, clothes, pins and so on. Parliament, with its power increasing and with popular support, called monopolists to account for the monopoly privileges they had been granted. Eventually the wide sweep of monopolies through the UK economy was reduced.

Patent law, like copyright, is sometimes justified by an appeal to the natural rights of creators. What the historical record shows though is that right from the beginning a ruthless trade morality drove the development and use of patents. Clearly, when English kings and later the colonial governments of America granted patents to those who imported innovations that had been invented abroad by others, they were not much concerned about the "natural rights" of the foreign inventor. Right through patent history all states kept a weather eye on the extent to which their patent system recognized the rights of foreign patent holders. When states did grant patents to foreigners they generally also insisted on the foreign patent holder "locally working" the patent within the state.

Patents were also an important tool of protectionism. Toward the end of the 19th century and into the 20th a number of states in Europe became afraid of the might of the German chemical industry. The Swiss in their patent law required inventions to be represented by a model. Since processes could not be represented in this way it meant that processes could not be patented. Swiss chemical manufacturers could continue to free-ride on processes developed by German manufacturers. With the threat of German import duties on Swiss coal-tar dyestuffs hanging over their head, the Swiss dropped this requirement in 1907.[31] The Swiss were not the only ones to hide a mercantilist devil within the detail of their patent law. The English, also worried by the impact of the German chemical industry on their own, did not allow the patenting of chemical compounds. We shall see later that when developing countries tried to protect their own industries using the rules of intellectual property they were slapped down by Western powers.

One of the important rhetorical victories that TRIPS represents is the belief that the absence of intellectual property protection is an impediment to free trade. To the uninitiated this belief represents something of a puzzle. The proliferation of monopolies in Elizabeth's time did not turn England into a model of free trade. It was precisely because the monopolies so liberally granted by the Crown interfered in trade and commerce that successive English parliaments worked toward their elimination. The 19th century also saw the patent system attacked on the ground that its operation was contrary to free trade. The basis of this attack lay in the fact that patentees could use the patent system to restrain the movement of goods across borders. In fact the link between patents and protectionism is to be found as early as 1833 when the states of the German Zollverein retained the discretion to prohibit the import of goods that were the subject of a domestic patent, thereby defeating the aim of creating a customs union. Free trade passions ran so high that for a while the future of the patent system dimmed a little. The Dutch repealed their patent law of 1817, the Swiss had in their constitution prohibited the government from adopting one, and there was even speculation in England that the patent system might be abolished. As it turned out, the Dutch eventually reenacted their law, the Swiss changed their constitution and the English stuck by their patent system. States realized that patent systems could be used to cloak protectionist strategies. There were also reputational advantages for states to be seen to be sticking to intellectual property systems. One could attend the various revisions of the Paris and Berne conventions, participate in the cosmopolitan moral dialogue about the need to protect the fruits of authorial labor and inventive genius, and make fine speeches condemning piracy, knowing all the while that one's domestic intellectual property system was a handy protectionist weapon.

Propping up the patent system and other intellectual property systems at the expense of free trade turned out to be something of a long-run miscalculation by states. During the 20th century the patent and copyright systems were colonized by big business, which routinely used these systems as the backbone of international cartels. These cartels exacted a heavy toll from states or rather from their citizens. Patents formed the basis of a cartel among pharmaceutical companies to raise the price of broad-spectrum antibiotics, causing countless thousands of deaths among people who could not afford to buy them.[32]

Copyright and trademarks are today routinely used by international business to segment global markets. The basic strategy is a simple one. It requires coming to an exclusive licensing arrangement with an agent in a country, working out a price that the market in that country will bear and using intellectual property rights to prevent someone other than the exclusive agent from importing the same *legitimate* product that has been released by the intellectual property owner more cheaply in another part of the global market. The intellectual property right is used by its owner to prohibit a parallel stream of importation into a market (generally referred to as the parallel importation issue). This strategy is normally accompanied by stories from corporate intellectual property owners about how the consumers in the country wearing the high prices are better off in terms of service, or how, in the case of copyright, multinational intellectual property owners use these profits to help to cross-subsidize the efforts of native authors. Developing countries are better off, runs the argument, because intellectual property owners will price more cheaply for their markets. Sometimes this is true and sometimes it is not.

A survey of a sample of prices of 16 proprietary drugs in Africa, Latin America and Organisation for Economic Co-operation and Development (OECD) countries showed that the average prices of some of the drugs were higher in African and Latin American countries than in OECD countries.[33] Once the intellectual property owner is given power over the movement of goods there is no guarantee that developing countries will be better off. During the course of our fieldwork in Australia when we asked the Copyright Law Review Committee whether they had come across any evidence that the "Big Seven" record producers used their profits to help struggling Australian musicians, the answer was none whatsoever. Similarly, the Australian consumer movement has always opposed the use of intellectual property rights to segment markets because there is no evidence that this brings anything other than higher prices for consumers. Intellectual property rights over the movement of goods in the global economy put too much power over price in the hands of intellectual property owners. Significantly, TRIPS does not set a global standard on the issue of parallel importation. Too many states opposed the idea during the negotiations. It remains an issue for another World Trade Organization (WTO) trade round.

These days the 19th-century history of free trade opposition to intellectual property rights has been conveniently elided from the international trade policy discourse on intellectual property. Monopoly rights, the exercise of which national parliaments struggled over the centuries to bring under democratic control, have been slipped into a world trade agreement. In the corridors of power that matter to the global economy, the WTO, the International Monetary Fund (IMF), Washington and Brussels bureaucrats participate in a trade "think speak" in which global monopoly privileges are entirely consistent with free trade and must be strengthened. During our interviews at the General Agreement on Tariffs and Trade (GATT) (before it became the WTO) we came across members of the Secretariat who conceded that there was something odd about placing TRIPS in an organization ostensibly dedicated to bringing down barriers to free trade. But as one member of the GATT Secretariat said, the Secretariat simply responded to the "imperatives of the negotiations" (GATT interview, 1993).

The key imperative of the Uruguay Round of trade negotiations became for the US a globally enforceable agreement on intellectual property. Before the Round had started such an agreement seemed against the odds. Support for it was not that great from Japan and Europe. There was a feeling that perhaps there should be a GATT agreement dealing with counterfeit goods. There had been lukewarm support for such an initiative in the dying stages of the Tokyo Trade Round. But very few people in the trade game would have bet on an agreement on the scale of TRIPS. It was an accepted part of international commercial morality that states would design domestic intellectual property law to suit their own economic circumstances. States made sure that existing international intellectual property agreements gave them plenty of latitude to do so. The rhetoric about piracy was recognized for what it was—rhetoric. Disgruntled authors and artists, clinging strongly to romantic notions of the "individual god author," were perhaps the only ones who were vehemently insistent that copying amounted to a universal moral offense. States did not go to the International Court of Justice about disputes over intellectual property treaties. In part this was because individual states realized they were not in a position to cast the first stone. No one had a clean slate when it came to respecting the intellectual property of foreigners. Certainly not the US, which was not a member of the Berne Convention, but whose publishers took advantage of its higher standards of protection "through the back door" method of arranging simultaneous publication in a Berne Convention country like Canada.[34]

TRIPS brought to an end this live-and-let-live attitude toward the international protection of intellectual property. Despite its legal and moral murkiness, piracy is drawn upon by corporate intellectual property owners when they pass judgment on the economic policies and behavior of states on the matter of intellectual property protection. States failing to meet the standards of TRIPS find themselves before a WTO dispute settlement panel. An agreement that in another era would have been rejected as a global charter for monopolists has come to be thought of as consistent with free trade and competition. The cost to business everywhere of this agreement has been increasing surveillance by the state on behalf of intellectual property owners. For some citizens it has meant new forms of servitude. When farmers farm with Monsanto's seeds their world changes. Seeds become patented technology. Farming becomes agricultural biotechnology. Farmers never own this technology. Instead they become its annual lessees under a system of patents and licenses. Farmers manage a technological system on behalf of a corporate entity that keeps a monitoring eye on their land and crops to make sure that its patents and licenses are being observed. It is a little like the feudal lord to whom obligations were owed when he allowed serfs to till his land, one point of difference being that the serfs had more rights over the seeds they used. The story of how TRIPS became part of a new global regulatory fabric and its consequences for citizen sovereignty occupies our remaining chapters.

CHAPTER 3

The Knowledge Game

KNOWLEDGE PROFITS

Knowledge is not only power. It is also the source of profits in modern global markets. At least this seems to be the conclusion that disciplines such as economics, management studies and international political economy are heading toward as they seek to conceptualize the economic and social transformations of the late 20th and early 21st centuries. The management guru Peter Drucker signals the direction of this new paradigm when he says that the basic economic resource in society "is and will be knowledge."[1] Yet, like Hegel's owl of Minerva, scholars are arriving at the realization of the existence of the knowledge economy after dusk. In one of the many paradoxes of management consultancy, consultants are hired by companies to tell those companies about the management of knowledge assets when companies have known since the beginning of the 20th century that the management of knowledge is and always has been the main game. The resolution of this particular paradox probably lies in the fact that knowledge about the knowledge game in the first part of the 20th century was confined to a few truly international industrial enterprises rather than companies in general. And as the circumstances of the knowledge game have changed, this industrial elite has changed the rules of the game.

LABORATORIES OF KNOWLEDGE

Many of the companies on Fortune's leaderboard of the world's largest industrial enterprises have a history stretching back to the beginning of the 20th century and in some cases further. When in 1905 three cousins of the DuPont family consolidated the US explosives industry under the Executive Committee of the E. I. DuPont de Nemours Powder Company, the DuPont company had already been in existence as a family firm for one hundred years.[2] The Computing Tabulating and Recording Company (CTR), which was renamed International Business Machines (IBM) in 1924 by its chairman Thomas Watson, had been founded in 1896 by Herman Hollerith, an engineer and inventor of a system of punch cards for the taking of census data.[3] Hollerith had called the company the Tabulating Machine Company and sold it in 1911 to Charles Flint, a financier, who renamed it CTR.

Some of these companies became what in modern parlance is called the "knowledge-creating company."[4] This was not the creation of knowledge for its own sake, but rather for the purpose of developing new products or improving existing ones. Research was seen as a vital way of protecting or growing a company. These early corporations organized themselves to create knowledge by means of industrial research laboratories. The laboratories were large-scale affairs. It was the inventor Thomas Edison who provided the model that the corporate giants of the 20th century were to follow. In 1876 Edison built a laboratory at Menlo Park, New Jersey. He staffed it with large numbers of scientists and tradesmen to work on a multitude of projects. Far from being the lone inventor, Edison in fact managed an "invention factory."[5] Its production goal was to produce "a minor invention every ten days, and a big one every six months or so."[6] It was the best-equipped facility of its kind in the US. There were other examples of the importance of research laboratories to industrial supremacy. The domination of the international chemical industry by Germany in the 19th century was built on an infrastructure of highly organized industrial research. The Germans had realized something that others had not—nature would give up its chemical secrets only under a collective systematic assault by large groups of scientists. The sheer number of tests required, for example, to find a successful dye meant the lone inventor had little chance of making discoveries of industrial interest. Once the knowledge had been discovered it had to be turned into a product and this required more interaction between scientists and those responsible for production. Large industrial laboratories linked to equally organized production and sales facilities that took care of the development side of the research, all coordinated by one management structure, became a fundamental pattern of corporate organization.

Early on, DuPont integrated scientific labor into processes of industrial production and market competition. In 1902 the company established the Eastern Laboratory. This was followed in 1903 by a second research facility known as the Experimental Station. Each laboratory was different in orientation. The Eastern Laboratory was dedicated to applied scientific problems, while the Experimental Station had a more basic research orientation in the area of explosives. DuPont management had determined that such a laboratory was crucial to maintaining its lead in the explosives business, especially its lead over the US military. If the latter achieved a superior in-house research and manufacturing capability it would probably have dispensed with most of DuPont's services. These two laboratories signaled DuPont's entry into the knowledge game. Over the years DuPont proved itself to be an adept at the game. Among other things, its laboratories delivered cellophane, rayon, Teflon, neoprene, nylon, Dacron, Lycra and Kevlar to the company. By 1958 DuPont dominated the US chemical industry. Knowledge continued to be its focus. It employed roughly 4 percent of the industrial chemists in the US, so many PhDs that it equaled about a third of the number in the US academic system and it spent, on average, about double that of its competitors on basic research.[7]

DuPont was not the only company whose business strategies pivoted around investment in research. Other companies also entered the knowledge game. General Electric's laboratory was established in 1900, AT&T set one up in 1907 and Westinghouse in 1903.[8] The more companies that went down the path of large-scale industrial research, the more that followed. By the end of the first decade of the 20th century Western Electric, Electric Storage Battery, International Harvester, Corn Products, General Chemical, Goodrich Rubber, Corning Glass, National Carbon, Parke Davis and E. R. Squibb all had large-scale research departments.[9] It was a pattern to be found in all industries. American Cotton Oil and National Lead had established labs to research their products in the 1890s. Between 1921 and 1941 the number of industrial research laboratories went from 300 to 2,200. These laboratories employed more than 70,000 research staff. In 20 years the US had built an industrial research structure that towered over that of other nations (with Germany perhaps the exception). Like a vortex this structure drew in much of the best and brightest scientific talent in the country, as well as talent from abroad. GE's lab grew from a staff of 102 in 1906 to 555 in 1929 and, by 1925, Bell Labs employed 3,600 with the physicist C. J. Davisson, the first Nobel Prize winner to come out of Bell Labs.[10] Graduates working for these large companies were given some of the best-equipped laboratories in the country and salaries exceeding anything they were likely to earn in the university system. Universities themselves became more and more dependent on funding from large corporations like DuPont. These companies understood that their needs for highly skilled scientific labor could be met only through healthy science faculties. Corporate funds flowed to universities.

Knowledge as the basic resource of economic production arrived before the great industrial production run of the 20th century. In essence, it laid the foundation for that run. Large, sophisticated laboratories staffed by thousands of researchers enabled the strategy of product diversification that characterized the chemical, electrical, automobile and machine industries. Chemical companies like Monsanto and DuPont started from a narrow technological base, the chemistry of saccharin in the case of the former and nitro-cellulose in the case of the latter. Research turned that base into many different product lines. Nitro-cellulose technology, for instance, gave DuPont "artificial leather, rayon and other textiles, paints, varnishes and dyes, cellulose, and plastic products."[11] This knowledge-based strategy of diversification brought with it a new form of corporate organization, the "integrated, multidepartmental enterprise."[12] Its basic form was that of autonomous divisions strategically coordinated by a general office. This structure was widely adopted by American companies as they set about the task of expanding into overseas markets after World War II.

The entrepreneurs of the great companies of the early 20th century understood the importance of knowledge better than most. The financier J. P. Morgan was a longtime supporter of Edison, investing heavily in his electric light companies and serving on the board of General Electric until he died in 1913.[13] Henry Ford also saw the importance of Edison's industrial laboratory to the industrial age: "It is the fashion to call this the age of industry...Rather, we should call it the age of Edison. For he is the founder of modern industry in this country."[14] Edison's laboratory was a footbridge between the world of scientific research and competitive advantage in the business world. In the hands of the corporate giants of the 20th century that footbridge became a multilane highway. Most of the traffic would come to travel in the direction of the business world.

For individual scientists who participated in the emerging systems of industrial scientific research there was only one tiny devil hidden among the corporate organizational detail governing their lives. Before they could publish anything they had to clear it with the lawyers. The lawyers often said no or placed limits on what they could publish. The scientists soon learned that all scientific communication with outsiders had to be vetted by their legal departments. They had joined a system in which knowledge was no longer thought of as a public good.

PATENT LOCKS ON PUBLIC GOODS

There is a well-known problem about public goods in economic theory. The market is not good at generating them because individuals find it hard to make a profit in their production. Knowledge is a case in point. Knowledge that is useful can be used over and over again without any individual consumer depriving another of the use of that knowledge. We can all simultaneously use the times tables. A problem arises if one person funds the cost of discovering the useful knowledge. How is that person to make a profit? Without some form of property right in the knowledge, others can appropriate the knowledge without any obligation to contribute toward the cost of its production. Patents are one form of social invention to deal with this problem.

A fairy story was used by the patent attorney profession to justify the patent system to outsiders. The patent, it was said, was a contract between the state and the inventor in which the inventor disclosed his or her invention to the world in return for a limited period of monopoly. Once the knowledge was made public everybody would have the benefit of it and, after the patent period had expired everybody could make the invention to which the knowledge related. In this way the story had a happy ending. The inventor benefited and so did society.

But the corporatized system of scientific research that the J. P. Morgans of the 20th century financed and the Henry Fords built had little time for fairy stories. The only ending the engineers of this system had in mind was one in which the items of knowledge that had turned a profit remained in private control for as long as possible. Here, corporations faced a problem, for patents typically could be held for only 16 or 17 years. The patent system had to be re-jigged so that it allowed corporations to retain control over commercially valuable knowledge for much longer periods of time. There were issues relating to the acquisition of knowledge. It was in the first instance the individual inventor who was entitled to the patent. This potentially gave individual employees some bargaining power. There were other problems. Before a patent could be granted to an inventor he had to satisfy the requirement of inventiveness. One could not get a patent monopoly for yesterday's mousetrap. But how high was the standard of inventiveness to be set? Just how creative did inventors have to be? How big a leap did they have to make in their particular field? It was also becoming clear that in industries like the chemical industry much of the work was time-consuming and tedious, requiring great resources rather than inventiveness. Finding a useful new dye required a lot of testing rather than invention. The same was to be true of the biotechnology and semiconductor chip industries later in the century. As some patent attorney agents in a 1993 interview remarked to one of us in a quiet moment of reflection, after the discovery of the DNA molecule and some of the early technology relating to recombinant DNA most of what had to be done in biotechnology was pretty well obvious, meaning noninventive. Setting the bar of inventiveness at too high a level would have meant, however, that many corporate players would have failed to obtain patents in these fields.

From the point of view of the corporate control of knowledge, the patent system was full of uncertainties. The public contract idea underpinning it, in which individual inventors had to make a genuine contribution to the industrial arts in exchange for a monopoly privilege from the state, suggested that patents should not be granted too easily. For corporations the patent system had really to function more as a public guarantee of returns on private investment than as an opportunity to make returns. The stronger the patent monopoly the more certainty there would be for these players. Whether or not stronger patents resulted in more innovation was another question. The main function of the patent system had to be investment guarantee.

PATENT LOCKSMITHS—THE PATENT PROFESSION

It was the patent profession rather than the corporations themselves that saw the potential benefits of the patent system to the corporate sector. In England at least, this profession had been born of the need by inventors for technical advice on the drafting of patent petitions and other documents.[15] This technical knowledge, along with the procedural intricacies of obtaining patents, allowed the profession over time to acquire enormous technocratic power, a power that was obscured by the mind-numbing technicality of patent "lore." It was they who devised the patent strategies that served corporations playing the knowledge game. It was they who campaigned for "reform" of the patent system. It was they who would, as the astute lackeys of the industrial research system, tilt, over a period of decades, the patent system in favor of private interests at the expense of the public interest.

One example of a highly influential figure in the development of a corporatized US patent law system was Edwin J. Prindle. Like his father he entered the patent bar, working in the US Patent Office till 1899. In 1905 he moved to New York where he established a successful patent practice. Prindle was a great lover of the patent system. He once observed in an address that:

> Our Patent System has been *the* primary factor in making the United States foremost among the nations in agriculture, inventing and manufacturing. While, of course there were other factors, the Patent System was by far the most potent one.[16]

Prindle was not, however, simply a starry-eyed patent enthusiast. As the secretary of the Patent Committee of the National Research Council he became the key player in shaping changes in patent procedure:

> He selected those who appeared before the various congressional committees in their hearings held in advance of and to guide their actions, and took charge of the witnesses so appearing. He assisted in preparing the provisions which eventuated in the Nolan and Lampert bills and he directed the operations in great part which led the technical and scientific organizations to take pronounced action on these bills.[17]

Aside from his position on the National Research Council, Prindle was, among other things, the president of the New York Patent Law Association, and the chairman of the Patent Committee of the American Chemical Society.

Perhaps more importantly it was through his writing that Prindle began to alert those in business to the full potential of the patent system. He wrote a highly influential set of articles on "Patents in Manufacturing Business" that were subsequently turned into book form. His main message was that corporations had to see the patent system as a fundamental tool of business:

> Patents are the best and most effective means of controlling competition. They occasionally give absolute command of the market, enabling their owner to name the price without regard to cost of production... The power which a patentee has to dictate the conditions under which his monopoly may be exercised has been used to form trade agreements throughout practically entire industries, and if the purpose of the combination is primarily to secure benefit from the patent monopoly, the combination is legitimate. Under such combinations there can be effective agreements as to prices maintained.[18]

Much the same conclusion was being reached in Germany. The German writer Hermann Isay observed in 1923 that "no other industries have at their disposal for cartelizing purposes as effective a device as the manufacturing industries have. This auxiliary device is the patent."[19]

Knowledge about patents became as crucial to corporations as knowledge about inventions. Having made scientific labor part of their internal structure via the mechanism of the industrial laboratory, corporations made

patent knowledge part of their internal structure by forming patent departments. Establishing patent departments was a natural extension of the multi-
department structure that corporations were in any case developing. Patent
departments were among the earliest departments created, at least in the
US. In England there were also some early examples of corporate patent
departments; British Westinghouse Electrical set up a patent department in
1897.[20] Where parent US companies had set up patent departments British
subsidiaries would often follow suit. Patent litigation between companies
was also sometimes a trigger for the establishment of a patent department.
Here again Edison had pointed the way, for he had at his Menlo laboratories appointed a patent draftsman.

Corporate patent departments and legal divisions became the overseers
of a corporation's most important assets—its intellectual property rights,
especially its trademarks, trade secrets and patents. Intellectual property
lawyers in these departments had several important functions. They functioned as patent police, keeping a watchful eye on the publishing behavior
of the scientists in the laboratory. For scientists, the path to scientific immor-
tality did not lie in having one's name on a lot of patent applications. Rather
it lay in publication in publicly accessible journals. Publication, however,
spelled death for a patent application. If even a hint of an invention was
thrown out in a paper that was published before a patent application had
been filed, that publication could be used to attack the patent.

DuPont's experience with some of its nylon patents reveals the hard-
nosed way in which the knowledge game was played using patents. A publication by a DuPont employee in 1931 relating to the making of nylon
allowed I. G. Farben in 1938 to develop nylon 6, somewhat undermining the
patent position DuPont had developed in relation to its own nylon
patents.[21] After that experience DuPont tightened its previously liberal policy on the publication of scientific papers by employees. Tough internal procedures were set up to scrutinize any proposed publication by a DuPont
scientist. Since lawyers generally think that too much caution is never
enough, the upshot was that some scientific papers did not get published.
DuPont began to get a reputation among the general scientific community
for feeding off the research efforts of others without returning anything to
that community.[22] Its obsession with patent protection conferred upon it the
reputation of being a free-rider.

But it was not only DuPont that set up rigid procedures for the surveillance of scientific publishing by research employees. All companies went
down this path. Each company knew that it had to have a strong portfolio
of patents so it could negotiate licensing deals for the use of technology
with other companies from a position of strength. Each company in this
game knew that it was unlikely to have all the technology it needed to manufacture a given product. "Nobody," as one patent attorney put it, "has it
all." This meant that it would have to license in the technology. It could be
sure of getting the license only if it had something to offer in return. Cross-
licensing, in other words, was really only a game for equals. Even more

importantly, each company knew that there was another calculation running silently in the background. In the biggest product markets, large companies would cross-license provided that they did not sense any weakness in the patent position of the other players. If they smelt a weakness and the market share they would gain by overturning the patent was large enough, it made sense to go after the patent in the courts. In this world it was dangerous for even the biggest shark to bleed in the water. Thus all companies carefully policed the publishing activities of their scientists.

Despite the best procedures things still went wrong; knowledge would slip through the net. In 1980 a researcher at IBM, Mark Levenson, discovered a way to eliminate the fuzziness of light that was being shone through tiny slits.[23] Computer chip manufacturers used this technique as part of a process in creating the complex microcircuitry of the chip. Levenson's discovery meant that they could work to ever higher levels of fineness and continue to use light in the imprinting process. Levenson wrote up the research and sent it to the lawyers. That was 1981. But the lawyers had met their quota for patent optics that year and so a patent was not pursued. The following year Levenson's discovery was included in a polymer patent, that quota not having been filled. For a variety of reasons the patent ended up being dropped. The knowledge was free to travel. Levenson masks, as they became known in the industry, turned out to be crucial. IBM was left in later years with the option of buying the technology from Toshiba.

Aside from vetting publication proposals from their own scientists, patent departments watched the publishing and patenting activity of other companies. One of their main jobs was to neutralize the effects of patents belonging to other corporations. Legal departments would carefully scrutinize the patents and patent applications of competitors, assessing them for strength and weakness. This information would be used in the bargaining and litigation games that corporations played with each other in their struggles to obtain or preserve "turf" in some domain of technological knowledge. Sometimes the patent knowledge would be used to overturn another company's patent and sometimes it would be used to counter the threat of litigation. A company might react to the threat of litigation from an opponent by saying "you claim that we are infringing your patent x, but we think you are infringing our patent y." The threat of mutually assured litigation costs saw many possible patent disputes quietly settled. In order to be successful in these negotiations it was vital for each company to acquire as much knowledge as possible about the other side's patent strengths, as well as maintaining a strong patent portfolio itself. Companies became systematic in the way they acquired patents, with companies like IBM setting themselves patent quotas in particular fields of technology.

The most important function of patent departments was, of course, to file for and obtain patents. It was the task of a patent department to weave a web of patents around a particular technology, a web so thick no one could steer through it, or even think to try. DuPont did this with cellophane, warning Union Carbide:

that any other company that tried to manufacture cellophane would be in difficulty with many patents in view of the long time we have been working on cellophane and the amount of work which has been done not only to strengthen the position with regard to cellophane but to build up a defensive patent situation as well.[24]

Drafting patent applications developed into a special kind of art. Since knowledge was the basis of competitive advantage, it followed for all companies that they should disclose as little of their knowledge as possible. But the patent system required the disclosure of the invention to the public. Over time the patent attorney profession developed two kinds of solution to this problem. Some of the core knowledge related to the invention was kept back from the patent system as private "know-how." Know-how was usually the subject of a separate licensing arrangement between commercial parties. Without the know-how a patent license was worth less and sometimes not much at all. The second solution to the problem of public disclosure was a drafting one. Patents were drafted in ways that satisfied the patent office, but were virtually useless to public readers of the documents. The best patent attorneys took the art of the "empty" but valid patent specification to spectacular heights. As we shall see a little later, many German chemical patents were drafted in such a way as to mask the working of the invention. During World War I, the Western allies confiscated patents belonging to German chemical companies, but to little avail. These companies had kept careful control of the know-how. The German patents did very little to help the US, British and French chemical industries and in fact after the war these industries went back to forming cartels, most notably with the German company I. G. Farben, such was its dominance in the chemical industry.[25] Patent offices around the world continue to stockpile patent documents that are misleading or incomplete. The main purpose of this documentation is not, however, to constitute a public domain of technological knowledge. As will become clear, its purpose is to service the administrative and coordination needs of global knowledge cartels.

Weaving patent webs around knowledge was not a strategy that DuPont or other US corporations dreamt up for themselves. They had learned it from the German chemical industry. The German chemical industry employed thousands of chemists and their output was measured by thousands of patents. Companies like Bayer and Badische Anilin Fabrik held hundreds of patents in the US. German industry held in total approximately 4,500 US patents, creating a "colossal obstacle to the development of the American dyestuff industry."[26]

The shift toward the use of patents by US business was swift. Two things happened. First, the number of patents being granted in the US went up. At the end of 1870, 120,573 patents in total had been issued. By 1911 that number had jumped to 1,002,478.[27] Second, the nature of patent ownership underwent a change. In the 19th century most patents were owned by individuals. Surprisingly early in the 20th century the bulk of patents came to be owned by big business. By 1930, for example, it was clear that of the patents being assigned before they were actually issued, most were going into the hands of US corporations.[28] Individuals continued to troop through the patent system, complaining no doubt about its procedures and costs in the way that "Old John" had in Dickens's *A Poor Man's Tale of a Patent*. The patent system was society's enticing promise of a just reward for an inventor's contribution to the public good. The promise of a golden patent continued to suck individual inventors into the patent system. The patent attorney profession, which had swollen in number to service the demands of big business, played the role of mythmaker, portraying the system as the servant of the heroic inventor. Underneath the promises the patent system was becoming the sophisticated bureaucratic arm of big business, a system that big players used to outmaneuver opponents or, where this was not possible, to unite with them.

Intellectual property rights and their globalization in the 20th century allowed business to echo a medieval form of organization—the guild. The knowledge guild based on intellectual property rights, we shall see in the next section, allowed international business to address two problems that had plagued it: the illegality of cartels and the problem of dishonest individual cartel members.

GLOBAL KNOWLEDGE CARTELS

Weaving patent webs was an expensive business, way beyond what small players could afford. But in the very large markets that companies like DuPont and AT&T played in, it was a comparatively small cost, especially in relation to the benefits that such a web might deliver. One of those benefits was that it enabled large corporations to divide international markets among themselves. Patents were not necessary to the formation of a cartel, but they were a very useful way of disguising and, most importantly, enforcing one. The need to disguise a cartel in the UK was less pressing since competition was understood to be an arrangement best left to the mutual understandings of gentlemen. Membership in one, like the membership in an exclusive club, was a sign of the highest success. In the US the hazard of cartel membership was greater. The real danger came from both state and federal legislatures, which had, in the face of public hostility to a cartelized US economy, enacted antitrust legislation. Business confronted by "trust busters" bent on smashing their cartels had to find another way to continue them. They were in the market for a solution to their problems, a solution that intellectual property lawyers were to provide in the form of the knowledge game.

In order to understand the genesis of the knowledge game we need to backtrack a little and understand the predicament of cartels in the US of the 19th century. Cartels are born of a desire by business to dominate markets, as opposed to the unpleasant fate of being dominated by them. Individual producers come to an arrangement under which they fix the price of a commodity or limit the production of that commodity. Cartels were omnipresent in 19th-century US business life. They were to be found in the lumber, woodware, flooring, furniture, casket, leather, petroleum, rubber, footwear, explosives, glass, paper, iron, steel, copper, brass, lead, metals and hardware industries.[29] Very often cartel arrangements would take the form of quite detailed articles of association. So, for example, the Kentucky Distillers in 1888 drafted an agreement determining that the quantity of whiskey to be made in 1889 was to be a maximum of 11,000,000 gallons, with a formula for deciding how many gallons each distiller was entitled to make.[30] The makers of gunpowder formalized arrangements among themselves in an agreement called "Articles of Association of the Manufacturers of Gunpowder." The purpose of the cartel was to fix the price of gunpowder:

> We, the undersigned, Manufacturers of Gunpowder, for the purpose of ensuring an equitable adjustment of prices and terms for sales of powder throughout the United States, hereby agree to the subjoined Articles of Association, to which we severally pledge for ourselves, and all under our control, *rigid and honorable adherence* [emphasis added].[31]

But the gunpowder cartel, the distillers' cartel and many others like them faced a problem that brought them undone. Individual cartel members did not always "rigidly and honorably" adhere to the articles of association. There was always the temptation for, say, a Kentucky distiller to make a few extra gallons of whiskey and slip it to some "good ole boys" a little cheaper. The more distillers who cheated, the more whiskey hit the market, thereby exceeding the cartel's limit on production.

All cartels faced the problem that individual cartel members might defect from the deals that had been agreed to by all the members. The defectors would manufacture more than their quota or sell more cheaply than was agreed. Loyalty was often a commodity in short supply among cartelists.

It was not possible to discipline the greedier members of a cartel by taking them to court, since courts would not enforce such agreements. The common law admittedly had no hard and fast rules about when it was illegal to create a monopoly, but when the contract in question limited supply or fixed the price of a commodity it was almost certain to be unenforceable.[32] Freedom of contract did not extend to the freedom to silence competition. What was known as the restraint of trade doctrine stood in the way of cartel members being able to go to the courts to solve their enforcement problem.

Cartel members turned to the use of the trust to help them deal with the problem of defection. The medieval device of the trust obliged the trustee (nominally the legal owner) to manage the trust on behalf of those in whose beneficial interest the trust was constituted. From the point of view of cartel members its chief virtue was that it allowed independent business entities to be centrally managed. Essentially, companies would transfer shares to a board of trustees who would then manage the trust on behalf of the companies. Crucially, price control and production could then be centrally managed. The first great trust to be formed for these purposes was the Standard Oil Trust Agreement of 1879. Under the terms of the trust 30 companies turned over their stock and interests to three trustees who would manage the trust for the "exclusive use and benefit" of the individuals named in the trust. John D. Rockefeller, one of the beneficiaries of the trust, got the lion's share of the benefits.[33]

Other gigantic trusts like the American Cotton Oil Trust, the Distillers' and Cattle Feeders' Trust and the Sugar Refineries Trust soon strode across the business landscape. The power of these trusts to determine economic and social life brought with it public outrage, not least because the cheaper prices that consumers were assured would follow the creation of these large efficient entities never came to pass.[34] Legislatures had to treat their connections with monopolists with great care. They also had to be seen to be doing something. Antitrust statutes prohibiting the use of trusts for the purposes of obtaining a monopoly were passed in a number of states including Maine (1889), Michigan (1889) and Kentucky (1890).[35] Senator Sherman introduced into Congress a bill that was passed in 1890—the Sherman Antitrust Act.

Some of the large trusts were declared illegal by the courts, most notably the Standard Oil Trust. It became clear to business that trusts were not the promised land for cartels. With public anger swirling around trusts, legislation permitting one company to hold the stock of a rival began to make its appearance in US states in the 1890s, "put quietly through under the cover of antitrust agitation, while the public, led by the newspapers, were looking somewhere else."[36] Again the idea was to use a legal device, the holding company, as a means of coordinating the members of a cartel. Holding companies, however, which were established for the purpose of achieving a monopoly, were declared illegal.[37]

Many US businesses having gone through a period of merger and consolidation (a response to trust busting) in the last decade of the 19th century stood, at the beginning of the 20th, profoundly transformed. Although many were dominated by a small group of individuals, they were no longer family businesses. They had begun a process of reorganization that would see some of them become great globally operating corporations. Creating new administrative structures to support their increased size and plans for expansion was one immediate problem that they faced.[38] They were also left with the problem of how best to organize and enforce a cartel. The cartelized US economy of the previous century had demonstrated to business that this was the best way to solve problems of overproduction and competition. The common law doctrine of restraint of trade stood in the way of the enforcement of articles of association setting up a simple price-fixing cartel. Similarly, trusts and holding companies had proved to be unreliable legal devices through which to effect a cartel. There was also the added complication that Congress had passed the Sherman Act. The act went further than the common law. Cartels faced the prospect of criminal prosecution under the act. At first, successful prosecutions under the act were slow in coming; concentrations of market power in excess of 70 percent and 80 percent were not considered violations of the provisions of the Act by the courts.[39] Slowly this changed. The Sherman Act proved to be a thorn in the side of big business over the coming decades.

The presence of a competition authority made the formation of international cartels a riskier proposition. The Antitrust Division had lawyers on its staff. Legal scheming to set up cartels could no longer be so transparent in the way that the use of articles of association or the trust had been. These contrivances were too easy for other lawyers to spot. Much denser legal thickets were needed to hide cartels from the eyes of competition lawyers. These thickets of rules also had to allow companies to fix price, control production and divide territories among themselves. As Prindle and others familiar with patent law had been arguing, patents offered large companies just these possibilities. Patents were a legally recognized form of monopoly that gave inventors a strong form of control over the production and price of the invention. Importantly, restrictions over price and production could form part of the patent license agreement. Such restrictions were in many cases regarded by the courts as a legitimate form of exploitation of a proprietary right. Attacking patent-based cartels was far harder for a competition authority, for now it had to face the argument that it was interfering in the use of private property. The legal representatives of owners of large intellectual property holdings in the 20th century worked very hard to remove the stigma of monopoly from intellectual property. They knew that once the veil of private property was drawn over what was essentially a state-granted monopoly privilege, it would be much harder for public authorities to question the nature of the business arrangements that individual competitors reached with each other using those privileges.

The knowledge game was not created overnight. Rather it evolved, its nature and complexity refined by many legal hands over the generations. The law was something of a contradictory resource for the designers of the knowledge game. There were patent law cases emphasizing the absolute nature of the patentee's monopoly, including the right to impose pricing restrictions and the fact that the exercise of patent rights did not contradict the Sherman Act. This line of authority had to be carefully nurtured.[40] Those cases elevating the public purpose of the patent grant had to be bypassed, left as tiny islands in a river that flowed only to strengthen the rights of the patent holder. Other aspects of the knowledge game also had to be improved. The essence of the knowledge game was to propertize as much knowledge as possible. Restrictions on patentability had to be removed. As corporate laboratories of knowledge ventured more and more into the biological sciences it became clear that the restriction on the patenting of discoveries would have to be overcome. How else could the players in the knowledge game come to have patent control over the genes to be found in nature? Patents were not the only building blocks of the knowledge game. Copyright and trademarks also became fundamental components of the game.

None of the early builders of the knowledge game saw it revealed in all its great detail. There was no prescient designer laying down a blueprint for future artisans to follow. Instead there was corporate strategy creating needs, above all the need to order markets; there was the contradictory, rule-bound complexity of the law; and there were entrepreneurial legal types like Prindle who saw in intellectual property rights developmental possibilities that would allow ordinary old-fashioned commodity cartels to re-establish themselves as knowledge cartels, but cartels nevertheless.

THE KNOWLEDGE GAME

The basic strategy of the players in the knowledge game came to this. Their laboratories would produce knowledge that would be developed into products, for which their legal divisions would secure an impregnable patent position. Use was also made of trademarks, trade secret law and copyright. The quest for knowledge was really the quest for monopoly. Competitors could be kept out or made to pay high royalties, depending on the way the numbers panned out. Alternatively, intellectual property rights and licenses could be used to structure a global knowledge cartel.

Commodity markets, so far as these knowledge players were concerned, were places to stay out of, for they were competitive markets, places where, for once, marginal cost did meet marginal revenue, where shareholders' expectations would be disappointed and the only benefits were to consumers and society. The onetime chairman of IBM, John Akers, once told a meeting that IBM would get out of the PC industry "if it ever became a 'commodity' business."[41] IBM, of course, had lived for many decades on profit margins in excess of 30 percent. Anything below double figures was a disaster. It was the same for other companies in the knowledge game. Once a market became a commodity market, that is to say an open market that others could enter, thereby removing the possibility of supranormal profits, knowledge companies left that market in a huff. So, for example, when parts of the plastics business turned competitive DuPont took its leave. Unable to achieve a dominant patent position in polypropylene DuPont abandoned its plans to manufacture it, and while it did manufacture linear polyethylene it took a long time to enter the market and then achieved disappointing results precisely because it was a competitive market.[42] It scaled back its efforts.

In the US, the knowledge game before World War II was confined to a relatively small number of players. In 1938 five industries employed 75 percent of the staff involved in industrial research: the chemical, power machinery, electrical, petroleum and rubber industries.[43] Each of these industries had its heavy hitters: DuPont, General Electric, General Motors, International Harvesters, United States Rubber and Goodrich and the various Standard Oil companies. These giants became dependent on a strategy of knowledge-led product diversification for their continued growth. After World War II they looked to new markets for these products.

American companies began a process of expansion, especially into Europe. The companies that made knowledge their focus became responsible for much of the investment in foreign markets.[44]

The knowledge game as it developed took on cooperative and non-cooperative dimensions. The cooperative knowledge game usually culminated in a cartel. The most obvious sign that a cooperative knowledge game was in swing between two or more corporations was the existence of an agreement on patents and the sharing of technical knowledge. Sometimes cooperation was achieved under the cover of apparently ferocious litigation. The Patent and Processes Agreement that DuPont concluded with the UK's Imperial Chemical Industries (ICI) in 1929 is a good example of the way in which patents were used to mask cartels. Before that agreement DuPont and Nobel (ICI's predecessor) had reached similar agreements in 1920 and 1926 on the exchange of patents and processes in relation to explosives. DuPont had been successfully prosecuted under the Sherman Act in 1913 for running an explosives cartel. The 1920 agreement was described by Sir Harry McGowan, the British chairman of Nobel who was used to the British version of competition, as "a camouflage" for all the relationships between Nobel and DuPont.[45] Back in the US, with one nervous eye on the Antitrust Division, DuPont strenuously denied the cartelish import of Sir Harry's words.

Patent-sharing agreements did exactly the same things that good old-fashioned cartel agreements did. They divided up territories, set prices and controlled production. The 1929 agreement between ICI and DuPont, for instance, divided the world into exclusive and nonexclusive territories. DuPont took North and South America for its exclusive use and ICI acquired the British Empire. Canada was shared between them by means of exclusive licenses. Only now the members of the knowledge cartel were no longer engaged in a conspiracy against the public, but they were rather exercising rights of private property. The failure to adhere to the terms of the agreement usually produced a breach-of-license issue and could be settled in court or, if privacy was important to the parties concerned, through international arbitration and mediation. Players in the knowledge game had, in other words, a way to deal with the enforcement problem that had beset the commodity cartels of earlier years.

The use of intellectual property rights to structure and enforce cartels spread between the two world wars. Cartels became, in the words of one study, the "outstanding characteristic of business."[46] Intellectual property became the outstanding marker of knowledge cartels.

During this period the knowledge game became a truly international game. The electric lamp cartel agreement, which was signed on 23 December 1924 by the world's leading producers (Osram, Philips, Tungsram, International General Electric), based its division of the world market on the exchange of patents. In 1919 General Electric had created a subsidiary, the International General Electric Company, assigning to it its trademarks and coming to a cross-licensing arrangement with it on the use of patents. The purpose behind this reshuffle of intellectual property rights was to use

International General Electric to negotiate market-sharing agreements with foreign manufacturers, ensuring that they did not compete in the US market. Ironically, one of the few sources of competition for General Electric came from the Soviet Union, which, because of its lack of Western-style intellectual property rights, meant that its manufacturers had trouble participating in knowledge cartels.[47] I. G. Farben used its stock of patents in synthetic rubber to strike deals with DuPont and Standard over the rubber markets. The tendrils of patent law reached into all aspects of the rubber business and related chemical industries. I. G. Farben agreed to pass on to Standard any patents it acquired in the chemical field of relevance to the oil business and in exchange Standard offered control to I. G. Farben of chemical patents that were not strongly related to the oil industry. Each player wanted to make sure that innovations in knowledge in its core areas of interest would flow back to it.

The partitioning of the world's markets using intellectual property rights occurred in all of the world's key industries between the wars. The rubber cartel, the nitrogen cartel, the aluminium cartel, the magnesium cartel and the electric light cartel were woven together through the thread of intellectual property agreements. Hardly an industry escaped the touch of intellectual property law. In the US motion picture industry the main players formed in 1908 the Motion Picture Patents Company. The company was a patent pool; only members of the company were licensed to produce pictures. The independents in the industry retreated from New York to a place called Hollywood where the cost of production was cheaper. For a variety of reasons the Patents Company lost its influence, but patents remained important, especially with invention of the "talkies." In the mid-1930s one commentator described the industry in the following way:

> The entire motion picture industry, therefore, through patent ownership, is indirectly under a monopoly control far beyond the early aspirations of the Motion Picture Patents Corporation...The peak figures in American finance, Morgan and Rockefeller, either indirectly through sound-equipment control or directly by financial control or backing, now own the motion picture industry.[48]

Copyright was also a means of ascension to the knowledge game. The American Publishers' Association, for example, used copyright to fix the retail price of books.[49] The motion picture industry used copyright licenses to fix the price of admission to cinemas.[50]

After World War II the knowledge game continued, the only real danger to its players coming from competition regulation and then only the US Antitrust Division. Most other countries had not made competition law enforcement a priority, even if they possessed a competition law. In fact, the Antitrust Division was sometimes the only hope of individuals working in the industries of small countries that were in the grip of a powerful global knowledge cartel. Australian booksellers found themselves in the thrall of just such a cartel. After the war US and English publishers entered into an agreement called the "British Publishers Traditional Market Agreement." Under the agreement British publishers agreed not to compete in the US market and in return they received the 70 or so countries that were or had been Commonwealth members. The Continent remained open for competition. Knowledge cartels featuring US and English players would often re-create an imperial past when they parceled up the markets of sovereign states. The Australian book market, of course, became the private hunting ground of members of the British Publishers Association. A situation in which British publishers placed a commercial filter over what books reached the Australian public and at what price deeply angered a bookseller in South Australia called Max Harris. He, along with some others, brought the existence of this agreement to the attention of the US Antitrust Division. Confronted by the prospect of an antitrust action, the US publishers ultimately agreed to a consent decree that broke the Traditional Market Agreement.[51] Not much changed in Australia, however. Under Australian copyright (derived largely from England) British publishers could still negotiate exclusive licensing arrangements for the importation of books into Australia. Australia remained a closed market. Even today its book market, like the book market of many countries, has copyright barriers that prevent it from being a fully open market.

The cooperative knowledge game never rested on foundations of deep friendship. Members of knowledge cartels may have swapped patents, but know-how was kept under tight wraps even among cartel members. It was a complaint of ICI, for instance, that DuPont was holding out on it in terms of communicating its research and therefore not honoring the spirit of the patent agreement between the two.[52] Knowledge cartels were not about sharing knowledge, avoiding the duplication of research, achieving efficiencies and so on. They were about the privatization of knowledge that would grant the holder of that knowledge the power to discipline markets. When the opportunity came to deprive others of their patent rights it was rarely neglected. Here we come to the noncooperative dimensions of the knowledge game.

World War I provided the US chemical industry with an excuse to strip German industry of key chemical patents. Prior to the outbreak of World War I, the US was heavily dependent on Germany for the import of dyestuffs and pharmaceuticals, as well as chemicals related to the manufacture of explosives. German industry had, as was mentioned earlier, locked up much of this crucial knowledge by means of patents: "These patents were obviously obtained and held [in the US] in order to prevent the formation of the American dye industry and to make impossible importation from other countries."[53] These patents, like modern biotechnology patents, were drafted in ways to achieve maximum coverage of chemical science. Trademarks and copyright were also part of the German defense structure. The goal of disclosure of the invention to the public was not uppermost in the minds of the patent attorneys who drafted these claims:

[I]t must be understood that many of these patents are bogus, that is to say, contain deliberate misstatements for the purpose of misleading inquiring minds as to the manner in which important products are manufactured by the firm. In fact, some German patents are drawn for the purpose of discouraging investigation by more practical methods: thus, any one who attempted to repeat the method for manufacturing a dye stuff protected by Salzmann and Kruger in the German patent No. 12096 would be pretty certain to kill himself during the operation.[54]

During the war these German intellectual property rights had been seized in the US under the Trading with the Enemy Act of 1917. The war had been a boon to the US chemical industry. The importation of German products into the US had ceased. Demand for these products had to be met by domestic manufacturers. US chemical manufacturers formed an association to exploit this market opportunity. Peace brought with it a problem. The monopoly they collectively acquired during the war in supplying the US market would be ruined once German industry began supplying the export market. US industry would once again find itself in competition with a formidable opponent. Prior to the war the German chemical industry was the most advanced in the world. Individuals from the US chemical industry working with the US Alien Property Custodian devised a plan to permanently acquire the German patents. Members of the chemical industry incorporated the Chemical Foundation in Delaware in 1919. The shareholders in this company were select members of the chemical club that had done so well during the war years. A list of desired patents to be seized and sold to the foundation was drawn up by members of the foundation. The patents were then sold to the foundation at a private sale at bargain-basement prices. The foundation acquired all the patents at a cost of US$250,000 or roughly US$50.00 per patent. Given that later the US government would introduce evidence that some of these patents like Salvarsan, neoSalvarsan and the Novocaine and Haber patents had an estimated value of US$18,000,000, the foundation on the day of the sale got a good deal.[55]

There were some minor irregularities that resulted in the US government bringing a suit against the foundation. A number of the officers of the Chemical Foundation also turned out to hold offices linked to the Alien Property Custodian. It was these individuals who had helped to fix the discount prices that the foundation paid for the German patents. The Alien Property Custodian himself, Francis Garavan, was, at the time he made the transfers, president of the Chemical Foundation. The US government lost its action in the Supreme Court, basically because different values apply when you are dealing with enemy property. The chemical industry, which had been outraged by what it considered to be its unpatriotic treatment by the US government, felt vindicated. The Chemical Foundation after all had been formed for a patriotic purpose. Its certificate of incorporation read that its purpose was to hold:

property and rights so acquired in a fiduciary capacity for the Americanization of such industries as may be affected thereby, for the exclusion or elimination of alien interests hostile or detrimental to the said industries, and for the advancement of chemical and allied science and industry in the United States.[56]

The problem, though, was that once the Chemical Foundation members got ahold of the patents they were very reluctant to diffuse their benefits through US industry. Cartelism is a highly addictive way of life.

The German chemical patents were at one level worthless. As the suit against the Chemical Foundation wound its way through the courts, the evidence showed that chemists following the instructions disclosed in the patents could not arrive at the promised result. The Germans had that valuable know-how. To an outsider, not in possession of this know-how, the patent was probably not worth even the US$50.00 per patent that the Chemical Foundation had paid. The French, for instance, had paid 2,500,000 francs in license fees for some German patents that they eventually had to abandon because they could not make them work successfully.[57] At another level, the German patents were worth their estimated millions. Competitors confronted by a thick wall of patents stretching over much of the chemical domain would often be deterred from climbing over it to do research in the field it made private. Testing such a large number of patents in court required money. By having so many patents held in different countries, the Germans could make it difficult for others to export to the markets of those countries. What the US had learned from World War I was, in the words of its president, that in the case of industries key to defense "too great reliance on foreign supply is *dangerous.*"[58] Foreign global knowledge cartels like the German chemical industry posed a real threat to US national security and economic interests. What US industry learned from German industry was that patents were matchless instruments of business domination. In the following decades the US patent profession put its energies into perfecting the use of this instrument.

THE CHANGING KNOWLEDGE GAME

After World War II, the knowledge game continued to bring great returns to those companies that had invested heavily in it. DuPont remained a leader in the synthetic fibers revolution. IBM became perhaps the best exemplar of the knowledge game. At its height, its spending on R&D roughly equaled one-tenth of all corporate expenditure on R&D in the US.[59] Its network of research laboratories had propelled it to a share of between 65 and 70 percent of the world's computer market (excluding communist bloc countries).[60] Surveys began to show that the US economy generally was building a comparative advantage in highly research-intensive industries: computing, electronics, chemicals, pharmaceuticals and scientific equipment.[61]

But there were different kinds of storm clouds gathering on the horizon that, as they started to roll in, made life for these successful players increasingly tough. To begin with, the costs of doing R&D continued to rise, but the returns from it began to drop. DuPont, worried by the trend, began an in-house analysis that confirmed its worst fears. R&D costs in the 1950s were three times what they were in the 1940s.[62] Despite spending more DuPont had fewer and fewer commercial products to show for it. Even worse, it was facing price competition. The great profits to be made in chemicals tempted more and more entrants. There were already established players like Dow, Monsanto and Union Carbide. Chemical knowledge continued to be diffused throughout the world by the universities, through journals and the career movements of chemical engineers and researchers. There were only so many patent battles that DuPont could fight and expect to win. The cozy cartelish way of life that predominated in the chemical industry prior to World War II had been given a nasty shock in the form of antitrust actions. Under Roosevelt, the Antitrust Division of the Justice Department was given more resources. The division, under its head Thurman W. Arnold, began some 180 antitrust actions between 1938 and 1942, about half the number of the previous 48 years.[63] This antitrust attack also made it dangerous for companies to acquire more knowledge by means of gobbling up smaller companies. It meant that they had to wear the cost of expensive research. The chemical industry was changing from a knowledge game to a commodity game. Nobody much liked this. The question was what to do about it.

In the case of DuPont, as with a number of other key chemical players, a strategic decision was taken to enter the life sciences business. Perhaps biology might deliver the kinds of profits in the new millennium that chemicals had in the first two-thirds of the 20th century. But before this shift could be made intellectual property protection for biological inventions would have to be much, much stronger. The knowledge game would have to acquire much tougher rules about who was to own the source of profits. Another strategy, the full force of which is only now emerging, was the decision by some corporations to do less basic research and rely on smaller companies and universities to do basic research. This required, however, the integration of universities into the knowledge game (see Chapters 10 and 14). They would, in effect, become the large-scale knowledge laboratories that the big corporate players needed in the knowledge economy.

Key players in the copyright industry were coming to similar conclusions about the need to change the rules of the game. The problem with copyright was that it was a leaky system. People could make use of bits of copyright information for free claiming that it was fair dealing, that the information was too insubstantial to merit protection or that what was being used was the idea and not the expression (copyright protects expression and not ideas). It would be preferable from the point of view of profits to have a world in which every single bit of information usage would attract a fee. The beauty of this is that information doesn't wear out. It could be endlessly recycled, repackaged and, provided the rules were properly defined, endlessly charged for. In this world every information transaction would attract a fee of some kind and the transaction would be repeated as many times as possible. In this world, unlike in the commodity markets, the consumer could never actually own the information, but merely pay for its use.

Bill Gates has shown a great intuitive understanding of the ways to use property in information to develop a pricing strategy. When in 1980 Gates of the fledgling Microsoft and Jack Sams of IBM were hammering out the deal for the supply of an operating system to IBM, Sams was expecting Gates to ask for a large one-off fee.[64] Instead Gates went for a small royalty on each IBM PC sold with DOS and a nonexclusive license thereby giving him the option of licensing other manufacturers. Similarly in 1985 when Gates was renegotiating with IBM over the provision of operating systems he more or less let IBM have DOS for free, but negotiated the right to charge other PC manufacturers for the supply of DOS. IBM agreed thinking it would always dominate the PC market. Once DOS became the standard in the PC industry copyright allowed Gates to maintain it as a proprietary standard. He was able to develop a pricing strategy based on use without ever parting with its ownership.

The knowledge game changed for other industries as well. The pharmaceutical industry, like the chemical industry, had gone through its happy times of cartels and price-fixing behavior. The discovery and patenting of broad-spectrum antibiotics, for example, saw a number of companies globally fix the prices of those drugs. But like the chemical industry, the pharmaceutical industry faced increasing R&D costs. The large industry players also faced competition from generic manufacturers. These manufacturers tended to service national markets. It was also becoming clear to the industry that the rate of discovery of new drugs based on the synthesis of chemical compounds had considerably declined.[65] Like the chemical industry, the pharmaceutical industry began to place its bets on the potential wonders of biotechnology. The leaders of this industry also wanted changes to the rules of the knowledge game. Sovereign states like India had used the patent system to develop a highly competitive generic industry that delivered quality drugs at cheap prices to its citizens. Indian patent law allowed pharmaceutical companies to obtain patents on processes, but not the products of those processes. The incentive for Indian pharmaceutical manufacturers was to make profits by finding cheaper and cheaper ways to make drugs.

The effect of permitting states like India to have a say about the rules of the knowledge game was an erosion of the corporate control of knowledge. The gaps in the patent system when it came to the global control of knowledge would have to be closed. In the international movie business states had quotas on the screening of foreign films, as a way of supporting their domestic film industry, thereby preventing the maximal exploitation of the copyright in US films. There was also the problem of copying. A way would have to be found to prevent states from interfering in the knowledge game to the detriment of its key corporate players. Another generation of designers would have to come forth and make their contribution to the hidden tapestry of the knowledge game so that the players in the game could continue to accrue the power necessary to discipline markets and, this time, states.

CHAPTER 4

Stealing from the Mind

MESSAGES

On 9 July 1982 an op-ed piece bearing the title "Stealing From the Mind" was published in the *New York Times*. Appearing under the name Barry MacTaggart, the then chairman and president of Pfizer International, its central charge was that US knowledge and inventions were being stolen. The culprits were other governments: Brazil, Canada, Mexico, India, Taiwan, South Korea, Italy and Spain. These governments, it was argued, designed laws allowing for US inventions to be "legally" taken. The World Intellectual Property Organization (WIPO) came in for criticism for "trying to grab high-technology inventions for underdeveloped countries" and contemplating treaty revisions that would "confer international legitimacy on the abrogation of patents."

Those at Pfizer who had been involved in the drafting of the piece had been hesitant about its release in the *New York Times*. The developing countries that were accused of theft were also important markets for Pfizer. Pfizer's strategists were also unsure about how the attack on WIPO would be received. This was an organization with a lot of developing country members. Thus far Pfizer's campaign to turn intellectual property protection into a trade issue had been confined to the usual Washington and business networks. Attacking WIPO in this highly public way was a new and risky step.

As it turned out, the company's strategists need not have worried. Expressions of support from many quarters including from within the US government rolled in. The op-ed piece had crystallized the views and feelings of many. "People came out of the woodwork," as one Pfizer employee told us in 1994. This response saw Pfizer push on with greater confidence with one of its goals, that of linking the issue of intellectual property protection to the trade regime. Two years after the op-ed piece, the US amended its Trade Act to allow a process of trade retaliation (known as the 301 process) to be used against countries that did not adequately protect US intellectual property rights. The proposal to do this attracted the support of important congressional committees. Pfizer had not achieved this legislative change single-handedly, but it had been one of the key players in obtaining a new direction for US trade policy. The op-ed piece also became a marker in another important way. It had cast WIPO as the representative of "international socialism" when it came to intellectual property rights. The support the op-ed piece had garnered suggested to Pfizer that it was not alone in its view that WIPO was running down standards of intellectual property protection. Even more importantly, it suggested that when the time came to move real standard-setting power over intellectual property away from WIPO, such a move would have advocates in US policy quarters.

As big a goal as getting better international protection for US intellectual property was, a few individuals at Pfizer had been tossing around an even bigger idea for the world's trade regime—the creation of a multilateral agreement on investment (MAI). This agreement would provide strong guarantees of security to individual investors, allowing them to invest in states free of the many restrictions that states had in the past placed on for-eign investment activity within their borders. Intellectual property would be one asset protected by such an agreement. Pfizer's challenge to WIPO was part of a broader strategy designed to secure a favorable investment regime for multinationals with global production needs. Pfizer saw, as one employee later told us, that the "locus" of where international intellectual property issues were debated had to be shifted. That new locus turned out to be the trade organization the General Agreement on Tariffs and Trade (GATT) and its successor, the World Trade Organization (WTO). WIPO would have to share its power and influence in the field of intellectual prop-erty standard-setting.

Nothing quite worked out, as we shall see, in the way the different par-ties involved in these trade negotiations expected. US business didn't get its multilateral agreement on investment (at least not yet), but it did achieve an agreement on intellectual property. The MAI, we were told in some 1994 interviews, would simply be a mopping-up exercise.

LAST RITES

After World War II, the US was clearly the world's most powerful economy. As the world entered a period of decolonization the sun began to set on the British Empire. More important than the loss of territory was the fact that the US dollar became the currency of world trade. The days when the Bank of England and London had presided over financial markets were a fading memory of the glory of empire. The new global financial institutions, the IMF and the World Bank, which had been created by states at Bretton Woods in New Hampshire in 1944, were to be located in Washington.

The period of reconstruction after World War 2 saw the US become a credit provider to Europe and Japan. Everyone wanted US dollars. US banks progressively expanded into overseas markets creating the era of multinational banking. US companies in knowledge-intensive industries (e.g., computing, electronics, chemicals, pharmaceuticals) began to establish overseas production facilities. US companies dominated the lists of the world's largest industrial enterprises. So, for instance, in 1962, 1967, 1972 and 1978 there were only two non-US companies in the list of the top ten of the world's largest industrial enterprises for each of those years. [1]

Possession of the world's largest companies and the world's biggest domestic market did not bring peace of mind to the US. There developed in the US in the 1970s and early 1980s a policy discourse of a US in decline. Loss of competitiveness became an issue. At first intellectual property did not feature in this talk of decline. That would come later. The fear about the loss of economic power was made more personal and therefore more real for the US through watching the "deindustrialization" of the UK, its onetime colonial master.[2] The UK, despite its commitment to free trade, was in deep economic trouble. Various statistics showed that it had declined dramatically as a manufacturing power (e.g., the level of the UK's manufacturing production in the mid-1980s was close to what it had been in the 1960s).[3]

Other data began to take on ominous significance. The massive share of world trade enjoyed by developed countries in the 1960s began to lessen in the 1970s. Developing countries like India and Brazil began to show leadership potential, albeit of a regional kind. At the same time new economic competitors emerged. The public images the US constructed of these rivals were neither friendly nor comforting. "The gang of four," "the Asian tigers," "the Dragon economies" could hardly do other than make the US uneasy about its share of world markets. Japan had already performed the economic miracle, but this was with US assistance and for all its economic prowess Japan seemed, when it came to global politics, to have embarked on a strategy of retreatism or nonintervention. Japan did not try to set the rules of the game; it tried to beat the West under its own rules. There was no guarantee that the new "tigers" would be so politically compliant.

Then the Japanese economic miracle began increasingly to wear on US nerves. Japanese manufacturing triumphs began to be seen as a portent of US deindustrialization. Public myths began to be constructed in the US about the "true" nature of this success. American ideas, American know-how were being stolen by the Japanese, it was widely believed. Like all public myths it had some basis in reality. Transistor technology had been patented by AT&T, but under US antitrust law it was required to issue patent licenses to qualified manufacturers. The Japanese company Tokyo Tsushin Kogyo Kabushiki Kasha (eventually to be known to the world as Sony) was granted a license by AT&T. The Japanese, in other words, acquired this US technology legitimately.[4] The trade surplus that Japan had with the US should have been welcomed for, if the theory of comparative advantage was right, it benefited both American consumers and in the long run the US economy. Instead, this trade surplus became a rallying point for protectionist elements within the US. US economists began to explore strategic trade theory. Various forms of "Japan bashing" began to occur, sometimes in crude xenophobic ways, which the mass media under the guise of reporting the news assiduously propagated (e.g., burly American auto workers smashing a Japanese car to pieces). Japan's trading successes gave protectionism within the US a strong political foothold. At the same time it helped the US economy by helping to keep down world interest rates, as well as enabling the Japanese to become lenders on world capital markets to countries like the US, which were becoming net borrowers of capital.[5]

By the time those who represented US intellectual property interests arrived on Capitol Hill to tell their story, they found an audience that was in the mood to do something concrete to remedy US economic problems. The story they would tell this audience was, in the style of Mark Twain, beautifully simple. Stronger property rights were needed to protect American ideas and industry. Better protection meant more jobs and these industries were the very ones that would restore the US to a positive trade balance with the world. It was always going to be a persuasive story. In the climate of insecurity about the political and economic future of the US, this story with its deeply nationalistic underpinnings made compelling listening. Its truth hardly mattered. In 1978 there was one Japanese company in the top 20 companies in the world — Toyota — and it was 20th. US economic hegemony was not really under threat. Perhaps what mattered about the story, though, was that it gave those in US policy circles a mission. The minority economies of the world like Singapore, Malaysia and Taiwan, which were not paying attention to US intellectual property rights, would be taught a lesson. Woven into the story was the protection of high technology, something that in the 1980s had become a symbol of a nation's economic and industrial virility. Absolutely crucial to the persuasive power of this story was economic analysis. The mode of analysis became the message. Economic reports turned the intellectual property story from one of moral transgression into the loss of markets and profit.

THE PROBLEMS

The scale and number of problems facing the US corporate elite playing the knowledge game at the end of the 1970s and early 1980s would test even their resources. Their private agenda was to take the knowledge game to new heights: expand the scope of its reach, prevent states from interfering in its rules and increase its profitability. Obviously they could not go to the US government and demand that it globalize intellectual property in order to allow the corporate knowledge elite to form new and better global knowledge cartels. An argument had to be found to persuade policy makers that intellectual property enforcement was the single most important issue facing the US economy, so important that the US government would have to stake the outcome of the entire Uruguay Round on a deal for intellectual property. Getting policy makers to go this far wasn't going to be easy. There were lots of other issues clamoring for attention during the 1970s and early 1980s: the breakdown of the Bretton Woods system of fixed exchange rates and the consequent problems of international monetary adjustment, OPEC and the oil crisis, the debt crisis and possible collapse of the world's banking system, to mention a few.

Even if one could persuade the US government of the foundational importance of intellectual property, what could the US do to improve standards of intellectual property protection? The US, after all, was only one country. In a forum like WIPO, where revisions to intellectual property treaties were discussed, it could always be outvoted by a large bloc of developing countries. The answer, which a small group of people had worked out, lay in the use of trade sanctions. The endless dialogue at WIPO would never produce the rules needed for a new knowledge game. But was it realistic to expect the US to use trade sanctions against other countries, countries with which it had important diplomatic ties that might easily be cut once the trade sword fell? It was not only Asian countries that would be labeled pirates, but European states like Italy, Spain, Greece and Portugal. In fact, most nations in one way or another were transgressors when it came to US standards of intellectual property. Could the US be persuaded to use its trade power against so many countries? There were other problems. It was one thing to beat up on minority economies like Singapore, Malaysia and Taiwan for being intellectual property pirates, but entirely another to take on Europe and Japan. For a while at least these last two would have to be allies, part of an intellectual property triumvirate. But how could the governments of Europe and Japan be persuaded to join what was essentially a cause of US business? A way would have to be found.

PFIZER'S WORLD OF IDEAS

Like most players in the knowledge game Pfizer had a long history.[6] It was incorporated in 1942 as Charles Pfizer & Company, but had earlier beginnings in a partnership between two cousins, Charles Pfizer and Charles Erhart. They had come to New York in the 1840s from Ludwigsburg in Germany, lured from their well-to-do background by the potential of the New World. The company's main product became citric acid. During the 1920s two of the company's chemists developed a fermentation process for using sugar and then molasses to obtain citric acid in large quantities. The deep-tank fermentation methods that the company developed for citric acid became the basis of the mass production of penicillin during World War II. Pfizer became the single biggest supplier of penicillin to Allies during the war. After World War II, Pfizer began, through a program of diversification, to climb up the ladder of the world's largest industrial enterprises. Much of its growth was based on the sale of its first major research success, the antibiotic Terramycin. The company would later be investigated by the US government for the part it played in a cartel that fixed the price of this and other antibiotics. It also branched out into consumer products, medical equipment, animal health products and specialty chemicals relevant to the food industry.

As a pharmaceutical company Pfizer understood better than most companies the importance of public policy to the operations of business.

The drugs that it sold in the US depended on regulatory approval from the Food and Drug Administration; its growth depended on keeping antitrust enforcement against its monopolistic practices at bay. Pharmaceuticals was also an industry in which there were genuinely global companies like Pfizer that had production facilities in many parts of the world and competed in many markets. Pfizer itself had 21 manufacturing plants located in less developed countries including India. Four out of its six R&D labs were located outside the US.[7] The sale of Pfizer's products both in the US and internationally was intimately linked to government decisions and government regulation. Taking a leadership role in influencing that regulation was something to which the company was culturally attuned by virtue of the products it sold. The company also had experience with the patent regimes of developing countries. During the war years Pfizer had been required to share its penicillin production techniques with other US manufacturers in order to meet the demand of the Allies. Facing strong domestic competition in the production of penicillin after the end of World War II, in the 1950s the company began a program of expansion into developing country markets. Pfizer's move into overseas markets was the idea of John "Jack" Powers Jr., who in effect globalized Pfizer as a firm. Out of his initiative was born Pfizer International. Manufacturing plants and distribution networks were established "in countries ranging from Argentina to Australia and Belgium to Brazil."[8] By 1957 Pfizer International had achieved more than its target of US$60 million overseas sales. More importantly, it had decided that it was worth persisting with developing country markets. The pharmaceutical markets of populous, less developed countries like India and China became long-term bets.

The long-term prospects of these markets, however, became clouded as countries like India began to develop technologically. Industrialization started slowly in these countries because they were preoccupied with throwing off colonialism and achieving political sovereignty. The overseas sales figures that Pfizer International achieved in the 1950s were in a sense a postcolonial legacy. Technological development could hardly take place in countries struggling to win their independence and create stable political institutions. The citizens of such countries still got sick. This meant that drugs had to be imported. National pharmaceutical industries either did not exist or were only in their infancy. In fact many people in Africa, India and South America relied on a variety of indigenous knowledge systems for their health-care needs.

The problem with importing drugs lay in their expense. In the 1960s India, despite having one of the poorest populations in the world, had some of the world's highest drug prices. There was price discrimination but not in favor of India's many poor. Pharmaceutical companies were instead aiming at the small but growing class of Indians who could afford Western prices. Achieving more affordable drugs became a priority in India and other developing countries. With political stability came a measure of technological development, a capacity to produce drugs locally. Governments of developing countries asked themselves a simple question: how might we use the patent system to help the production of cheap drugs in our country? This led India down the path of designing a patent system that helped to meet the demand by its population for cheap drugs.

During the 1950s when Pfizer had ventured into developing country markets, patent protection was less important to it because countries like India did not have the technology or know-how to copy its products. Patents, as with all intellectual property rights, only matter when competitors acquire the capacity to copy and distribute to markets. As India and other developing states began to acquire technological capabilities, Pfizer's bet on these markets began to look shaky. It began to look especially shaky as India and others passed patent laws aimed at fostering a local pharmaceutical industry. The patent law in countries like India did not allow for patents on pharmaceutical products and would permit patents on pharmaceutical processes for only five to seven years. The idea behind the product/process distinction was that Indian pharmaceutical manufacturers would have an incentive to find cheaper and cheaper processes for the production of drugs. Developing countries also made use of compulsory licensing regimes to bring down the price of essential drugs.

As these policies began to bite, Pfizer was faced with unprofitable operations in these countries. In the words of Edmund Pratt, the CEO of Pfizer from 1972 to 1991, "[w]e were beginning to notice that we were losing market share dramatically [in developing countries] because our intellectual property rights were not being respected in these countries."[9] Lack of respect on the part of developing countries did not necessarily imply illegality, but rather that developing countries were adjusting the rules of the patent game to serve their local industries in exactly the same way that, as we saw in Chapter 2, Western states used intellectual property for their own protectionist ends. The loss of market share in developing countries did not really impact on Pfizer's overall profitability. Pratt again: "Fortunately, we were doing well in our other operations so it didn't affect our overall performance dramatically."[10] The world's biggest pharmaceutical markets remained the US, Japan and Europe. Pfizer's own sales in developing markets were never much more than 10–12 percent of its total sales.[11] Nevertheless these less developed countries were nibbling at the edges of the global knowledge game. Among other things, they were providing pharmaceutical products to their populations at very cheap prices. Not only that, but some countries like India were also supplying neighbors like Nepal. Pharmaceuticals from India were also finding their way into African states. The presence of these cheaper manufacturers in the world had the potential to raise embarrassing questions within Western markets about the nature of the connections between patents and the price of drugs. Witness the following statement from a Western doctor who had worked in Nepal:[12]

> Having just returned from medical work in Nepal, I am intrigued by the Association of the British Pharmaceutical Industry's statement that "the

pharmaceutical industry in the UK is highly competitive especially in terms of prices." Most of the drugs available in Nepal are manufactured in India and their efficacy in clinical practice I have found to be the same as their UK equivalents but the price is about one-tenth to one-twentieth of the UK price. Any argument about research and development costs can hardly apply to such humble drugs as paracetamol.

Raising these kinds of issues was something that no global knowledge cartel could tolerate. Developing countries had to be disciplined.

Toward the end of the 1970s an internal discussion began to take place in Pfizer about the next round of GATT trade talks. People in business generally saw trade talks as being about tariff barriers and related export–import issues. In many ways the whole GATT paradigm was somewhat removed from the needs of players in the knowledge game. The GATT related to goods crossing borders, not knowledge. The problem of nontariff trade barriers was only dimly perceived. Intellectual property protection was not a subject that the GATT dealt with in any significant way. The conversation within Pfizer arose in response to a question: what would be needed to truly liberalize the world trading order? The answer, which would lead the company into a major national and ultimately global lobbying campaign, took the form of a radical idea, that of linking the trade regime to investment. A truly liberal world trade order was about much more than just goods and services crossing borders. It would involve liberalizing the opportunities for investment, removing the structures and restrictions that currently functioned within states to limit the opportunities of global investors. A liberal trading order should essentially become a liberal investment order. Of course, the investment issue meant different things to different companies, a "real semantic issue" as one informant put it. For Pfizer, the investment issue translated into globally enforceable intellectual property standards, standards that would protect its knowledge in whichever jurisdiction the company went. The liberal trading order that was being envisaged, though, was not simply one in which restrictions on investment were lifted. Rather it was about changing the nature and source of the restrictions. States like Canada, for instance, had for a long time interfered in the investment equation of an international pharmaceutical company by having compulsory licensing schemes for patents including drug patents. From the point of view of a global knowledge player like Pfizer a liberal trading order would place investors first by removing these kinds of restrictions. The 1982 op-ed piece had signaled this when it complained about the compulsory licensing schemes of India and Canada, pointing out that in the case of the latter's scheme the royalty was "a meager 4 percent."

The chairman of Pfizer from 1972 to 1992 and CEO from 1972 to 1991 was Edmund T. Pratt Jr. Now retired from Pfizer he retains the title of emeritus chairman, and participates in the distinctive American philanthropic tradition that has benefited many educational institutions in the US. In 1998 he donated US$12 million to the University of Long Island. Under

Pratt's chairmanship, Pfizer developed a strategy of growth based on product innovation. Pfizer became one of the biggest spenders on R&D, investing in the order of 15–20 percent of sales back into research. Its strategy of investment saw its sales go from US$1 billion in 1972 to more than US$6 billion in 1990. According to its website it now has more than 60 new products under patent. By 1999 it had become the world's third largest pharmaceutical company. Pratt's more significant achievement from a historical and institutional perspective lies in the contribution he made to the globalization of intellectual property rights. Those who worked with him described his intellectual, business and political leadership on the issue of trade, investment and intellectual property as "crucial" (1994 interview). In later years he reported that the fight for global intellectual property protection was one of "the highlights of my career."[13] Also involved in the campaign were Ted Littlejohn, responsible for much of the detail of it, as well as its intellectual content, Gerry Laubach and Michael Hodin. Hodin had been hired by Pratt to work on public policy issues. Under the direction of these men Pfizer's public relations department became a public affairs division. Public relations was about image, about obtaining favorable publicity, giving information about product releases and so on. Public affairs was about influencing the public policy agenda and ultimately securing the right regulatory outcomes. In order to do this Pfizer had to enter "the world of ideas" (1994 interview). Bringing about change in public policy was not just a matter of a snapping of the corporate fingers. Other business leaders would have to be convinced, a corporate consensus would have to be built, policy analysts would have to lend legitimacy to the proposed new direction and finally the whole thing had to be politically salable in Washington.

Pfizer entered the world of ideas at different levels both within and outside government. Pratt began delivering speeches at business fora like the National Foreign Trade Council and the Business Round Table outlining the links between trade, intellectual property and investment. As a CEO of a major US company, he could work the trade association scene at the highest levels. More importantly, as we will see in the next section, he found his way to the chairmanship of the Advisory Committee on Trade Negotiations. This enabled him to have an input into the trade policy process. He was by all accounts a forceful articulator of an argument. The president of one US business organization described a speech he heard by Pratt on the issue of connecting trade and intellectual property as a "table thumping affair" that won strong approval from its business audience. Other Pfizer senior executives also began to push the intellectual property issue within national and international trade associations.[14] Gerald Laubach, president of Pfizer Inc., was on the board of the Pharmaceutical Manufacturers Association and on the Council on Competitiveness set up by President Ronald Reagan; Lou Clemente, Pfizer's general counsel, headed up the Intellectual Property Committee of the US Council for International Business; Bob Neimeth, Pfizer International's president was the chair of the US side of the Business and Industry Advisory Committee to the OECD. Like the beat of a tom-tom, the message about intellectual property went out along the business networks to chambers of commerce, business councils, business committees, trade associations and peak business bodies. Progressively Pfizer executives who occupied key positions in strategic business organizations were able to enroll the support of these organizations for a trade-based approach to intellectual property. With every such enrollment the business power behind the case for such an approach became harder and harder for governments to resist.

Pfizer also began to engage with those groups that developed ideas and theories as part of the public policy process. Ideas about trade and investment needed analytical backing and justification. Working with such groups was, as one Pfizer interviewee remarked, a way "to extend your tentacles." With the planning being done by Ted Littlejohn of Pfizer, the company went after some of the biggest and most respected think tanks in the US. High on its list were influential conservative think tanks like the Heritage Foundation, the American Enterprise Institute and the Hoover Institution. The Heritage Foundation was important because President Reagan was known to listen to it. Pfizer wanted to engage widely with the world of ideas and did not want to be seen "just talking to the choir" (1994 interview). It also targeted think tanks that it saw as being in the centre or even slightly to the left of American politics, think tanks such as the Brookings Institution. The goal was to generate a broad-based discussion among policy analysts of the trade and investment issue. Pfizer pushed the intellectual property issue through the various think tanks by making direct financial contributions to them, funding specific projects or supporting conferences.

In some ways this was a dangerous but necessary strategy. Most of the think tanks were, in terms of their objectives, committed to principles of free trade. Given intellectual property's protectionist history and monopoly nature the process of analysis that Pfizer sponsored might easily have gone wrong. There were various ways around this problem, including picking one's think tanks carefully and encouraging projects that looked at the growing importance of trade in intellectual property rights as opposed to the effects that intellectual property monopolies might have on trade. More subtly, Pfizer set out to locate the intellectual property issue within a frame of reference of its own devising. This frame of reference was made up of fundamental liberal values, such as the individual right of property ownership, the right to a reward for labor, and fairness. Contained in it were appeals to the pride that existed in US high-technology achievements and most US think tanks of both right and center have objectives that are very much about the US national interest. American companies were portrayed as embattled innovators facing an uncertain future in a world where rapacious developing countries were ignoring the fundamental rules of business fair play. Once intellectual property was connected to the protection of high technology people began to link it to national and military security. Part of national security was securing intellectual property protection for the knowledge industries that gave the US its technological superiority. Slowly but surely intellectual property protection assumed a permanent place in official discourse and thinking.

The message of "Stealing from the Mind" was that governments of other countries were stealing from the minds of individual US inventors by denying them patent protection. Of course by the time evidence came out that individual pharmaceutical companies were stealing from the collective knowledge of indigenous peoples—the collective mind of the non-Western other—the ink had long dried on TRIPS. Pfizer had managed to create its own turf on the intellectual property issue. As a Pfizer employee pointed out, that is fundamental to winning a campaign on any major issue.

It was not just a matter of Pfizer gaining turf. Others had to lose theirs, especially the intellectual property lawyers.

One of the paradoxes facing Pfizer strategists was that they needed the technical abilities of intellectual property lawyers, but at the same time they needed to neutralize them as a political force. As one Pfizer employee pointed out, "if the Turks propose a new intellectual property law I give it to our experts and ask them what it means." But at the same time intellectual property lawyers had over the years made slow progress with intellectual property globalization, especially on the enforcement front. For decades intellectual property experts from many countries had regularly gathered in WIPO's imposing, art-laden building near Lake Geneva for long days of speech-making. The developing countries would speak about technology as the common heritage of mankind, the Europeans about the moral rights of authors and the need to maintain the integrity of the intellectual property system and the Americans about their own distinctive traditions of intellectual property. Afterward smaller groups of conference participants would gather in Geneva's restaurants and, over wine, reiterate to their fellow diners, who weren't really listening, the many fine points of principle they had made in their interventions on behalf of their countries. It was a comfortable, secure world in which it was easy to believe in one's importance, the only real hazard being the tedium of diplomatic protocol and ceremony.

It was exactly because so many intellectual property experts were embedded in the traditions, not to mention perks, of existing intellectual property organizations that "they did not see the possibilities" and "had got nowhere with the issue" (1994 interview). So while Pfizer saw the need for the technical expertise of the intellectual property community, they also saw, in the words of one Pfizer employee, that "at another level we had to take it from them" (1994 interview). Figuring out its relationship with intellectual property experts became one of Pfizer's great challenges. Figuring out its relationship with WIPO was easy. After Pfizer's failure to persuade WIPO to do anything about patent protection under the Paris Convention, a treaty that WIPO administered, Pfizer decided to shift the issue to another forum. In the words of Lou Clemente, Pfizer's general counsel, "[o]ur experience with WIPO was the last straw in our attempt to operate by persuasion." [15]

GETTING ON COMMITTEES

It is one thing to have the idea of linking investment and intellectual property to the trade regime and entirely another to turn this idea into a negotiating objective and then an international legal reality. Real power in the modern world, as much of this book shows, comes from sitting on committees that filter out other interested decision makers or parties from key decisions, but that in some way or another can be read as representing the excluded. In such committees power becomes concentrated in the hands of the few. Its exercise is democratically legitimated by the symbolic links the committee retains with the many that are excluded from the real decision making. The Advisory Committee on Trade Negotiations (ACTN) was just such a committee.

ACTN was a pipeline for US business to the US executive on trade issues. Its function was to advise the US Trade Representative (USTR) on where, in the eyes of the private sector, US economic interests really lay (see Chapter 7). ACTN was a direct line of communication between business and the bureaucratic center of trade policy. As the Uruguay Round unfolded, ACTN became one of the key portals of influence in developing the US stance on intellectual property.

Pratt became a member of ACTN in 1979. Michael Hodin, the vice president of public relations at Pfizer, had been hired by Pratt in the late 1970s. Hodin had worked in the trade area and knew the Capitol Hill scene. Pratt took over the chairmanship of ACTN in 1981 and for the next six years presided over its work program. The internal discussion that had been going on in Pfizer about the integration of trade, intellectual property and investment now had an official and influential outlet. In the next GATT round US trade negotiators would have to make decisions about trade-offs in order to get the best possible deal for the US. The message from ACTN was that the industries most in need of protection in the US were those with big intellectual property portfolios. Pharmaceuticals, semiconductor chips and the copyright in icons like Mickey Mouse were what mattered most. Old-fashioned manufacturing and agricultural industries would have to take a back seat in the negotiations.

ACTN established a task force on intellectual property. The recommendations of the task force became over time the basis of US strategy and action on intellectual property (described in more detail in Chapter 7).[16] In effect the US negotiating position had to become, "no IP, no trade round." And at the bilateral level it had to be prepared to wield the stick of trade sanctions. One important step that ACTN took in ensuring that intellectual property and investment remained a priority during the negotiations was to see to the creation of a special position within the United States Trade Representative's office called the Assistant Secretary for International Investment and Intellectual Property. The task force set about developing an overall trade-based IP strategy consisting of three parts:

- **Multilateralism:** to develop in the context of the upcoming GATT round an intellectual property (IP) code containing good standards of IP protection, which was binding on all parties to the negotiations and was tied to a dispute settlement mechanism.
- **Bilateralism:** to begin bilateral negotiations with countries that did not sufficiently protect US IP with a view to obtaining agreements from those countries for better protection.
- **Unilateralism:** if necessary, to make use of the fact that many "pirate" countries traded in the US market to threaten or actually impose trade sanctions on those countries if they did not enact and enforce higher standards of intellectual property protection.

Obtaining a strong multilateral agreement on intellectual property was a long-term strategy, while the use of bilateral negotiations and unilateral trade tools could provide an interim strategy for improving intellectual property protection abroad. All three parts of the strategy were important and all three had to be pursued.

The overall strategy for intellectual property, the working out of which we will describe in the following chapters, was the product of a remarkably small group of men. At Pfizer it was Edmund Pratt, Ted Littlejohn, Michael Hodin, Gerald Laubach, Robert Neimeth and Lou Clemente. Outside Pfizer another player in the knowledge game, IBM, had also been taking a strong interest in the possibility of a trade-based approach to intellectual property. It had engaged an economist, Jacques Gorlin, to write a paper suggesting in detail how a trade-based approach might be developed for the copyright protection of computer software. Like Hodin, Gorlin had a background in trade. In autumn 1984 he left his government position to write the strategy paper for IBM. John Opel, a chairman of IBM in the 1980s, headed ACTN's task force on intellectual property. Gorlin became a consultant to ACTN on the intellectual property issue in the mid-1980s. Many of the strategies that Gorlin had written about in his paper for IBM found their way into the work program of ACTN. When Pratt and Opel established the Intellectual Property Committee (IPC), Gorlin became its consulting economist. As we shall see in Chapter 6, the IPC became another elite committee that made the TRIPS agreement a reality. When in 1994 we interviewed a former US trade negotiator, he remarked that "less than 50 individuals" were responsible for TRIPS. Fewer than 50 individuals had managed to globalize a set of regulatory norms for the conduct of all those doing business or aspiring to do business in the information age. For this research we managed to interview perhaps half of these individuals in our effort to make sense of the remarkable TRIPS story.

CHAPTER 5

The Illusion of Sovereignty

SOVEREIGN POVERTY

In 1959 approximately half the Brazilian population were living on annual incomes of between US$50 and $100.[1] This group of people could not afford to buy books, even if they had been cheap. But they were not, least of all for people in developing countries. For a long time copyright had been used by Western publishers to run cartels. Books were at their cheapest in the US where publishers from time to time faced antitrust actions and a more competitive domestic market than elsewhere in the world. London book publishers dominated the book markets of the British Empire and then the Commonwealth. After World War II, New York and London publishers came to an agreement not to compete on each other's turf. Known as the British Publishers Traditional Market Agreement, it placed the book market of many developing countries under the influence of London publishers.

The achievement of sovereignty by developing states left them with many responsibilities, including that of educating their populations. Here they inherited a problem of enormous magnitude. For the most part their former colonial masters had not been interested in programs of mass education. To the extent that colonial authorities did provide education it was of a general liberal arts kind. Training local people in science, technology and engineering was quietly neglected. Colonies were seen essentially as sources of raw materials.[2] Education in colonial countries was part of the system of domination, a way of keeping the indigenous masses away from the knowledge relevant to development. It was also used to create an educated local elite, which was then enrolled in the task of maintaining a country's colonial status. In India this policy produced a class of "baboos," locals who could read and write English for the purpose of carrying out menial administrative tasks.[3] One estimate is that India, Pakistan and Indonesia entered independence with considerably less than one-fifth of their respective populations being literate.[4]

Fundamental to any system of mass education is access to textbooks at prices that libraries and students can afford. Developing countries faced massive textbook shortages. Indigenous authors and titles were in short supply. UNESCO statistics[5] show that the total number of titles (including nonperiodical publications like pamphlets) in India in 1960 was 10,741 and in Indonesia for the same year it was 1,114. For other developing countries it was far lower: 153 for the Philippines in 1959 and 608 for Burma in 1959. Bearing in mind the populations of these countries, one can see that book production was very low. Importing books from the West was not an affordable option. The prices being fixed for books by London and to a lesser extent New York meant that sufficient quantities of books could never be imported to meet the needs of a mass education system in developing countries. Far from encouraging investment in education, copyright was the invisible but effective servant of Western colonial power.

Another option was to "pirate" the textbooks by printing them without the permission of Western copyright owners. Here, though, many developing countries faced a fundamental obstacle—a shortage of paper. In developing countries the amount of paper available for consumption per head was extremely low. Domestic production was virtually nonexistent and developing countries did not have the necessary foreign currency reserves to meet the cost of importing the amounts they needed. The shortages of paper led the Conference on Pulp and Paper Development in Asia and the Far East in 1960 to observe that educational programs in developing countries would be jeopardized unless the growth of a paper industry was encouraged.[6]

In thinking about how to overcome the legacy of ignorance left to them by colonization, developing countries began to look to the rules of international copyright. They reasoned that it might be possible to modify the existing copyright regime in ways that took account of their educational needs. They turned out to be wrong. Their proposals triggered in the 1960s what is referred to as the "crisis of international copyright." The crisis consisted of developing country proposals for rules of international copyright that gave them access on better terms to books published in the West.

The demands for change by developing countries took the form of proposals to revise the Berne Convention for the Protection of Literary and Artistic Works 1886 (Berne Convention), the preeminent treaty for the regulation of copyright relations among states. By 1960, many developing countries were members of the Berne Convention. In fact large numbers of them had been included in Berne's territorial reach during the heyday of colonialism. Four major colonial powers ratified the Berne Convention in 1887, the year in which it came into force: France, Germany, Spain and the UK. Under Article 19 of the Berne Act for the Convention, these states had the right to accede to the Convention "at any time for their Colonies or foreign possessions." Each of these colonial powers took advantage of Article 19 to include their territories, colonies and protectorates in their accession to the Convention. The UK accession, for example, included "the United Kingdom of Great Britain and Ireland and all the colonies and possessions of Her Britannic Majesty."[7] The accession of colonies is complicated because the colonial powers used their power under Article 19 at different times. For example, India and Australia were excluded from the initial UK declaration. They were the subject of a separate declaration in 1912 after their permission had been obtained.[8] The general trend, however, was very clear. More and more colonies were drawn into the Berne system, especially after another two colonial powers, the Netherlands and Portugal, joined it in 1914.

Even after developing countries became sovereign states it proved hard to leave Berne's embrace. The prospect that developing states might leave a system that paid no regard to their economic development needs stimulated the secretariat of the Berne Union (BIRPI)[9] into taking, in the words of the Chief of BIRPI's Copyright Division, "all appropriate action with a view to avoiding a constant and significant geographical shrinking, to the prejudice of the interests of authors."[10] The question of whether newly sovereign states are bound by treaty obligations acquired at a time when they were of a lesser legal status is a complicated question of international law. On this issue BIRPI became a model of proactivity. It took a highly flexible, creative and at times inconsistent approach to complex questions of state succession in international law. It invented the "declaration of continued adherence" even though such a declaration was not expressly recognized in the Berne Convention and wrote to developing countries suggesting that this be used.[11]

The former colonial powers also continued to watch over their former colonies. They lent their expertise to these newly independent states when they needed it. Expertise in copyright law and policy was the province of Europeans in top hats from the metropoles of Paris, London and Berlin, who were steeped in natural rights jurisprudence, the intricacies of copyright law and treaty negotiations and who in turn were watched over by hardheaded publishers who knew the trade stakes. When 11 sub-Saharan states joined Berne they were:

> so totally dependent economically and culturally upon France (and Belgium) and so inexperienced in copyright matters that their adherence was, in effect, politically dictated by the "mother country" during the aftermath of reaching independence.[12]

The Berne system was run to suit the interests of copyright exporters. Each successive revision of Berne brought with it a higher set of copyright standards. For instance, under the Berne Act of the Convention, duration of copyright remained a matter of domestic law, but in the Brussels revision of 1948 a term of life of the author plus 50 years was made mandatory. The more and more rights that accrued to copyright holders the better, because it meant that there were more and more uses of a copyright work for which a charge could be made. For copyright exporters this translated into trade gains. By the time many countries shed their colonial status they were confronted by a Berne system that was run by an Old World club of former or diminished colonial powers to suit their economic interests. Beneath the dissembling rhetoric about the need to protect authors and provide incentives lay a harsh global economic reality of a cartelized publishing industry, price fixing and world market-sharing agreements.

At the time of the Stockholm Revision Conference in 1967, 24 of the 57 members of the Berne Convention were developing countries.[13] They had entered the revision process with a view to obtaining a better deal for copyright importers. In this way they were swimming against the protectionist tide of international copyright history. Developing countries wanted a better deal on translations, on the duration of copyright, on the broadcasting of copyright works and the use of copyright for educational purposes. Things began amicably enough with both BIRPI and UNESCO playing a supportive role in relation to the developing countries' agenda. But as developing country ideas were made concrete in the form of a draft Protocol to the Berne Convention, opposition from the publishing business to those ideas solidified. Heading the opposition were British publishers, the biggest exporters of copyright in the world.[14] Their attacks on developing countries were veiled by a sermonizing discourse on the need to protect the exclusive rights of authors. India in particular, because it had taken something of a leadership role, came in for stick because it had failed to convert to the cult of the author:

> Since, as we know, the Convention of the Berne Union is entirely based on the principle of the author's exclusive right it is to be wondered what India is doing in that Union.[15]

The provisions of the protocol were said to "steal, or authorize the stealing of other people's property: the intangible but precious property of authors, composers, artists, and publishers."[16]

The Stockholm Conference produced a Protocol Regarding Developing Countries, but it proved to be of no use to developing countries. Developed countries were under no obligation to ratify the protocol and no major copyright exporter ever did.[17] Rather than risk a collapse of the Berne Union a compromise was reached in the Paris Revision Conference of 1971. An appendix was added to the Berne Convention containing special provisions for developing countries. Highly complex, they had little positive impact on the ability of developing countries to get access to copyright material on affordable terms. For approximately ten years, developing countries had been working their way through the intergovernmental committees, study groups, committees of governmental experts and consultative committees that constituted the labyrinthine structure of international copyright treaty negotiations with little to show for their efforts. Their need for textbooks remained. By 1975 the student populations of some developing countries had increased by 150 percent on what it had been in 1965.[18] The capacity of governments in these countries to fund this demand for education had not always increased. In some cases, for complex reasons having to do with shocks in the world economy, the debt burden and the structural adjustment policies of the IMF and World Bank, it had actually decreased.[19] It was also obvious that Western publishers would not tolerate any significant change to the intellectual property arrangements that underpinned their business.

One group of countries, the future "tiger economies" of Asia, had studied the Stockholm process and drawn their own conclusions. Some of these countries (Korea, Malaysia, Singapore, Thailand) had attended the first copyright seminar ever organized in Asia by BIRPI in New Delhi in January 1967.[20] At the seminar many country delegates reported that copyright law was being examined in their country. The Malaysian delegate pointed out that a copyright bill had been drafted for the purpose of enabling Malaysia to accede to multilateral copyright conventions.[21] Shri Prem Kirpal, the secretary and educational adviser to the government of India, asked the Western copyright establishment to recognize the problem of developing countries in having "to develop adequate means of educating a large number of people" and to:

> consider not only the rights which an intellectual creator ought rightly to have over his works in the interest of society but also the interests which the society may have in using his works.[22]

This plea fell on deaf ears at Stockholm. After Stockholm it would have been very hard for developing countries to conclude anything other than that international copyright was a trade game, the rules of which were run by key copyright exporting nations. If they were to meet the educational needs of their populations they would have to do so outside the Berne system.

As Korea, Malaysia and Singapore began to develop they, along with others, began to copy Western textbooks. They were branded "pirates" by the US. At this time most of these countries were not in breach of international copyright obligations because they were not members of the Berne Convention. (Nor were they members of the Universal Copyright Convention, the other major copyright convention.) The legalities of developing country actions, though, were largely irrelevant to those in the US who were behind the branding strategy. Creating a pirate identity for these countries would make it easier to persuade Congress and the president to take action against them when the time for action came. The US itself did not join Berne until 1989. Singapore joined in 1998, Korea in 1996 and Malaysia in 1990. Indonesia's membership in the Berne Convention was made retroactive by BIRPI to 1949 when in 1956 the Netherlands informed BIRPI that it took the view that Indonesia was bound by virtue of the 1949 Charter of Transfer of Sovereignty. The gains of this to Dutch publishers were by all accounts considerable.[23] In 1960 Indonesia formally denounced the Convention (it became a party again in 1997).

It is worth asking why Western publishers did not take the longer view of international copyright and developing countries. They might have reasoned that by coming to special arrangements with developing countries over copyright they were encouraging the growth of a market that would one day repay their investment. Developing countries were willing to pay royalties, but clearly in countries where the annual income of many people was less than US$100 per annum not much could be afforded. The answer to our question lies in the ruthless cartelist logic that informs the global use of intellectual property rights. Cheaper texts in developing countries might find their way back onto Western markets. Concessions to developing countries might also lead to questions about the global role of copyright in maintaining prices. Ultimately, for cartelists holding global monopoly privileges the logic is to enforce higher prices and make sure that the cartel's arrangements stay intact. Better to hang on to the certainty of monopoly than risk the uncertainty of virtue. This meant insisting publicly on the primacy of the author's exclusive right above all else and never conceding for a moment that copyright might be an instrument of rational economic planning and development, which different countries at different times might, for the sake of the welfare of their populations, choose to use differently. When individual publishers broke ranks and made individual arrangements with developing states as did Macmillan Co. with Ghana, northern Nigeria, Zambia, Tanzania, Uganda and Lesotho, they came in for the severest criticism from their publishers' association. The shared business values of publishers, their tradition of cartelism and the ideology of the god-author combined to prevent them from creatively engaging with the problems of developing countries.

If the benefits of the international copyright regime were not obvious to developing countries this was even more true of the international patents regime. This particular regime revolved around the Paris Convention of 1883, which had formed the International Union for the Protection of Industrial Property. Patents, if they confer net benefits on any country, are likely to do so on countries that have a strong industrial base. International patent protection, that is to say the recognition of a country's domestic patents in foreign countries, is likely to interest only those countries that have large export markets in patentable technologies. All developed countries during the course of the 20th century had trodden warily before recognizing the rights of foreign patent holders in their domestic markets. The words of Lloyd George, president of the Board of Trade in 1907, capture the trade fears that existed:

> Big foreign syndicates have one very effective way of destroying British industries. They first of all apply for patents on a very considerable scale...A British inventor makes a bona fide discovery. He attempts to patent it...But the moment he does so this powerful foreign syndicate brings an action against him for infringement of patent...At the present moment many British industries are bound hand and foot by the working of the patent system. Many British industries have been completely wiped out by privileges conceded by British institutions to foreigners.[24]

Similar fears exist today in relation to the patenting of the human genome by US and Japanese industry. A recent EC report warned of the aggressive patenting practices of US companies and questioned the "European preference for putting DNA sequence into the public domain."[25]

For developing countries there were really only two questions to ask about the international patent system.[26] First, would the recognition of foreign patents bring welfare gains of some sort to their population? Second, would the recognition in foreign countries of patents held by their own citizens provide them with significant gains? The answer to the second question was clear enough. Most developing countries had agricultural economies and therefore little to gain from a regime favoring exporters of patentable technologies. Even those developing countries whose economies were becoming more reliant on manufacturing (for example, Korea, Singapore, Taiwan) had not all that much to gain because they were operating in sectors of manufacturing where patent protection was less important. What really mattered to all these countries were lower tariffs rather than higher standards of patent protection.

Even if there were no export gains from the international patent regime for a developing country there might have been import gains if, by extending patent protection to foreign patents, it thereby stimulated the production overseas of inventions that were really needed by that developing country. The areas in which this was most likely to be true were pharmaceuticals and chemicals since it is in these sectors that patents have the greatest effect.[27] But here the role of the patent system had been and continues to remain disappointing from the developing country perspective. The patent system has not, for example, stimulated the invention and production of the kind of drugs that developing countries need. Pharmaceutical companies carry out R&D in those markets where the returns are likely to be the greatest. This market rationality explains why only 1 percent of the new chemical entities marketed between 1975 and 1997 related to tropical diseases.[28] Western tourism in developing countries is a large part of the explanation of why we have the malaria drugs that we do. The bulk of the world's population lives in developing countries where tropical diseases are a problem, so demand is not the issue. Rather it is the ability to pay. The poor by definition have no or little ability to pay. When they do pay it follows that they pay more as a percentage of their income than the rich do for pharmaceuticals. The following statistical snapshot on annual drug expenditure per capita reveals something of this: Japan US$411, US US$191, Germany US$111, Mozambique US$1, Bangladesh US$1 and India US$3.[29] In short, it will be more profitable for a transnational pharmaceutical company to invest money in R&D on slimming pills for Westerners than on a tropical disease.

But it was not just that the international patent system led by the Paris Union had failed to deliver benefits to developing countries. There was some evidence that it had done actual harm. We have already mentioned in Chapter 2 the role of patents in the cartel over antibiotics, a cartel that affected the price of these drugs in developing countries. Synthetic hormones and quinine are other examples of essential medicines the supply of which has been affected by international cartels employing intellectual property rights.[30] Even more strikingly, the international patent regime resulted in developing countries facing higher drug prices than those in developed countries. For example, in 1961 a US senate committee led by Senator Kefauver observed that India faced some of the highest drug prices in the world. India in fact had a patent law before many European countries, having acquired one in 1856 while under British colonial rule. From that time on British manufacturers used the patent system to obtain the best possible prices in the Indian market. After India's independence in 1947 two expert committees conducted a review of the Indian patent system. Unsurprisingly, they concluded that the Indian patent system had failed "to stimulate inventions among Indians and to encourage the development and exploitation of new inventions."[31]

The response of Indian policy makers was to draft another patent law. Passed in 1970 the new law followed the German system of allowing the patenting of methods or processes that led to drugs, but not allowing the patenting of the drugs themselves.[32] Patent protection for pharmaceuticals was granted for only seven years as opposed to 14 years for other inventions. This law opened the path to a highly successful Indian generics industry, which began to produce essential drugs at a fraction of their price in Western markets. It also earned India the label of pirate. During this time India was not a member of the Paris Union for the protection of industrial property (India joined in 1998).

Other developing countries, however, had joined the Paris Convention. By the mid-1980s two-thirds of the members of the Convention were developing countries.[33] This change in membership of the Paris Convention meant that its reform could no longer be dictated by the developed countries. The Paris Union, once a quiet club devoted to the elevation of the international patent regime, became a battleground. Developing countries pushed for access to the technology of multinationals on favorable terms. The fiercest debates took place over the revision of compulsory licensing of patented technology.[34] For the US, developing country proposals for exclusive compulsory licensing amounted to little more than expropriation of US intellectual property rights. The revision of the Paris Convention, which had begun in 1980, was never completed. In the eyes of key industry players like Pfizer, WIPO had failed. Even more dangerously, countries like India had shown that developing countries could lower standards of patent protection and still have a thriving generics industry. Other countries like Brazil, Argentina and Mexico were also limiting the scope of patentability in the pharmaceutical and chemical sectors. By now the Asian tiger economies were experiencing hypergrowth. Competition for the members of the knowledge cartels that we described in Chapter 3 was looming from all directions. They understood best of all the real price of the end of colonialism—the loss of power to frame the rules that would regulate the capacity of others to compete in the knowledge game.

MOST WANTED

In March 1992 Jack Valenti, president and chief executive officer of the Motion Picture Association of America (MPAA), testified before the Senate

Finance Committee.[35] The committee wanted to know about the importance of processes under the US Trade Act 1974, commonly referred to as 301 and Special 301. Valenti concluded his presentation by saying that "without 301, American intellectual property is undone."

Certainly 301 had been important to the motion picture industry. Valenti had described the American TV program and movie as the USA's "most wanted" export. Not quite everyone did want it, or at least not all of the time. Most states had some kind of trade barrier in place when it came to importing movies and TV programs, usually in the form of screen and television quotas. They may have been big stars but, in Paris, Donald Duck and Mickey Mouse had to make space for French movies about existential despair. Such quotas were perfectly permissible under the General Agreement on Tariffs and Trade (GATT). The architects of the GATT had seen that culture follows the film and therefore appreciated the need for a multilateral trade regime to give states some flexibility about the levels of trade in foreign films.[36] Aside from these market access problems there were other problems the US film industry wanted to fix. An increasing part of the industry's revenue was coming from overseas markets. Piracy, according to the industry, was a major threat to it. Every videocassette that was pirated in Italy, Greece, Thailand, Singapore and elsewhere represented lost export dollars. How the figures on piracy were arrived at we shall see in the next chapter. There was also a deeper, more complicated issue that was given less publicity. Copyright is made up of a bundle of rights such as the right to reproduction, the right to perform the work in public, the right to broadcast it and so on. Clearly the more types of rights that the copyright owner could acquire the more market uses of the work he or she could control through the mechanism of licensing. Other countries had to be persuaded to recognize new types of rights such as the right to rent the copyright work. Films had also become giant advertisements for merchandised goods. The right to reproduce and distribute such goods was fundamentally dependent on the rules of copyright. Stamping out copyright piracy was thus only part of the story. More important was the creation, enforcement and globalization of copyright and trademark standards that would serve Hollywood's overseas business interests long into the future.

THE CARIBBEAN

One place in which piracy of motion picture intellectual property was rampant was the Caribbean. The Caribbean Basin states had in the 1980s an excellent communications system based on a microwave system that was linked to global communication networks. Some of these states were using their systems to transmit signals of US movies without the approval of the owners of the copyright in the films. An opportunity to prevent this practice came in the early 1980s when the US began to think of a strategy for dealing with Caribbean states that rested on encouraging processes of liberalization in those states.[37] In 1983 President Reagan signed into law the Caribbean Basin Economic Recovery Act of 1983. Under the act, states of the Caribbean would be given duty-free privileges for their goods in the US market if they met certain criteria. The president was obliged to refuse a country this benefit if a government-owned entity in it was broadcasting copyrighted material without the consent of the US copyright owners.[38] Other provisions required the president not to designate a country for benefits if it had taken steps in relation to intellectual property that amounted to the nationalization or expropriation of that property.[39] The act gave the president some flexibility to overlook a state's record on intellectual property on the grounds of national economic and security interests. But it was also made clear in the background reports relating to the act that the president was not to do deals with Caribbean states that would lessen the protection of US copyright owners.[40]

Some Caribbean states like the Dominican Republic found themselves having to acquire copyright law in a hurry in order to get entry into the US market on favorable terms. Finding the necessary local expertise to do the job was something of a problem since intellectual property protection had not been a high domestic priority. US copyright experts soon found themselves on flights bound for the Caribbean, where they drafted the necessary legislation. Inevitably, they produced laws based on US models. The process of imprinting US intellectual property standards on the world had begun.

Of itself the Caribbean Basin initiative on intellectual property was not particularly economically significant. Ronald Reagan, perhaps remembering his thespian roots, had helped out the movie industry by approving legislation that allowed the US to pull a trade lever against Caribbean states if their hotels continued to intercept satellite signals of US movies without paying a license fee. This market was not vast. In any case the hotels presumably would pass on the cost of the license fees to their customers, many of whom would have been visiting US tourists.

The deeper significance of the events in the Caribbean Basin lay in the realization by key individuals in the US that the rules of trade and intellectual property could be rewritten in order to form a global partnership between the trade and intellectual property regimes. This partnership could bring with it access to new markets and vastly increased royalty incomes. Nor was this partnership aimed exclusively at developing country markets. The largest markets for the Hollywood merchandising machine remained Europe and Japan. As Jack Valenti had pointed out in his 1992 testimony, American movies and TV programs captured 40 percent of the Japanese market, a figure that the US car industry could only dream about. Similarly, the US computer industry led by IBM and Microsoft was not content to follow the cosy copyright partitioning arrangements of British and US publishers. It wanted the European and Japanese markets. Although they never quite grasped the fact, European trade negotiators had more in common on intellectual property standards with their developing country counterparts than they realized. The US initiative on intellectual property was aimed at European and Japanese markets as much as it was at the tiger economies of Asia.

The Caribbean Basin initiative thus marked a beginning. In the words of one the players we interviewed, it was "part of a new fabric" (1993 interview). It was also something of a trial run for the forthcoming bilaterals with the more important developing countries as well as for the forthcoming Uruguay Round negotiations. But there was a long, long way to go. Persuading the Caribbean states to adopt intellectual property protection was, like the invasion of Grenada, comparatively easy in the scheme of things. The Caribbean states were not powers in the geopolitics of intellectual property. It would be harder to deal with the lead countries of the developing world. Nor was obtaining the cooperation of Europe and Japan on the inclusion of intellectual property in the Uruguay Round a foregone conclusion. Creating an agreement on intellectual property within the framework of the GATT rules was not exercising European minds. They were not, so far as American corporate strategists were concerned, thinking "out of the box" on the issue of international intellectual property protection (1994 interview). The GATT was about lowering tariffs and generally persuading countries to treat the products they imported in no less favorable a way than they treated their own products so that all products could move freely across borders. Intellectual property law did not fit well into this framework, because at its heart it was about rules that conferred opportunities for monopolies, the very kind of rules the GATT regime was designed to reduce. To the free trade eye it looked odd to have a body of rights in the GATT allowing their owners to restrict the circulation of products and to segment world markets.

Within the corridors of Brussels at the beginning of the 1980s there was no push by Europe's bureaucratic elite to make an agreement on intellectual property a major negotiating objective of the forthcoming trade round. They would have been happy with a side code in the GATT that dealt with the problem of counterfeit goods. European luxury brands were, after all, the subject of copying. Side codes on matters such as dumping and subsidies were already in use as devices within the GATT regime. The foundation for a code of some kind on intellectual property had been laid in the Tokyo Round (which concluded in 1979) where the US in particular had been successful in pushing for the recognition of the need for an anticounterfeiting code. The Europeans were also more sensitive to developing country complaints about the basic unfairness of the existing intellectual property regime. US trade negotiators were openly critical of what they saw as European softness on the issue.[41] But the Europeans realized that imposing harmonized intellectual property standards on developing countries via the GATT regime would carry with it complex diplomatic costs. By the mid-1980s, however, US industry wanted much more than a simple side code on counterfeit products. A comprehensive agreement on intellectual property was now part of the US agenda. Europe's top civil servants would have to be persuaded that an agreement on intellectual property was fundamental to the entire Uruguay Round.

CHAPTER 6

The Bilaterals

THE TRADE DEFENSE INITIATIVE

Trade policy has its mood swings. During the middle 1980s the mood in the US Congress was decidedly protectionist. Worsening trade deficits and loss of jobs in manufacturing made it easier to believe in the possibility that the US might, sooner rather than later, become a felled economic giant. The trade deficit had gone from US$31 billion in 1980 to US$170 billion in 1987.[1] During this time the manufacturing trade balance had swung from a US$27 billion surplus to a US$138 billion deficit. The US had financed this by borrowing from foreign creditors, thereby becoming the world's largest debtor nation. The human cost of this, as one senator observed in 1989, was that somewhere between 2 and 4 million Americans had lost jobs in this seven-year period.[2] These blunt statistics spoke to Congress. As an angry protectionism grew so did the tough talk and the desire for action. It was a good time for intellectual property lobbyists to be on Capitol Hill peddling the idea that better intellectual property protection would allow the US to reap the benefits of high-technology growth and bring more jobs for Americans. As one lobbyist explained, the link between intellectual property rules and high-tech growth was a powerful piece of symbolism with appeal in offices that mattered (1993 interview). The other obvious advantage of linking intellectual property to high technologies, especially the semiconductor chip, was that it blurred the line between protecting US economic security and US national security.

Ronald Reagan was also the right man to be president so far as the intellectual property lobby was concerned. He had stepped easily into the role of "cold war warrior." He could also probably be persuaded to play the role of "trade warrior." This would require him to approve trade sanctions on countries that were sailing under the flag of intellectual property piracy. The Reagan administration had also signaled a certain skepticism about the usefulness of multilateral fora to the US. Over a period of 18 months it had reviewed its participation in 19 international organizations and concluded that six of these had "serious problems of politicization."[3] One of those organizations, UNESCO, saw the US withdraw from membership in 1984. This was just the kind of hard-nosed approach the intellectual property lobby wanted to import into bilateral negotiations with "pirate" states.

Persuading Congress to pass the necessary changes to the Trade Act, which would give the United States Trade Representative (USTR) the authority to proceed against developing countries, was also an achievable goal. Few congressional representatives knew anything about intellectual property law, but they could not help noticing some of America's wealthiest companies becoming fervent about the issue of better intellectual property protection. There was always the possibility of these companies contributing to a re-election campaign. Before long Congress also became fervent about the issue of intellectual property. Soon the Hill was awash with protectionist bills, many of which contained provisions related to intellectual property. Intellectual property law, which for so long had languished in the shadow land of technical legal obscurity, was striding rapidly into the limelight.

The year 1984 turned out to be an important one for US trade law. The link between trade and intellectual property that had been made in the Caribbean Basin legislation in the previous year found its way into the Trade and Tariff Act of 1984 (which amended the Trade Act 1974). As one Washington lobbyist told us: "It was the Motion Picture Association that introduced an amendment to the Bill" (1993 interview). Beneath the legal language there were two simple approaches at work: the carrot and stick approach and the big stick approach.

THE US GENERALIZED SYSTEM OF PREFERENCES

A system known as the Generalized System of Preferences (GSP) allowed the US to develop a carrot and stick approach to the globalization of the standards of intellectual property it wanted.[4] Under the US GSP program, designated beneficiary countries were able to export eligible products into the US on a duty-free basis. Ironically, the idea for a GSP had been developed by the UN Conference on Trade and Development a few decades earlier. As one of its Indian architects explained to us, it was an attempt to create real bonds of trade between developed and developing countries (1995 interview).

The US GSP program had begun in 1976 and was authorized by the US Trade Act. When the GSP began working, protection of intellectual property was not a criterion of eligibility for receiving benefits under it. By 1984 roughly 3,000 products from 140 developing countries and territories were part of the scheme.[5] These developing countries were more dependent on being able to trade in the US than the US was on maintaining trade relations with them.[6] The GSP program had to be renewed by Congress on a periodical basis. In 1984 the GSP was due to expire in one year. The intellectual lobby noticed that in the words of one copyright lobbyist, "major pirates in SE Asia were dependent on GSP" (1993 interview): Argentina, Brazil, Egypt, India, Indonesia, Singapore, South Korea, the Philippines, Taiwan, Hong Kong and Thailand were among those on GSP benefits. In 1984 business organizations such as the Recording Industry Association of

America, the Association of American Publishers and the International Anticounterfeiting Coalition paraded before congressional committees arguing that a country's GSP status ought to be conditional on it protecting US intellectual property.

The Trade and Tariff Act of 1984 brought the same kind of language that had been used in the Caribbean Basin legislation into the GSP program. The president now had to look at a country's conduct on intellectual property in deciding whether it would receive or continue to receive GSP benefits. States complying with US demands on intellectual property would be rewarded with GSP benefits while those that did not might lose them. The idea of linking trade and intellectual property in the Caribbean Basin initiative had had immediate effects:

> Jamaica had no intellectual property law,[7] but they wrote one [with our help]. Similarly the Dominican Republic. I sat down with their lawyer and together we wrote their copyright law. The US Trade Representative asked me to come down to the Dominican Republic because the USTR knew nothing about IP, only trade. The US ambassador in the Dominican Republic was uncooperative and unhappy that I was upsetting his diplomatic relationships. I worked independently [of the USTR] too (1993 interview, US lobbyist).

The amendment to the US GSP program in 1984 also had an effect. For many developing countries gaining access to the closed and subsidized agricultural markets of developed countries was the main game. The whole point of the GSP system was to improve this access. At a meeting of the GATT Committee on Trade and Development in November 1985 some developing country representatives had suggested that the US was using its GSP system in a way that was "quite alien to the spirit and purpose of the generalized system of trade preferences in favor of developing countries."[8] The US, through its 1984 GSP amendment, had sent a warning shot across the bows of those developing countries trading in its markets. At least some of them began thinking about a change in course on the intellectual property issue.

It was not all plain sailing for the intellectual property lobby on the amendments to the GSP. They had to push for the renewal of the GSP program because the more old-fashioned, protectionist elements in the Congress wanted its removal (1993 interview). Why give countries competing with US manufacturers duty-free import privileges in the US market? The intellectual property lobby took a different view. Old protectionism was about keeping your rival's goods out of your domestic market. New protectionism in the knowledge economy was about securing a monopoly privilege in an intangible asset and keeping your rival out of world markets. But that meant persuading your rival to play by rules recognizing your "right" to the asset.

It was vital to keep the GSP intact and use it against developing countries where necessary. The argument of principle used by opponents of the GSP was that it benefited newly industrializing economies like Singapore most and they needed it least. But these were precisely the countries the intellectual property lobby most wanted to influence.[9] Extending the GSP was not permanent but a new world intellectual property order might be a permanent structural change for the wealthier developing countries. If a country could be persuaded to enact domestic intellectual property laws recognizing the rights of US intellectual property owners it would give those owners the following options:

1 A US company could allow foreign competitors to use its intellectual property under license, in which case the US company would be earning a royalty income.
2 A US company might choose to exploit its intellectual property in the foreign market itself, in which case it would be earning export dollars for the US.
3 A US company might choose to relocate its production facilities in the relevant foreign market because of more favorable labor and tax conditions, safe in the knowledge that its intellectual property could not be purloined by local rivals. It could then, among other things, export goods with an intellectual property content back into the US market. This would do little for American jobs or even the tax revenues of the US government. The multinationals for which better intellectual property was being designed could always play complex transfer pricing games with their income, games in which even the Internal Revenue could suffer losses. Because the value of a piece of intellectual property, like copyright in new software, was hard to quantify, it could be sold into a tax haven at a low price and sold on from the tax haven at a high price, thus shifting taxable profits to the haven. The intangible nature of intellectual property makes it difficult for tax authorities to prove that a valuation is wrong. Global intellectual property was to become a boon to global tax planners. In extolling the virtues of globalized intellectual property protection for the US economy the intellectual property lobby drew little attention to this third option.

Once the revised GSP program was in place it was used in the manner of a carrot and stick. Singapore was given a favorable GSP package in 1987 because of its good efforts in copyright especially, while Mexico (1987), Thailand (1989) and India (1992) came in for GSP losses (US$50 million, US$165 million and US$80 million, respectively) because they failed to meet certain standards of intellectual property protection.

SECTION 301

Section 301 of the Trade Act was also amended in 1984 to make it clear that the president had the authority to deal with states that failed to provide "adequate and effective" protection for US intellectual property. The intellectual property language of the Caribbean Basin legislation was also recycled in Section 301 of the Trade Act. This was because some of the same people were involved in the drafting (1993 interview). Under the 301 process an unfavorable finding could see the president authorize the withdrawal of trade benefits to a country or impose duties on its goods. The USTR was also given the power to "self-initiate" a 301 action against a foreign country. Intellectual property slowly but surely was being placed at the heart of those legislative provisions that guarded US commerce. The simple message, which was repeated again and again on Capitol Hill, was that American commerce was a commerce of ideas and creativity in desperate need of protection from thievery. As we shall see in the next section this message was reinforced with statistics that at first glance seemed impressive.

The 1984 trade amendments had given legal backing to a bilateral process of ratcheting up standards of intellectual property protection in other countries. The process had a chance of success only because other countries wanted to get their hands on the vast US market. As long as these countries calculated that the cost of complying with US demands on intellectual property was outweighed by the benefits of access to the US market then the 301 process would bring positive results. But as Jacques Gorlin, a key player in all this, had pointed out, there was the danger of an overreliance on bilateralism.[10] Lead pirates like Singapore, Hong Kong, Korea and Taiwan were developing fast and would in time lose their GSP status or it would cease to matter to them. (In January 1988 President Reagan announced that Taiwan, Hong Kong, South Korea and Singapore would go off GSP benefits in 1989.[11] All four states, which had enacted intellectual property laws a little earlier, expressed disappointment. Even after they went off GSP the US had the option of pursuing a 301 action against them.) There was also the problem that the president might balk at the last moment in authorizing sanctions against another sovereign state over the copying of cartoon videos in the interests of some greater diplomatic objective such as national security. Pushing multilaterally for higher standards of intellectual property protection was really the crucial, long-term objective.

In 1988 the 301 process was the subject of further refinement. To the existing procedures was added what came to be referred to as "Special 301."[12] Special 301 was a public law devoted to the service of private corporate interests. Under its terms the USTR had to identify those countries that denied "adequate and effective protection" of intellectual property rights or that denied "fair and equitable market access" to US intellectual property owners. Countries with the worst records on intellectual property were to be tagged "priority foreign countries." This in turn led to a 301 investigation of their laws and practices on intellectual property.

The USTR had to draw on the expertise of other departments in order to be able to do what Special 301 required of it. More and more people walking the miles of corridors in federal government buildings found themselves carrying files related to intellectual property. Surveillance and monitoring of intellectual property had been turned into an obligatory routine as opposed to something that the USTR might occasionally do. Every year, after the submission of the National Trade Estimate to Congress, the USTR under Special 301 had 30 days in which to identify the year's gallery of intellectual property rogues. There were reporting obligations to Congress. Special 301 procedures had tighter deadlines than other 301 investigations. The aim was to have an investigation last no longer than six to nine months.

The Special 301 process was set up in a way that allowed the USTR to respond to the differing dynamics of each country negotiation on intellectual property. Within the process there were three important categories: priority foreign country, priority watch list and the watch list. A country put on the watch list was being sent a message about its unsatisfactory practices on intellectual property. It knew it was on the 301 conveyor belt that led to trade sanctions. Regular contact with the USTR was the first stage of the process. Typically, at this point the target country would make some promises about investigating the USTR's complaints. If a country did nothing to shut down its levels of piracy it would be upgraded to the priority watch list. Typically, for such a country the USTR had formed some set of precise objectives that the relevant country had to begin to work toward. Saudi Arabia, for example, was in 1993 shifted from the watch list into the priority watch list because it was not a member of the Berne Convention and had a poorly drafted and badly enforced copyright law. Priority foreign countries were those on trade's death row. These countries had, in the words of the legislation, "the most onerous or egregious acts, policies, or practices" when it came to intellectual property. Countries in this category lived with the possibility of trade retaliation by the US.

Although this chapter focuses on the use of 301 against developing countries it is worthwhile pointing out that its purpose was to bring *all* of the United States' trading partners up to a standard of intellectual property protection satisfactory to the US. It was, after all, Japanese and European companies rather than Brazilian and Indian ones that offered US companies the most serious competition. Japan was the first to feel the heat of the 1984 amendment to 301. In 1984 US trade officials pressured Japan to drop its support for special laws for software protection and use copyright law instead (see Chapter 11). With the recent amendment to 301 lurking in the background Japan complied. Japan appeared on the 1989 Special 301 watch list for intellectual property misbehavior, as did Canada. No Western state, however, in 1989 made it into the more serious priority watch list. Europe especially was an ally in the multilateral game we describe in the next three chapters.

DESIGNERS, LOBBYISTS AND PETITIONERS

Linking intellectual property to trade had been the work of a few key individuals. Pfizer, led by Edmund Pratt, as we saw in Chapter 4, had played a central role in pushing the linkage between intellectual property and trade.

Under Pratt's leadership the Advisory Committee on Trade Negotiations (ACTN) had argued that the US government should develop an integrated multilateral and bilateral intellectual property strategy based on trade linkages. Jacques Gorlin, adviser to ACTN, headed the Intellectual Property Committee, the key lobbying body on the industrial side of intellectual property. It had been the Motion Picture Association that "wrote" an amendment to the Caribbean Basin legislation of 1983 that tied trade concessions to intellectual property. Eric Smith, a key figure in this period, had helped to put this language into the GSP program. It had been Smith and another copyright lawyer, John Baumgarten, who had a significant influence on the framing of the language of 301 (1993 interview). The 301 system that became the basis of the USTR's bilateral negotiations was the brainchild of a small group.

The reworking of the US Trade Act in the 1980s to accommodate intellectual property was accompanied by the formation of two business organizations, the Intellectual Property Committee (IPC) and the International Intellectual Property Alliance (IIPA). Both became pivotal actors in the bilateral and multilateral strategy that had been developed for the globalization of intellectual property rights. The IPC was formed in 1986. Its principal aim, as we shall see in Chapter 7, was to ensure that the Uruguay Round produced an agreement on intellectual property rights that was satisfactory to its corporate members.

The IIPA was established in 1984 to represent US copyright industries. Unlike the IPC it did not deal with the industrial side of intellectual property. Its executive director and general counsel was Eric Smith. The IIPA was then, and probably remains, the single most powerful copyright lobbying organization in the world. Its membership consisted of eight trade associations:[13]

1 the Association of American Publishers (the principal trade association of the book publishing industry with roughly 230 corporate members);
2 the American Film Marketing Association (124 members responsible for the production and licensing of independent English-language films);
3 Business Software Alliance (established in 1988, its members, which included Apple, Microsoft, Lotus and Novell, were then responsible for 75 percent of the world's prepackaged software);
4 the Computer and Business Equipment Manufacturers Association (representing companies from the computer, business equipment and telecommunications sectors);
5 the Information Technology Association of America (more than 500 members dealing with all aspects of information technology);
6 the Motion Picture Association of America (the trade association of the American film industry, functioning as the lobbying arm of the seven largest film producers);
7 the National Music Publishers' Association (more than 500 members that were owners of copyright in musical works—described as the "eyes, ears and

voice of the American music publishing association." Its subsidiary Harry Fox Agency, Inc., acted as licensing agent for US music publishers.); and

8   the Recording Industry Association of America (comprising US record companies that at the time accounted for approximately 50 percent of world annual recording industry trade).

When banded together these eight trade associations represented some 1500 companies, which in 1990 accounted for 3.3 percent of US GDP. They represented "the leading edge of the world's high-technology, entertainment and publishing industries."[14]

The IIPA was effective because its members stuck together and agreed to move quickly. When the wily prime minister of Singapore, Lee Kuan Yew, attempted to play the software, record and book interests against one another ("I'll give you what you want, but not them"), they said, "I'll stand with my brethren" (1993 interview). We were told of one intellectual property industry association that the alliance:

> kicked out in effect because they were too slow in making decisions. We need unanimity, rapidly achieved. So we cut them off so we could be more effective and move faster. We can't wait or the window of opportunity will be passed (1993 interview).

In commenting on the more limited success of the US trade union movement in linking labor standards to trade and the total failure of the environmental movement to secure a "green 301," one IIPA leader said: "The problem with the greens is they're not as united as we are."

Many of the members of the IIPA had been around for some time. The Motion Picture Association had been established in 1922. Some companies, like Microsoft, were newcomers. They all had in common the fact that digital technologies had the potential to transform the market structures in which they operated. No one in the recording or film industry could fail to notice how their products once in digital form could be delivered in a variety of different ways. The worrying possibility for these established companies was that they might not be the ones doing the delivering, having been swept away by one of those entrepreneurially driven "creative gales of destruction" that the economist Schumpter said typified the evolution of capitalism. One way to avoid possible extinction was to design intellectual property rules that would prevent these companies from losing the core intellectual assets of their business. Bill Gates had shown in the 1980s how it was possible to protect intangible assets using copyright. Once DOS and then Windows became the industry standard, copyright law could be used to hold at bay those other entrepreneurs who wanted to enter software applications markets that Microsoft wanted to reserve for itself. The companies and trade associations paying dues to the IIPA were not just interested in a copyright regime that secured export markets, but also one that helped to maintain the industrial pecking order within the world economy.

Once the 301 system had been put in place, those who had lobbied for its creation became its biggest users. A 301 action could begin with the USTR or alternatively any "interested person" could file a petition asking the USTR to launch an investigation under 301.[15] Petitions could also be filed to deny GSP benefits to a country. The IIPA became, as we shall see in the next section, an "interested person."

PINOCCHIO'S NOSE

The 301 process began with dialogue between the US and the target country, but at base it was a mechanism of economic coercion. It was a process in which countries were routinely threatened with trade sanctions. Since threatening other countries carried diplomatic costs there had to be some evidence to support the allegation that a country did in fact have egregious policies and practices when it came to protecting US intellectual property. There also had to be some sort of procedure for obtaining this evidence. Procedural due process was not an unimportant idea in US domestic law.

Under Special 301 the USTR had a lot of work to do. More was needed than just an allegation of piracy against a country by a US company. Before the USTR could identify a country as a priority foreign country under Special 301, it had to analyze that country's intellectual property law, examine its practices and attempt to work out the impact of those laws and practices on US trade. When USTR negotiating teams traveled to places like Seoul, Singapore and Rome to meet with officials, those teams had to be able to point to numbers on piracy indicating serious trade losses for the US. When the USTR Carla Hills sent a US team to Rome in 1992 to meet Italian authorities to discuss the piracy of Disney movies, it helped to know from the Motion Picture Association that the US industry was losing US$224 million annually to Italian pirates, that 80 percent of video outlets in Italy were part of the piracy enterprise and that Italy was second only to Taiwan in terms of the overall losses it was causing to US copyright industries. There was little hope otherwise of getting the attention of Italian officials and even less chance of being taken seriously.

Putting numbers on piracy was useful in other ways. It created a fact for public consumption. The numbers could be publicly circulated in the US to confirm the pirate image of a country. For this purpose the numbers were regularly fed to the US and foreign press. If the USTR finally did impose trade sanctions the numbers on trade losses helped to provide a justification for those sanctions. The numbers could also be used by the USTR as the basis on which to calculate the size of the penalties that would be imposed under 301.

Then there was the simple psychological truth that people liked numbers. Of course, they had to be simple, big numbers—ones that educated people could easily remember and trot out in a conversation to make a point and show their command of the facts: "Trade losses in 1992 in these countries [28 pirate countries identified by the IIPA] exceeded US$4.6 billion."[16]

The resource implications of obtaining hard data on piracy were staggering. So far as the US copyright industry was concerned there was hardly a country in the world not pirating US intellectual property. The USTR was of a similar mind. In 1989 a USTR "Fact Sheet" stated that "no foreign country currently meets every standard for adequate and effective intellectual property protection."[17] Certainly the pirates were not confined to Southeast Asia and the Caribbean. Italian pirates came in for bitter denunciation from the Motion Picture Association (MPA), especially after they violated *Snow White*'s copyright. Greece, Poland, Russia and Spain were examples of other European piracy trouble spots.

The USTR's office was not particularly large or well resourced. Nor was it filled with social scientists who knew all about the collection and analysis of quantitative data. The 301 system required the USTR to survey the laws and economies of nations as they related to intellectual property all around the world. This was in addition to the work that the USTR carried out in its more traditional sectors such as agriculture and textiles. Moreover, the data needed to reach a judgment under 301 were inherently difficult to obtain. How was one to measure the losses US industry was suffering at the hands of copyright pirates in other countries? Was it plausible to assume, for example, that every pirated videocassette of a US movie in Italy cost the US film industry a theater ticket? Was it plausible to assume that most of the illegal videocassette market was related to US movies? In Italy, for example, not everyone was using videocassettes to copy *Snow White* and other Disney classics. A considerable part of this market was devoted to copying "red light" porn movies of European origin.[18] Pirated pornographic material has historically always formed a significant part of the market. No doubt the US porn industry, the biggest in the world, also suffered at the hands of video pirates, although this tended not to be publicly stressed by the US film industry.

Right from the beginning the IIPA realized that it had to deliver economic analysis in order to make persuasive the political argument to act against intellectual property pirates. One of its first significant achievements was the preparation of an economic report on piracy in 1985, "Piracy of US Copyrighted Works in Ten Selected Countries." It made a "big hit" in Congress (1993 interview). The IIPA also filed it with the USTR in response to the USTR's request for information concerning the use of 301 and the GSP. The report marked the beginning of a symbiotic relationship between the two organizations. The USTR needed the data provided by the IIPA in order to be able to convince the trade negotiators of other states that there really was a piracy problem, as well as to justify the making of threats if the problem was not fixed. The IIPA needed the USTR to issue those threats if the overall intellectual property strategy of which the IIPA was a part was ever going to succeed.

As the 301 process was fine-tuned during the 1980s the relationship between the USTR and the IIPA became one of close cooperation. At the beginning of each year the USTR would place a request for information in the Federal Register for the purposes of determining which countries were to be on what Special 301 lists for that year. The IIPA would respond by filing a detailed analysis of each problem country's practices on intellectual property along with estimates of the size of market losses to the relevant US copyright industry (see Figure 6.1). So, for example, in 1993 the IIPA identified 28 problem countries that were responsible for a trade loss of US$4.63 billion.[19] The IIPA would then make recommendations about which countries were to go on what lists. The countries with the worst record would be put on the list of priority foreign countries. Taiwan and Thailand had regular spots on this list. Other nations would find themselves recommended for inclusion on the priority watch list or the watch list. Occasionally, the IIPA would send a positive signal to a country by suggesting its removal from the watch list. For example, Malaysia in 1991 was taken off the watch list by the USTR at the suggestion of the IIPA because it had made genuine efforts to deal with the piracy problem. If a country slackened off after its good efforts it would find itself back on a list. Malaysia was back in IIPA's bad books in 1993. It was a question of getting a good 301 report card every year.

Figure 6.1 *"Special 301" in Action*

USTR—Request in Federal Register for Written Submissions under Special 301
(usually in January)

⑤

Lobby Group (e.g., IIPA) files its Special 301 recommendations and estimates as to trade losses on intellectual property
(around February)

⑤

USTR submits the National Trade Estimate report to the president and various congressional committees (contains analysis and estimates of trade losses on intellectual property with information being drawn from, among other sources, private sector trade advisory committees and interested persons)
(on or before 31 March)

⑤

USTR has 30 days in which to identify foreign countries under Special 301, including priority foreign countries (around 30 April). Sources of information for this purpose include information received from interested persons such as the IIPA

⑤

USTR has 30 days to initiate a 301 investigation from the date that a country is identified as a priority foreign country unless the USTR determines it would be detrimental to US economic interests to investigate

The IIPA delivered more than just numbers to the USTR. If, for example, the Singaporeans passed a copyright law in response to 301 pressure, how would the USTR know whether this law was adequate and effective? The USTR was not teeming with intellectual property experts, especially ones on Singaporean law. What if the law had not been passed in English? Here the IIPA would perform a service. It would get an expert to do a legal analysis of that law and then ship that analysis into the USTR's office (1993 interview). In the USTR's busy office the delivery of this kind of prepackaged analysis was invaluable.

Over time the IIPA and the USTR got to know each other's views. They were in frequent contact via phone and meetings, exchanging information, plugging each other into the politics of their respective decision-making processes, working out which countries they were going to hit and which to leave alone for the time being. The views of those in the USTR began to correspond with those of the IIPA. There was nothing surprising in this. US corporations, the most moneyed on earth, had sent the USTR a simple message at the beginning of the 1980s: no deal on intellectual property, no Uruguay Round. Whatever trade package US trade negotiators brought back had to contain an agreement on intellectual property. Otherwise there was no prospect of negotiating through Congress the necessary legislative approvals for the implementation of the Uruguay Round package. Deep cooperation with the intellectual property lobby made a lot of sense as far as the USTR was concerned. Without the backing of this lobby there would be no mega-multilateral trade deal that represented the summit of every trade negotiator's career. The intellectual property–trade linkage brought the USTR into closer association with the most powerful corporations in the US, thereby increasing the status and power of the office. The decision to impose trade sanctions under the 301 process was not a decision for the USTR to make alone. It was ultimately the decision of the National Economic Council (NEC), an interagency body on which all major US government agencies had a representative. The USTR's connections with powerful corporations on the issue of intellectual property protection helped to give weight to its recommendations about what to do. Generally, the decisions of the NEC were resolved along the lines of the USTR's views (1993 interview).

At a more personal level it also dawned on people within the USTR's office that their knowledge of the trade game would be valuable to companies with large intellectual property portfolios. Trade negotiators were given medals and certificates in recognition of their successful efforts in a trade negotiation. While it was nice to have these adorning an office wall, they didn't in the long run quite match the salary and share packages negotiators might get if they were recruited by a US multinational to advise on trade-related intellectual property issues. When, for example, Jack Valenti flew to Geneva to thrash out aspects of the Uruguay Round negotiations with French film producers, the advisers he took with him were former USTR employees. There were incentives for individuals within the USTR to really deliver on intellectual property.

The USTR came to rely heavily on the figures on piracy provided to it by US companies and business organizations like the IIPA. How did the IIPA and other influential intellectual property lobbyists like the Business Software Alliance arrive at figures of trade losses like US$47 million in Bulgaria in 1992 and US$490 million in Russia in the same year? The IIPA represented a membership of some 1,500 companies, these companies having offices all over the world. The companies formed for the purposes of gathering data on piracy a "gigantic worldwide network" (1993 interview). Assisting this global private surveillance machine were the US embassies. Improving intellectual property protection became a part of their diplomatic activities. Commerce and diplomacy became even more intertwined. These embassies collected information on a country's practices on intellectual property that was fed back to the USTR. US embassies in various pirate countries provided visiting USTR teams with briefings and support when those teams came to exert bilateral pressure on a country.

Each year the IIPA would put out the word among its members—"where are you having problems?" Individuals working for companies in problem countries or individuals who traveled regularly to these places would send in their estimates of loss of corporate profits due to piracy to company headquarters and eventually this information would find its way to the relevant trade association of the industry and ultimately to the IIPA. Data were drawn from a wide variety of sources. Publishers traveling to book fairs would complain to each other about book piracy in various markets and some of these complaints would end up in an IIPA report. Naturally, no large company wanted to be seen to have a small estimate. It implied that its products were not worth pirating. It also meant that the company's problems would be put down the queue of 301 priorities by the USTR. Company employees working in developing country markets could also blame large-scale piracy for slow progress on sales. The incentives to be generous in one's estimate of the piracy problem were strong. There was no real downside to overestimating the size of the problem. Who was going to contradict the figures being put forward? For reasons that we have explained, the USTR had no rational reason to do so. The media simply reported the facts. The countries on the receiving end of the 301 process had doubts about the figures that USTR negotiating teams were throwing at them. An Italian government report suggested that reliable estimates of the Italian video piracy problem could not be made using the assumption that every illegal cassette amounted to an unsold theater ticket. There were lots of reasons why Italians were not particularly avid theatergoers. The report went on to put US losses at 15–22.5 billion lire per year, whereas the MPA's estimate was 279 billion lire per year. The discrepancy between the US and Italian estimates in fact became evidence in the eyes of the MPA that the Italian government lacked the necessary commitment to tackle the theft of intellectual property.

Privately there must have been the occasional doubt about the estimates being provided by US industry to US officials. Witness the following exchange in a 1993 interview:

Drahos: How accurate do you think are the industry figures on piracy?

US Department of Commerce official (smiling): Trade organizations have a varying degree of commitment to accuracy.

A little skepticism was warranted. After all, the facts and fact sheets were sourced from a faction—the intellectual property lobby. Reservations about the size of the piracy problem tended to remain in the realm of private thoughts. Publicly and officially a picture was painted of foreign governments tolerating rampant piracy. Individual estimates that had drifted into the offices of intellectual property lobbyists from far-flung corporate offices were written into analyses and sent on to the USTR and other areas of government. They became part of officialdom, making their way into government reports. The estimates grew ever larger:

> Foreign pirating reduces the revenues of the US software industry by several billion dollars. One personal computer manufacturer has commented that it has lost 80 percent of its potential revenue in Southeast Asia to competitors who have illegally copied its intellectual and industrial property.[20]

The IIPA was not the only business lobbyist playing the numbers game. The Business Software Alliance (BSA), a member of the IIPA, had an aggressive strategy for the enforcement of intellectual property rights in software. Like the IIPA, it hired Economists Incorporated to write reports about the importance of the software industry to the US economy.[21] Economists Incorporated described the problem of software piracy as "ubiquitous."[22] The estimated annual worldwide loss to industry of US$10–12 billion was the BSA's figure.[23] Even though there was some occasional skepticism within the USTR about the BSA's quantification of software piracy losses, it did not stop the USTR from using those figures in calculating the punitive duties it could threaten China with under the 301 process (1994 interview). They were, after all, the only figures that were available. The IIPA and the BSA aggregated the estimates they received and sent the results into a loop consisting of Congress, the USTR and other relevant federal government departments, the media and consulting economists. A process of constant recycling followed and after a while these estimates came to be seen as hard facts. The same intangibility of the value of intellectual property that made it ideal for tax games also made it ideal for political games.

By the early 1990s the USTR, the intellectual property lobby and the companies for which they worked had a closeness born of participation in a common crusade. When the Disney Corporation was in agony over the unauthorized broadcast of *Snow White and the Seven Dwarfs* in Venice in 1991 the then USTR Carla Hills wrote to Frank Wells, the CEO of Disney, saying that, largely in response to Disney's needs, a USTR team had been sent to Italy to see what could be done. The letter ended with, "We now have their attention and we will keep up the pressure."[24] The intellectual property lobby reciprocated these feelings of solicitude:

I cannot laud Ambassador Carla Hills too highly. In a global nest of complex-ities, she has been a mostly triumphant captain. She has been thoroughly sup-portive of the MPAA's and the International Intellectual Property Alliance's objectives...But in resources USTR is thinly clad. It has a tiny band of profes-sionals, not enough to man all the barricades...MPAA believes USTR needs more support staff.[25]

Washington lobbyists do not always push for an increase in the size of a government bureaucracy!

THE WOLF AT THE DOOR

Between 1985 and 1994 (the year in which TRIPS was signed as part of the Final Act of the Uruguay Round) the USTR brought Section 301 actions dealing with intellectual property against Brazil (1985, 1987 and 1993), Korea (1985), Argentina (1988), Thailand (1990 and 1991), India (1991), China (1991 and 1994) and Taiwan (1992).[26] Given that by the end of 1994, 95 Section 301 actions had been initiated, the launching of 11 Section 301 actions related to intellectual property against seven countries would seem to be a modest use of coercive power. Further, in only one of those cases, that of Brazil in 1987, were punitive tariff measures actually imposed. In the case of China in 1994 the USTR did increase duties on more than US$1 bil-lion worth of Chinese imports as from 26 February 1995, but on 25 February 1995 an agreement was reached between the two countries and so the duties were not imposed.

Section 301 was much more about barking than biting. For any country, even one as powerful as the US, aggression brings costs. Trade relations between states depend on open lines of communication between trade offi-cials, and on good professional relations that enable those officials to nego-tiate trade deals that bring them professional credit and promotion. In the community of trade negotiators what really counts are deals that allow trade to happen, not decisions that disrupt trade relations. Countless con-versations, official and nonofficial, are required to smooth the way for traders wishing to get their goods past the border of another country. Once one country resorts to actual coercion in attaining a trade objective it is a very public admission of failure. Trade thuggery rips apart the webs of dia-logue on which trade negotiators rely to manage their long-term negotiat-ing objectives, leaving them the difficult task of reconnecting those delicate strands for future negotiations. Closing deals, the mark of every good nego-tiator, as our informants told us, becomes much more difficult.

It was not only trade people who would have to wear the costs of bullying on the intellectual property issue. International trade relations on intellectual property were part of a larger set of international trade issues that were in turn part of an even broader set of international economic, foreign and defense issues. In such a world of complex interdependency the USTR could hardly go around lashing out at "pirate" countries whenever the private sector demanded it. To some extent at least the US had to remain concerned with its image and appeal among developing countries. The use of 301 had to be tempered by diplomatic wisdom. Intellectual property was nested in a much larger game of complex interdependency meaning that it made no sense to punish every single transgression of US intellectual property. The Caribbean states, after having signed up to the Caribbean Basin initiative, did little to protect US movies, something to which the USTR, much to the annoyance of the IIPA, turned a blind eye:

> IIPA expresses concern that USTR has never formally acted upon, or even acknowledged, any petition filed to remove countries from the CBERA [Caribbean Basin Economic Recovery Act] program for violations of intellectual property rights of the US copyright industries. It notes that USTR has not promulgated procedures for receiving and acting upon petitions to revoke, suspend or withdraw CBI beneficiary country status. IIPA suggests that additional Congressional direction may be appropriate.[27]

Similarly, when the USTR Carla Hills in April 1990 did not designate any country as a "priority foreign country" under Special 301, the IIPA was openly critical, claiming that it threatened "the credibility of US trade policy."[28] The IIPA's enthusiasm for the use of the trade fist was readily understandable. It was a single issue lobby and it had to justify the dues its corporate members paid. Trade sanctions, as far as it was concerned, were the most effective way to get quick action from a country on intellectual property. As a single issue lobbyist it had the most to gain from the use of coercion and the least to lose. The individual company members of the IIPA were also happy for the IIPA to be seen as the bully. Companies such as IBM with offices and markets in developing countries did not want to be too closely linked to the use of 301. There was always the possibility that they might be the subject of some sort of counterretaliation by a developing country. IBM in particular concentrated on achieving a multilateral solution to its intellectual property problems leaving the IIPA "to beat up on" individual countries (1993 interview).

The aim of the 301 process was to push and prod developing countries into accepting intellectual property rules that would allow their economies to be integrated into a global knowledge economy being led by US entrepreneurs. For this purpose it was more important to give countries the feeling that their behavior on intellectual property was the subject of constant surveillance. The watch list method under Special 301 did precisely this. Dozens of countries were listed under Special 301 once it was introduced in 1988. No country was exempt from the watch list process with both Australia and Europe appearing on it. Once under surveillance a country found itself drawn into an atmosphere of threat, with the possibility of a 301 action lurking in the background. Rather than risk a full-blown dispute with the USTR, countries would attempt to do something on intellectual property to appease the USTR and avoid a really bad 301 assessment. Every year as the deadline for the USTR's Special 301 review approached countries would rush through some amendment to their intellectual property law, perhaps put a few more pirates in jail, increase penalties or take some other action, all in an effort to demonstrate their commitment to respecting US intellectual property. With both bilaterals and the GATT, the IIPA position was: "We'll *not* negotiate on standards of IP. We'll negotiate on *time* to meet them. Any watering down of IP standards and no deal, no GATT" (1993 interview).[29] The annual 301 report card handed out by the USTR to each country looked at the progress that it had made since the previous year and hinted at what might happen if a country did not become a better student. Good pupils were given encouragement and the delinquents chastised; everybody was told how they could do better. The following are taken from the USTR's *2000 Special 301 Report*:

> Ireland: However, Ireland's commitment to enact comprehensive copyright legislation has not been met...The US government remains hopeful that Ireland will take steps necessary to complete the legislative process in the very near future, but will feel compelled to consider other options in the face of any further delay.

> Kuwait: Kuwait has been lowered to the watch list this year in recognition of its efforts over the past year to address concerns regarding its intellectual property laws and enforcement actions.

> Latvia: Although Latvia has made progress in improving its intellectual property rights regime since it became a member of the WTO in February 1999, there is still much room for improvement.

The watch list mechanism has in this regard proved to be surprisingly effective, as this observation from a USTR official shows:

> One fascinating aspect of the Special 301 process occurs just before we make our annual determinations, when there is often a flurry of activity in those countries desiring not to be listed or to be moved to a lower list. IP laws are suddenly passed or amended, and enforcement activities increase significantly.[30]

Sovereign states, no matter how big or small, are caught up in a global surveillance network consisting of American companies, the American Chamber of Commerce, trade associations and American embassies, a network that gathers and reports on the minutiae of their social and legal practices when it comes to US intellectual property. The pressure to improve one's protection of intellectual property is relentless. US officials traveling to Thailand take the opportunity over lunch to tell Thai judges from the Intellectual Property and Trade Court that they should hand out genuinely deterrent punishments to the intellectual property infringers currently before them. The judges listen to these insistent remarks with the civility that is characteristic of Thai people's treatment of guests, knowing that if they do not comply their government will receive a report card like the following:

Thailand's intellectual property record over the past year has improved moderately. The intellectual property courts are imposing criminal penalties; however, these are often not sufficient to deter infringement and are often suspended pending appeal.[31]

The countries against which 301 actions were taken in the 1980s and early 1990s were specially chosen. These bilateral actions were part of a coordinated strategy that had a multilateral dimension, a dimension we explore in the next chapter. As we have pointed out elsewhere the US:

> targeted its Section 301 action on forms of conduct that it was seeking to control through the Uruguay Round, such as disrespect for US intellectual property laws and restrictions on US foreign investment.[32]

In Chapter 5 we saw that India had during the 1960s, 1970s and 1980s led developing country resistance to Western business initiatives to ratchet up standards on intellectual property protection. Brazil had also been a resister in the 1960s, attempting to turn the UN into a forum to reexamine critically the patent system. Korea, worryingly for the US, was making strides in the manufacture of semiconductor chips and showing every sign that its markets, like Japan's, would remain beyond the reach of US knowledge companies. As one Korean negotiator told us, Korea was being called a "second Japan" by US negotiators (1995 interview): Brazil, India, Korea—all three developing country leaders—all three the subject of 301 investigations.

In 1985, the year after the amendment to Section 301 of the Trade Act to include intellectual property, the USTR self-initiated two 301 actions. The first on 16 September was against Brazil's policy on informatics and the second on 4 November 1985 was against Korea for its lack of effective protection for US intellectual property rights. The action against Korea produced the first significant bilateral deal on intellectual property.

A number of US industries were unhappy with Korea. The Motion Picture Export Association (MPEA) had trouble distributing and showing its movies there. When its movies were shown it was by pirates rather than authorized distributors. Authorized distributors came in for a tough time in Seoul; "thugs and goons" intimidated the patrons of theaters in which MPEA movies were shown, on one occasion releasing snakes into the theater (1994 interview). The takings in these theaters were not great. The MPEA had filed its own 301 petition on 10 September 1985, but withdrew it on 25 October 1985, after a Korean minister traveled to Jack Valenti's Washington office and spent four days settling a deal that was acceptable to the MPEA (1994 interview). Pharmaceutical companies had gripes about the Korean patent system and the US semiconductor industry saw Korea as a major center of piracy of US chips. Korea itself had aspirations to join the OECD. It was an emerging economic power. Much of its success was built on trade with the US. In 1985 the US was Korea's number one trade partner; 35.6 percent of Korea's trade was conducted with the US.[33] The USTR needed a strong victory under its new 301 procedure for intellectual property and Korea represented its best chance of success.

The bilateral negotiations were described by one US negotiator who was involved in them as "slow and painful" (1994 interview). The US had had discussions with Korea over the intellectual property issue prior to 1985. Each side knew the other's arguments. The US argued that it was in Korea's interests to have stronger copyright protection. The Koreans replied that stronger protection would raise consumer prices and, in any case, changing the attitude of Korean people toward intellectual property was a task beyond the capacity of government. Copying within Korean culture was a compliment to the author. The last defense in particular made US negotiators take deep sighs before restating the US position. The USTR adopted another tactic to neutralize the cultural claim. Copyright in Korea and other Asian countries was typically administered by departments of culture. US trade officials pointed out to Korean trade negotiators that officials in the Korean department of culture were, by seeing copyright as a cultural rather than economic tool, getting Korean trade into a lot of hot water. Would the US really be forced to close its huge markets to Korea because some officials from cultural affairs were insisting that in Korean culture copying brought pleasure and honor to the author? Once the USTR put together officials from Korean trade ministries and culture ministries it did not take long for the former to pull rank on the latter. Korean culture was not a big export earner and trade negotiators everywhere move in a practical milieu. As one lobbyist put it, 301 was in effect a "wake-up call [to] get senior people in developing countries to think about the issue" (1993 interview). Putting the blame on officials from cultural affairs was also a useful negotiating tactic in that trade negotiators from both sides could blame an absent party. Absent parties from the closed rooms of trade negotiations generally are a handy negotiating convenience in trade talks. When US negotiators made threats at an early stage about what would happen to Korean exports if the Koreans did not comply on intellectual property they also said that they had little choice in the matter because of the pressure they were under from US industry (Korean negotiator, 1995 interview).

On 21 July 1986 the White House announced that it had reached an agreement with Korea on the protection of US intellectual property. It was signed on 28 August 1986. Korean officials we spoke to described it as a "dividing line" in Korean intellectual property history. A former US negotiator said of it that it "became the blueprint for other agreements plus the GATT" (1994 interview). The USTR Clayton Yeutter, in a lunchtime talk to the American Intellectual Property Law Association on 9 October 1986, described it as sending a message to GATT members and the rest of the world.[34]

There was little attention to legal niceties in the agreement. It was not a treaty or even a memorandum of understanding. It was simply a deal in which US companies wanted money for their patents, protection for their trademarks, the pirates jailed and Koreans to open their markets, culture and wallets to US copyright and patent products, and that was that. What stuck in Korean minds was the millions of dollars handed over by Samsung to Texas Instruments. Patents soon became a "number one priority" for companies like Samsung. They could see that building up a patent portfolio of thousands of patents, many of them of doubtful validity, and then springing them on competitors was going to be an important route to profits in the future.

The 1986 agreement marked the beginning of an American intellectual property tutelage for the Koreans. Their drafts of new intellectual property laws were reviewed by US experts and comments provided to Korean drafters with a speed that surprised those drafters (1994 interview). Getting intellectual property legislation on the books was merely the beginning. The US also put pressure on the Koreans to close operations like Tower Publications, which were copying US copyright products without permission. The USTR continued to apply bilateral pressure under Special 301 procedures and US business continued to petition for the use of 301 against Korea. Bristol Myers filed a 301 petition in 1987 alleging inadequate enforcement of a particular patent. Squibb Corporation and Bristol Myers both filed petitions in 1988 on patent protection issues. The MPEA also filed a petition in 1988. These petitions were withdrawn when Korea offered to settle the actions.

Korea tried to keep the terms of its deal with the US a secret, but eventually news of the deal leaked into the other embassies. Europe and Australia, among others, which in other contexts bemoaned aggressive US unilateralism, showed up on Korea's doorstep demanding a similar deal from the Koreans for their own industries. These officials saw no inconsistency in publicly criticizing the US for trade bullying while privately riding on its coattails. In fact the EC made it a practice to obtain a copy of the agreement that the US obtained from Asian countries in its bilateral negotiations and then attempt to get similar terms. It never did better and normally did worse (1993 interview).

These days the Korean commitment to intellectual property is impressive. Korean officials will tell you of the enormous potential benefits of the system. There is the occasional glum note as when a trade negotiator in 1995 told us that Korea would go into a trade deficit with the US.[35] There is also a note of realism about what intellectual property represents: "Intellectual property is really an issue of survival within the world system" (1995 interview). It is the price that countries have to pay, largely to US companies, to enter the world trading system.

The 301 action against Brazil in 1987 was unusual because it culminated in 1988 with the imposition of US$39 million in tariff penalties on Brazilian products being imported into the US market (the tariffs were lifted in July 1990). But it also illustrates how important US bilateralism was to the multilateral strategy we will be discussing in the next chapter. Brazil had chosen not to have patent protection for pharmaceutical products. It was not alone in adopting this type of patent law. Argentina, Mexico and the Andean Pact countries had all decided not to protect pharmaceutical inventions or to offer only weak protection. The aim was to keep the price of pharmaceuticals as low as possible. For the US there was the danger that a developing country leader like Brazil might in the context of the GATT negotiations team up with India and lead a developing country bloc on the issue of the patenting of pharmaceuticals. If, however, Brazil and some of the other South American states had bilaterally been pressured into adopting US-style patent laws on pharmaceuticals then in the context of the GATT they would only be agreeing multilaterally to patent standards to which they had already bilaterally agreed. As one former US trade negotiator put it: "Each bilateral brought that country much closer to [the] TRIPS agreement, so accepting TRIPS was no big deal" (1994 interview). (Aside from Brazil, the Pharmaceuticals Manufacturing Association also filed a petition in 1988 against Argentina, which was withdrawn when Argentina agreed to modify its patent law.)

Breaking Brazilian resistance on pharmaceutical patents was absolutely crucial. It would send a message to other South American states and deprive India of a potential ally in the TRIPS negotiations. When on 20 October 1988 the US president proclaimed the tariff increases on Brazilian paper products, non-benezoid drugs and consumer electronic items, the Brazilians were faced with a cost-benefit calculation. The cost of not complying with US wishes was roughly equal to the death of their markets in the sectors affected by the tariffs. At that time almost 25 percent of Brazilian trade was with the US. The gain of complying with US wishes was the termination of the tariff penalties and keeping their markets. Compliance would also get the rod of 301 action off their backs for a while. Under Special 301 a foreign country could not be identified as a priority foreign country if it entered into good faith negotiations or made significant progress in bilateral or multilateral negotiations on intellectual property.[36] Thus the payoff to the Brazilians was the removal of tariffs, the recovery of their markets and the end of further threats under the 301 process on this particular issue.

The Brazilians did not cave in immediately. Countries do not like being coerced and Brazilian politicians realized that the issue of cheap drugs was important to the Brazilian people. Brazil's AIDS population kept increasing. Brazil commenced an action against the US arguing that the use of 301 was illegal under GATT. Some US trade experts had reached a similar conclusion.[37] Most 301 actions would have been illegal under GATT. But then, as an IBM lawyer pointed out to us when we raised this issue in a 1994 interview, the US could always block GATT dispute panels on the use of 301 "while the tariffs did the job for you." The longer Brazil resisted, the less likely it would be to get its US markets back and, in any case, it faced a long, uphill battle trying to get justice in a trade system that was more about power than playing by the rules. The Brazilians began to draft the necessary legislation in 1990. In 1996 a "Fact Sheet" on Special 301 put out by the USTR stated that Brazil had taken "the admirable step of enacting a modern patent law."

In 1991 India was also on the receiving end of a 301 action on intellectual property. But as one Indian negotiator explained, India hardly cared about this. No Indian politician could afford to be seen domestically as part of a bilateral deal in which the Indian market was handed over to an American pharmaceutical Raj. India had a large domestic economy and so it placed less weight on its trade relationship with the US than did Brazil. It was the multilateral game, which we describe in the next chapter, that eventually brought the Indian tiger down.

In Central and Eastern Europe, US bilateralism was important in the 1990s, but EC bilateralism even more so because of the interest these states had/have in meeting the conditions of admission to the EU: "Central and Eastern European countries are in the sphere of influence of the EC Patent Office under the PHARE Program" (1993 WIPO interview). Our interviews with strategic major players suggest that the third major economic power, Japan, has not been a lead actor in shaping IP bilateralism.

China had been the target of US bilateralism on intellectual property since the 1979 trade agreement between the US and China. In that agreement and through subsequent 301 actions the US tried to push China into granting US standards of protection to US copyright, trademark and patent owners. The US could also exploit China's desire to enter eventually the WTO system (China became a WTO member in 2001). Naturally, it was important for the US to secure better protection for its intellectual property in China. More fundamentally, it wanted to ensure that the Chinese entrepreneurs of the future would respect the rules of global information capitalism. China was an old civilization, but was becoming a young, aggressive market society whose entrepreneurs might be reluctant to recognize the authority of US information capitalists over the knowledge that mattered in global markets:

> It's ridiculous for these stinking foreigners to pick on China like they do. We're just following the general trend by pirating some of their stuff. And they're up in arms, carrying on about intellectual property infringement and making a fucking stink all over the world about us.
> Foreign devils are just plain unreasonable. To be honest, they've been ripping off the Chinese for ages. What's all this stuff about intellectual property? Whose ancestors got everything going in the first place?[38]

The US itself, we saw in Chapter 2, was no great respecter of European intellectual property. Because the US sees the dangers to it of a market society born of a rejection of traditional authority over property rights in the capital of information, the US has kept up constant bilateral pressure on China to adopt and enforce intellectual property standards, signing Memoranda of Understanding with China in 1989, 1992 and 1995. Nowadays trade sanctions hang over China like a sword of Damocles. Under Section 306 of the US Trade Act the US continues to monitor China's progress on intellectual property rights. Monitoring means that the "USTR will be in a position to move directly to trade sanctions if there is slippage" in China's enforcement of bilateral intellectual property agreements.[39]

Perhaps the most stunning achievement of the 301 system has been its continued growth and use in the period after the creation of the WTO. There were intimations that the creation of a WTO dispute resolution system would see the US ease off on aggressive unilateralism. But, if anything, 301 has acquired a more machine-like efficiency in the post-TRIPS period. The USTR Charlene Barshefsky used Special 301 announcements to publicize the actions that the US would take in the WTO against countries on intellectual property. The symbolism of these announcements is interesting. The WTO dispute resolution system is treated as part of the US 301 process. This process has impressive bureaucratic scale. In her *2000 Special 301 Report* Barshefsky pointed out that more than 70 countries had been reviewed under Special 301. She named 59 foreign countries that failed to meet satisfactory standards of intellectual property; 59 countries that had been graded and listed; 59 countries whose laws and practices on intellectual property had to be watched, analyzed and acted upon. A system like 301 costs a lot to run. It is only really possible because corporate America picks up the tab. It provides the global surveillance network, the numbers for the estimates on piracy and much of the evaluation and analysis. The US state in return provides the legitimacy, the bureaucracy that negotiates, threatens and if necessary carries out enforcement actions. It is a system with complete bipartisan support in the US. The Clinton administration, ignoring or perhaps not knowing the implications of stronger intellectual property rights for human rights like health and education, strengthened 301 by introducing immediate action plans for foreign countries on intellectual property rights as well as out-of-cycle 301 reviews, pushing developing countries into accelerating their implementation of TRIPS and letting big business know of the "Administration's continued commitment to aggressive enforcement of protection for intellectual property."[40] In 2000 the Clinton administration had to backpedal a little on 301 in the case of sub-Saharan Africa. The deaths from HIV-AIDS there were making the commitment to aggressive enforcement of intellectual property look bad.

US bilateralism on intellectual property rights remains relentless. As the course for the first WTO trade round in the new millennium is plotted the US continues to negotiate bilaterally ever higher standards of intellectual property protection. The Free Trade Agreement it signed with Jordan in 2000 contains, for example, higher standards of patent protection than are to be found in TRIPS. With the WTO experiencing a crisis of legitimacy and with all eyes upon it, the US has shifted the intellectual property game back to the bilaterals. The bilateral strategy of the 1980s described in this chapter is being repeated. From the Caribbean Basin legislation to the GSP to 301 and on to TRIPS, "There was a success breeds success thing" (1993 interview) for the Washington legal entrepreneurs and the US, then European, then Japanese business leaders to whom the entrepreneurs explained their own interests.

CHAPTER 7

Agendas and Agenda-setters: The Multilateral Game

THE GATT

Writing in somewhat miffed tones in 1992 the director-general of the World Intellectual Property Organization (WIPO), Arpad Bogsch, pointed out that the GATT was not even a proper international organization.[1] Since it was, in the words of one US negotiator, about "to take the pen out of his hands" on the writing of intellectual property standards, its status as a noninternational organization must have made Bogsch's loss of power even more galling (1994 interview). The status problems of the GATT trace back to the meeting at Bretton Woods, New Hampshire, in 1944 where, in addition to currency regulation (the IMF) and development funding (the World Bank), states also decided that the cause of free trade would be best served by the creation of an international trade organization. By 1948 a draft for an International Trade Organization (ITO), known as the Havana Charter, had been completed. Congress, the home of US trade policy, was worried by the sovereignty implications of an ITO and so refused to ratify the charter. Instead, on 1 January 1948, a treaty came into force, the General Agreement on Tariffs and Trade. States became contracting parties rather than members since there was no international organization of which to be a member. The GATT was applied provisionally by the contracting parties. A GATT secretariat was built by Sir Eric Wyndham White (himself given the title of executive secretary rather than director-general)[2] but it existed in a legal netherworld, an organization without international legal personality. Existing merely as a contractual arrangement the GATT gave its parties maximum flexibility when it came to obligations of trade. That suited the world's most powerful legislature.

By the time of the Uruguay Round, GATT negotiations had been successful in producing a reduction of tariffs on industrial production. The Tokyo Round alone had seen a 35 percent reduction in the industrial tariffs of major economies. Progress on other barriers to trade such as national rules on technical standards, subsidies and customs valuation had been much slower. States had in the Tokyo Round (1973–79) begun to inch their way toward reducing these kinds of barriers by means of side codes, the Code on Standards enjoying the widest membership. Membership in these codes was open to all countries of the GATT, but there was no obligation to join. During the Tokyo Round the US had pushed for the inclusion of a counterfeiting code to deal with cross-border movements of counterfeit goods. The owners of well-known trademarks were becoming increasingly worried by the unauthorized use of their trademarks on goods manufactured in developing countries. The biggest concern was that these counterfeit goods would find their way back into those markets normally exploited by the trademark owner. Alarmed by the prospect of a world full of cheap imitations, trademark owners and their attorneys, invoking the rights of consumers to have the genuine Rolex, began to agitate for some kind of international solution. Trademark attorneys were important players in these early moves on exploring ways to achieve better international protection for trademarks, especially the attorneys who worked for cigarette companies. These companies, more than most others, were in possession of global brands that they wanted to make globally safe. Developing countries remained unsympathetic to the plight of Western owners of luxury brands. Trade maneuverings by nations are rarely morally consistent. For years the Western multinationals that controlled the packaging and distribution of food had made extensive use of the territorial insignia of developing countries such as Darjeeling tea and basmati rice without much regard for whether the products they were distributing actually originated from these regions. No one in the West considered this a problem.[3]

Developing countries countered the proposal to include a code on counterfeiting in the GATT by arguing that it was WIPO that had primary jurisdiction over intellectual property matters. WIPO, after all, was the specialist UN organization for intellectual property. The GATT's reach over intellectual property issues was only tangential to its jurisdiction over trade in goods. Article IX required contracting parties to cooperate with each other on the misuse of trade names and Article XX of the GATT, the article dealing with general exceptions to GATT, with some qualifications allowed parties to take measures that were necessary for the protection of intellectual property (Article XX [d]).[4] In the hundreds of decisions by GATT panels only three had involved intellectual property, with the US as defendant each time.[5] Intellectual property was hardly mainstream for the GATT. As far as developing countries were concerned the plausibility of their jurisdictional argument was strengthened by the fact that developed countries had successfully used precisely the same argument to keep UNCTAD out of significant involvement with the intellectual property field.[6] Here, as we shall see, developing countries underestimated the malleability of liberal legal discourses. UNCTAD, despite its trade and development brief, did not have competence over intellectual property, but the GATT did.

Despite some support from the EC, Japan and Canada, there was no mention of a code on counterfeiting in the declaration dealing with the results of the Tokyo Round. Encouraged by the International Anticounterfeiting Coalition, a key international business organization comprising global trademark owners, the US kept pushing on the counterfeit issue. It and a number of other parties circulated in 1979 a draft entitled "Agreement on Measures to Discourage the Importation of Counterfeit Goods."[7] Ultimately this did not lead anywhere much. The issue of counterfeit goods in trade was formally mentioned in the Ministerial Declaration of 29 November 1982, which in turn led to the formation of a Group of Experts on Trade in Counterfeit Goods in 1984.[8] This group reported in 1985 suggesting that something had to be done, and referred the policy issue about which body was to take action back to the GATT council. In short, the US had received the bureaucratic bounce-around on the issue of counterfeit goods.

By now the key players in the private sector were thinking in much bigger terms about the connection between the trade and intellectual property regimes. Edmund Pratt had taken over the leadership of the strategic Advisory Committee on Trade Negotiations (ACTN), the committee that, as we saw in Chapter 4, advised the president on trade policy. As discussed in Chapter 6, the US had remodeled its trade legislation to create the link between the 301 process and intellectual property. And as we shall see later in this chapter, a massive lobbying campaign was under way to build an international business coalition that would pressure governments to negotiate an agreement on intellectual property in any forthcoming trade round. The failure to achieve the agenda on the protection of counterfeit goods had led to a much bigger agenda-setting exercise. The experience of the Tokyo Round and its aftermath had confirmed that leaving state representatives or international secretariats to deal with intellectual property issues would bring little or no results. Developing countries were not in the mood to accept intellectual property as an agenda item for a future multilateral trade negotiation. They were primarily interested in getting better deals on agriculture and textiles and showed little interest in the "new themes" GATT agenda being pushed by the US. Developing country resistance to the inclusion of intellectual property would have to be broken by a combination of raising the costs of resistance and increasing the rewards of agreement.

THE WIPO TALKSHOP

By the mid-1980s US private sector disillusionment with the WIPO secretariat and WIPO as a forum for getting things done on intellectual property was running high. The copyright crisis of the 1960s was still recent history and strong copyright protection was becoming absolutely crucial to the US computer industry. WIPO's contribution to the Expert Group on Counterfeits had been to send along a representative to participate in discussions, although according to the Group of Experts' report his participation was minimal.[9] Patents, the backbone of the Western pharmaceutical domination of the world of prescription drugs, were under threat in the Diplomatic Conference for the Revision of the Paris Convention for the Protection of Industrial Property.[10] During the 1970s reductions in patent terms and the abolition of protection for pharmaceuticals were among the kinds of reforms to be found in places such as India, Brazil, Argentina, Mexico and the Andean Pact countries. A thriving generics industry developed in these countries. The US went into the Paris Diplomatic Conference in 1980 hoping to obtain higher standards of protection. Instead it found itself having to defend the existing Paris Convention standards. Moreover, in the words of one commentator, the US at these revision conferences found itself "alone and almost isolated."[11] This was the last straw for the US pharmaceutical industry. WIPO, it concluded, was no longer a forum that could be trusted to deliver the standards it needed.

WIPO's deepest failure from the US perspective lay in the area of enforcement. The general view in the US private sector was that even if one could get a treaty through WIPO there would be little point if the treaty standards were not enforceable. As it happened, intellectual property treaties like the Berne Convention had an enforcement mechanism in the form of a possible action in the International Court of Justice (ICJ). But as Jacques Gorlin had pointed out, in the 37 years since that possibility had presented itself in the Berne Convention the ICJ had not heard one dispute.[12] This had much to do with the "live and let live" attitude adopted by states in WIPO. There were conflicts, of course, between states over levels of intellectual property protection, with the North–South divide being particularly strong. WIPO's response to these kinds of problems was to manage the conflicts through the creation of groups of experts and committees to examine the issues. Conflict was thus contained rather than resolved.

Countries from the South were brought into the intellectual property fold through a process of "persuasion and advice" (WIPO, 1993 interview). WIPO staff would patiently explain the long-run investment benefits of a good intellectual property regime to developing country officials and the advantages in joining the WIPO-administered treaties. "What are your fears?" WIPO officials would ask developing country officials (1993 interview). One fear was that developing country officials would not be able to find the budgets to attend the frequent diplomatic conferences and expert meetings in Geneva and other places in Europe. Here WIPO was able to render assistance. It was and is the wealthiest UN organization because of the fees it collects under its international registration services. In 1990, for example, it collected fees of 54,850,000 Swiss francs under the Patent Cooperation Treaty.[13] (WIPO's pool of capital continued to grow. In December 1997 its total reserve funds amounted to 313,022,413 Swiss francs.) Under its development program WIPO would target selected developing countries for assistance and pay officials to attend WIPO meetings (1993 interview). More and more developing country officials with generous per diem allowances under their belts found themselves in business class flying to the right hotels to attend meetings of status on the WIPO calendar. The symposia on geographical indications, which were held in Bordeaux and other places in France, attracted a lot of interest.

WIPO was successful in expanding the membership of the conventions it administered, no small achievement given that one would not have expected countries such as Barbados, Costa Rica and Rwanda to have made membership of these conventions a priority in the 1970s and 1980s. This success brought with it a problem. As the number of developing countries joining WIPO grew, the task of the WIPO secretariat in managing conflict grew increasingly difficult. "As a rule we try to achieve consensus," a WIPO official told us. But there was little hope of achieving consensus between the numerous states of the South, which were intellectual property importers, and a few wealthy states, which were intellectual property exporters, especially in the 1970s and 1980s when developing countries were claiming that much technological knowledge was in fact the common heritage of mankind. Moreover since Western intellectual property systems did not recognize the intellectual property of indigenous people, the states of the South were participating in a regime that by definition made them part of the intellectual property poor. When in the early 1980s the US began to push for a multilateral trade round that included intellectual property, this was the clearest possible signal that WIPO was in danger of being abandoned by the US as a forum.

The danger was real. After World War II the US had pursued a policy of international forum shifting in order to secure the results it wanted in various international regimes.[14] An example close to home, as far as WIPO was concerned, was the withdrawal of the US from UNESCO in 1984. UNESCO had been useful to the US in sponsoring the development of the Universal Copyright Convention (UCC) in the 1940s, a convention the US had wanted.[15] UNESCO served as the UCC's secretariat when the UCC came into effect in September 1955. The US withdrew from UNESCO because developing countries were using it as a forum to push a program called the "New World Information Order." UNESCO was also not the right forum for the US agenda on copyright. UNESCO was a place where developing countries linked copyright to education and other human rights, a perspective with which the US was not particularly comfortable. Moreover, after the copyright crisis of the 1960s many developing countries, which were members of Berne, wanted to join the UCC because it was better suited to their needs as importers of educational materials. The US, despite not being a member of the Berne Convention, was not particularly happy with this potentially serious weakening of Berne and took steps to ensure that the Berne Convention remained secure.[16] By the 1980s it became clear that Berne was the main game for US copyright interests. These days there is a small copyright unit in UNESCO carrying out mainly technical assistance work.

The WIPO secretariat was well aware of the importance of the US to the maintenance of the organization's status and power. Over the years it had done its best to push consensus in the direction of US interests. With its considerable financial resources WIPO was able to fund flattering studies of intellectual property. More generally, WIPO contributed in various ways to the creation of a specialist intellectual property community that was useful to the US and other key players on difficult technical issues related to patent harmonization, copyright and satellite transmission and so on. So why, when confronted by the US initiative at the GATT, did WIPO not do more to develop an effective dispute resolution mechanism?

The answer has much to do with the director-general of WIPO seeking reelection to office.[17] Clearly, the chances of a director-general persuading developing countries, which formed a majority in WIPO, to reelect him were slim if WIPO was a forum in which they were being successfully beaten up over the piracy issue by their former colonizers. The very first user of any effective WIPO dispute resolution mechanism would have been the US. The minute that TRIPS came into force the US began to use the WTO dispute resolution mechanism to obtain compliance with its provisions. It remains to date the biggest litigator under TRIPS. From the point of view of gathering country votes it was better for the director-general to continue to manage and contain conflict within WIPO while doing his best to steer consensus in ways that favored the US, whose support was also needed for reelection purposes. The levers of a very personal self-interest thus shaped a macro outcome.

Criticism of the organization by outsiders was simply not tolerated. The power to reward was an effective tool in this regard. Those who took positions disliked by WIPO knew that they would not be invited to join WIPO's expert committees and participate in the policy formulation process. A door leading to the status and recognition of working for a UN organization would be quietly clicked shut. Those experts who found themselves sharing WIPO's views found themselves in demand. They would be invited to play a role in the international treaty revision process. In this way WIPO over time carefully forged and managed a group of like-minded technical experts who understood WIPO agendas perfectly. It was these experts who produced the complex background legal papers needed in any treaty revision process and who helped to lay the juristic foundations for expansionist desires of business owners of intellectual property. These experts also became missionaries, traveling to exotic developing country locations where intellectual property law was largely unknown.

The WIPO secretariat was seen as being a jealous guardian of its power over intellectual property standard-setting, even to the point of being high-handed with states during negotiations. The following remarks from a US trade negotiator reveal a fairly widespread perception:

> In WIPO the secretariat does the writing and then goes to countries. The secretariat creates the document—pleadings, and intervention are needed by countries to change it. In the GATT process the secretariat writes down what trade negotiators decide for countries. [GATT] is much more country driven (1994 interview).

During the 1980s WIPO watched the US agenda-setting exercise at the GATT. Within the constraints of its membership the WIPO secretariat did the best it could to deliver those intellectual property standards the US wanted. For example, in a very short space of time WIPO was able to produce a draft treaty on protection for integrated circuits. The Treaty on Intellectual Property in Respect of Integrated Circuits (IPIC) was opened for signature on 26 May 1989. But by now it was too late. The US initiative at the GATT was in full flight. In US eyes the compulsory licensing provisions of the IPIC were too generous to developing countries. Developing countries led by Brazil this time had proved highly effective critics of the draft treaty. The US never ratified the treaty, in fact almost no country did. Instead, those provisions that passed muster with the US semiconductor chip industry were incorporated by reference into TRIPS and there, as we shall see, the compulsory licensing issue was fixed up to the satisfaction of US industry.

As the Uruguay Round progressed and it became apparent that the absence of a dispute resolution mechanism was a major problem for WIPO, a Committee of Experts on the Settlement of Intellectual Property Disputes between States was formed. It began meeting in 1990. There was always the chance of the Uruguay Round talks failing in which case WIPO would have the only dispute resolution game in town. The committee did produce a draft treaty by 1991, but by then a draft of TRIPS was all but complete. When in 1995 TRIPS came into force WIPO's draft treaty on dispute settlement was still a draft. It was still a draft when in 1997 Kamil Idris replaced Arpad Bogsch as director-general of WIPO.

GETTING INTELLECTUAL PROPERTY ON THE TRADE AGENDA: THE QUAD AND THE IPC

Developing country leaders like India and Brazil opposed US efforts to deepen GATT involvement with intellectual property issues. Their argument in essence was that WIPO should be left to deal with intellectual property standard-setting and that the trade dimensions of intellectual property should be dealt with by UNCTAD. Intellectual property with its close connections to technology transfer and development fell squarely within UNCTAD's remit. This blocking strategy by developing countries proved effective as long as there was no unified push by the US and Europe on the inclusion of intellectual property in the next trade round. Developing countries thus continued to run with the jurisdictional argument put up by their experts, but without a real fallback strategy.

As we saw in Chapter 4, a small group of individuals in the corporate sector had begun to think in much bigger terms about possibilities at the GATT. The wider US business community was in a receptive mood for new thinking about the international regulation of intellectual property. Pratt, with the assistance of other senior executives within Pfizer, began to put himself forward within business circles as someone who could develop US business thinking about trade and economic policy. In 1979 Pratt became a member of ACTN and in 1981 its chairman. ACTN had been created in 1974 by Congress under US trade law as part of a private sector advisory committee system. The purpose of this system was to "ensure that US trade policy and trade negotiation objectives adequately reflect US commercial and economic interests."[18] ACTN existed at the apex of this system. Under its charter, its membership of no more than 45 had to be drawn from a range of sectors including labor, industry, agriculture, small business, service industries, retailers and consumer interests.[19] During the 1980s representatives from the most senior levels of big business within the US were appointed by the president to serve on the committee (Pratt was appointed by President Carter). The committee was a purely advisory one, but with its direct access to the USTR and the duty of advising him or her on US trade policy and negotiating objectives in the light of national interest, it was an extremely influential committee. Out of this business crucible came the crucial strategic thinking on the trade-based approach to intellectual property. With Pratt at the helm, ACTN began to develop a sweeping trade and investment agenda. During Pratt's six years of chairmanship, ACTN worked closely with William E. Brock III, the USTR from 1981 to 1985, and Clayton K. Yeutter, the USTR from 1985 to 1989, helping to shape the services, investment and intellectual property trade agenda of the US.

A Task Force on Intellectual Property was established within ACTN. John Opel, the then chairman of IBM and another key member of ACTN, headed this task force. Jacques Gorlin was also a consultant to ACTN. His paper, "A Trade-Based Approach for the International Copyright Protection for Computer Software" (1 September 1985), which was produced for IBM, had synthesized the key strategic ideas on bringing intellectual property into the GATT. In Phase 1 of its work program the task force recommended that:[20]

- the link between trade and intellectual property be recognized and that its legitimacy be accepted by the intellectual property community;
- as an interim measure the US pursue bilateral and unilateral efforts to improve intellectual property (IP) standards in problem countries;
- work on a counterfeiting code continue;
- a broader IP code with minimum standards and dispute settlement procedures be developed;
- the negotiations take into account the hostility of certain developing countries and that consideration be given to pursuing negotiations of an IP code on a plurilateral basis among like-minded developed countries;
- a rapprochement be sought between the WIPO and GATT secretariats;
- the USTR draft a policy statement making clear the importance of the IP issue to the US and that the USTR establish a separate policy committee on IP.

In March 1986 Phase 2 of the task force's work program was finalized. Its recommendations included:[21]

- the development of an overall IP strategy by the US government and endorsed by the president and cabinet;
- the need for a massive consensus-building exercise, especially with the US's major trading partners in the first instance. The task force welcomed the consensus among the Quad group (the US, EU, Japan and Canada) to get IP on the agenda for the next trade round, but pointed out that that consensus had to be expanded to include developing countries;
- the need for a massive capacity-building exercise funded by both government and the private sector that would bring developing country officials and members of local legal professions in those countries into the Western IP community;
- the use of Section 301 and the Generalized System of Preferences to link access to the US market to improved IP protection, including any other "stick" measures such as the use of US votes at the IMF and the World Bank when voting on access by countries with poor IP protection to those facilities;
- membership of the Berne Convention by the US in order to give it a stronger voice in WIPO;
- the need to continue supporting WIPO since, more than any other organization, it had the technical expertise to develop IP regimes as well as money to fund technical assistance programs that would spread the institution of intellectual property to developing countries.

ACTN's basic message to US government was that it should pull every lever at its disposal in order to obtain the right result for US intellectual property. There were a lot of possible levers. US executive directors to the IMF and World Bank could ask about intellectual property when casting their votes on loans and access to bank facilities; US aid and development agencies could use their funds to help spread the IP gospel. Over time the message was heard and acted upon. Provisions protecting intellectual property as an investment activity were automatically included in the Bilateral Investment Treaty program that the US was engaged in with developing countries in the 1980s. Means of influence of a personal and powerful kind also began to operate. According to Jacques Gorlin in his 1985 analysis of the trade-based approach to IP, Shultz, the US secretary of state, discussed the IP issue with Singapore's prime minister Lee Kuan Yew.[22] President Reagan in his message to Congress of 6 February 1986 entitled "America's Agenda for the Future" proposed that a key item was much greater protection for US intellectual property abroad.[23] The ground was being prepared for intellectual property to become the stuff of big-picture political dealing and not just technical trade negotiation.

As far as ACTN was concerned, folding intellectual property standards into the GATT was the single best way in which to spread those standards.

Realistically, ACTN realized that the negotiation of a broad intellectual property agreement would be a long process. But this process would not start unless intellectual property was put on the agenda of the next trade round. For this to happen a Ministerial Conference of Contracting Parties of the GATT would have to issue a declaration containing, among other things, a form of words opening the way for the negotiation of an IP code. Here ACTN ran into a fundamental problem. Both Opel and Pratt had been pushing the IP agenda with the USTR, at first with William Brock and then his successor Clayton Yeutter. In 1981 Brock had formed the Quadrilateral Group (Quad) of countries for the purpose of trying to develop a consensus for a new round of multilateral trade negotiations. In the early 1980s there were differences of view between Europe and the US on the desirability and content of a future trade round. Without the agreement of the US and Europe the prospects of a multilateral trade round getting off the ground were slim. The Quad consisted of the US, the European Community, Japan and Canada. Once these countries had achieved a consensus on an agenda for a multilateral trade round the round would most likely begin. Yeutter saw the centrality of intellectual property to the round, but the problem was, as he explained to Pratt and Opel, that when he went to meetings of the Quad there was no real support from the other Quad members to merge IP and trade. "In 1986 the USTR said: 'I'm convinced on intellectual property but when I go to Quad meetings, they are under no pressure from their industry. Can you get it?'" (1994 interview).

Both the EC and Japan favored the more modest approach of a code on counterfeiting. Business in these countries did not have so direct a role in the development of the trade agenda, and European and Japanese business was not giving intellectual property the same priority as members of ACTN. Business in Europe had access to the commission, but that access tended to travel through a route of procedural steps involving national business organizations, UNICE (the Union of Industrial and Employers' Confederations of Europe) and the 113 Committee (the committee dealing with Community commercial policy matters). In the US there was also a formal consultative business structure that Congress had set up under the Trade Act, of which ACTN was a part. But this consultative structure did not discourage the direct access of US lobbyists to trade policy makers and negotiators. IP lobbyists did not find themselves having to talk to US trade officials from a distance. Access to officials, as more than one US lobbyist said to us, was never a problem. In Japan, the relentless search for consensus meant that Japanese business and the Ministry of International Trade and Industry (MITI) never operated too far apart from each other, making it difficult for Japanese business to take on the kind of agenda-setting role that US business played in relation to intellectual property. EC bureaucrats were less keen on trying to harmonize intellectual property standards via the trade regime. They had had some experience of the difficulties of trying to harmonize intellectual property standards in Europe. Some states, such as Germany and the UK, were keen on higher standards while others, such as Spain and Italy, were not so inclined. The view coming out of the EC at this time was to press on with the initiative on counterfeiting in the GATT (a lot of luxury European trademarks were the subject of counterfeiting) and make a general IP code a much longer-term priority. In Japan, the corporations and MITI adopted something of a wait-and-see attitude toward the US initiative. The case for global intellectual property standards was not clear, especially for some sectors of Japanese industry. As so often in the past, the Japanese simply sat back, watching and waiting for others to take the lead.

The problem facing Pratt and Opel was clear enough. They had to convince business organizations in Quad countries to pressure their governments to include intellectual property in the next round of trade negotiations. That meant first convincing European and Japanese business that it was in their interests for intellectual property to become a priority issue in the next trade round. Without such a consensus, developing countries would win with their jurisdictional argument. The time frame for the consensus-building exercise was roughly six months. The Ministerial Conference to launch a new trade round was scheduled to take place at Punta del Este in Uruguay in September 1986. The USTR had been working hard to convince the remainder of the Quad of the IP issue, but it had to become much more than just a talking point at the Ministerial Conference.

Pratt and Opel's response was swift. In March 1986 they created the Intellectual Property Committee (IPC).[24] The IPC was an ad hoc coalition of 13 major US corporations: Bristol-Myers, DuPont, FMC Corporation, General Electric, General Motors, Hewlett-Packard, IBM, Johnson & Johnson, Merck, Monsanto, Pfizer, Rockwell International and Warner Communications. It described itself as "dedicated to the negotiation of a comprehensive agreement on intellectual property in the current GATT round of multilateral trade negotiations."[25] Jacques Gorlin became its consulting economist.

Europe was the key target for the IPC. Once Europe was on board, Japan was likely to follow, or at least not raise significant opposition. Canada, despite its Quad membership, was not really a player. It was the support of European and Japanese corporations that was crucial. What followed was a consensus-building exercise carried out at the highest levels of senior corporate management. CEOs of US companies belonging to the IPC would contact their counterparts in Europe and Japan and urge them to put pressure on their governments to support the inclusion of intellectual property at Punta del Este. Small but very senior and powerful business networks were activated. The IPC also sent delegations to Europe in June 1986 and Japan in August 1986 to persuade business in those countries that they also had an interest in seeing the GATT become a vehicle of globally enforceable intellectual property rights. The IPC's efforts in the lead-up to Punta del Este brought it success, for both European and Japanese industry responded by putting pressure on their governments to put intellectual property on the trade agenda.

At the time of this consensus-building exercise there were considerable differences between US, European and Japanese businesses. There was, for example, an open patent war between US and Japanese corporations.[26]

Companies such as Texas Instruments aggressively pursued their patent rights against Japanese corporations in the courts. For years US corporations had made plain their frustrations with the slowness of the Japanese patent office (this issue actually led to the US placing Japan on its 301 watch list in 1989). Patents had become more strategically important to large Japanese companies, but the patent "flooding" practices of these companies was something they had learned from US companies. The Japanese response was in large measure a defensive one. IBM had dominated the computing industry as no other corporation and Microsoft's march to dominance of the software industry was well under way. Fujitsu and Olivetti were simply not in the same league and in fact, in the fight over the terms of the European Software Directive, lined up against IBM and Microsoft (1993 interview). Japanese views on copyright and computer software did, in the words of one US member of the IPC, create "tensions" (1994 interview). In light of all of this one might have expected a skeptical reaction to the IPC's line that an IP code in the GATT would serve the interests of European and Japanese industry. The fact remains, however, that US, European and Japanese companies were able to set aside their differences. From 1986 onward they worked together to make an IP code in the GATT a reality.

Perhaps what US CEOs were able to sell to their European and Japanese counterparts was a vision of a globally secure business future. Ultimately, US corporations might do best out of the globalization of intellectual property standards. A world in which US corporations were dominant but European and Japanese corporations still remained powerful players and strategic partners was preferable to a world in which corporations from all these countries faced competition from increasingly efficient developing country manufacturers. It made sense for the most powerful corporations from the world's three strongest economies to collaborate on a project that would enable them to lock up the intangible assets of business in the new millennium and allow them to use those assets to set up production facilities wherever it suited them best. The international character of their production along with their need to capture new markets became the basis of the mutual interest needed for an alliance between them. In the final analysis European and Japanese business probably reasoned that even if the fruits of cooperation with US business might not be shared equally they would all benefit from fencing off the orchard for themselves. And there was also the enticing prospect for all multinationals that a GATT-based IP regime would be enforceable against states.

PUNTA DEL ESTE

The US delegation that traveled to Punta del Este in September 1986 to attend the Ministerial Conference was accompanied by advisers from the IPC. Ed Pratt headed the group of private sector advisers to the US delegation. As was expected, a group of key developing countries resisted the US proposal on intellectual property rights and their enforcement. These countries stuck to their argument that the GATT was not the appropriate forum for the development of IP standards. The US private sector advisers worked the various country delegations, seeking to build maximum support for inclusion of intellectual property in the Ministerial Declaration. Despite the long hours of negotiation both inside and outside the negotiating rooms, a form of words acceptable to all was not found. A form of words under the heading "trade-related aspects of intellectual property rights, including trade in counterfeit goods" made it into the Ministerial Declaration on the Uruguay Round of 20 September 1986.[27] The IPC, in its description of Punta del Este, described the Ministerial Declaration as "including a strong negotiating mandate for intellectual property in the new round."

Revisiting the words of the declaration one is struck by how weak a mandate it seems. The first paragraph speaks of the negotiations clarifying GATT provisions and elaborating "as appropriate new rules and disciplines"; the second of developing a multilateral framework for the trade in counterfeit goods; and the third of the negotiations being without prejudice to complementary initiatives taken in WIPO and elsewhere. As Daniel Gervais observes, the entire edifice of TRIPS rests on the words "and elaborate as appropriate new rules and disciplines."[28] Developing countries may have thought they were giving away very little with these words. But ultimately the exact phrasing of the Ministerial Declaration was an irrelevancy. In the culture of the trade negotiator all that mattered was that a subject matter had been put on the dealing table. Any agreement on intellectual property would not be constrained by the words in the Ministerial Declaration, but rather shaped by negotiating context. US negotiators simply needed to get intellectual property onto the agenda at Punta del Este. That was all the mandate that was required. Against the background of US 301 unilateralism, the issue of what had been decided in the Ministerial Declaration would quietly fade away. Years later a developing country official involved in evaluating the US proposal prior to Punta del Este told us that US officials had given assurances that developing country jurisdictional arguments against the GATT dealing with intellectual property would be revisited, but had also said that there should be some discussion of the substantive issues (1999 interview). The jurisdictional issues were never revisited in any serious way. Developing country objections on the issue of competency of the GATT to deal with intellectual property had been managed rather cleverly, he concluded.

CHAPTER 8

Persuasion and Principles

BECOMING A COMMUNITY

As far as the Intellectual Property Committee (IPC) was concerned Punta del Este had been a great success. Developing countries saw things differently. They continued to persist with their objections about the competency of the GATT to deal with intellectual property. Their objections fell on deaf ears. In 1988 a senior US trade negotiator was describing the issue of competency as a "red herring."[1] The US and Europe were becoming increasingly unified on the need for some kind of code on intellectual property in the GATT. At the same time the US was turning up the heat bilaterally on the intellectual property issue (see Chapter 6). The European Community, despite its protestations about the use of 301 by the US, had in the same year as the US reformed its trade law to accommodate intellectual property (1984) and created its own version of 301 in the form of the "new commercial policy instrument" to protect the Community's intellectual property interests.[2] It moved against Indonesia and Thailand for record piracy, as well as suspending Korea's GSP privileges for failing to provide satisfactory intellectual property protection for European companies. With the US and European Community united, the intellectual property issue was not going to leave the trade arena. In effect, developing countries were being given a choice between a bilateral or multilateral negotiation. They were outgunned in the case of the former and not collectively prepared in the case of the latter.

It was one thing to place intellectual property on the negotiating table and entirely another to achieve the outcome the IPC wanted. Furthermore, in this particular negotiation, the last thing the IPC wanted was a compromise. This was not like a negotiation over the price of a house in which the two parties start out with different price bids and eventually agree to split the difference. Meeting developing countries midway on the intellectual property issue was not an option.[3] It was also clear that developing countries saw the existing intellectual property regime as already excessively tilted toward the interests of developed countries. A common sense of fair play was hardly likely to eventuate in the context of negotiations over intellectual property to help draw the parties together. The failed attempts to revise the Paris Convention for the Protection of Industrial Property (Paris Convention) showed just how very different were the perceptions of what was a fair deal in international intellectual property negotiations. There was also the danger that, left to their own devices, US negotiators might end up making too many concessions in order to achieve a final deal on intellectual property. This was a much stronger possibility in the case of European negotiators. In the run-up to the Ministerial meeting at Punta del Este, Europe had showed some hesitancy on the need to push for a negotiation on intellectual property beyond one dealing with counterfeits in international trade (1994 interview). Clearly, US and European trade negotiators would need some help.

After Punta del Este, the then USTR Clayton Yeutter made a suggestion to the members of the IPC about what to do next. Edmund Pratt explains:

> Having been successful in getting "TRIPS" on the GATT agenda, government asked the US private sector to provide specific proposals for an agreement, and to form an international private sector consensus to achieve it.
> In conjunction with more than a dozen companies from all relevant sectors of US business, Pfizer and IBM co-founded the Intellectual Property Committee or IPC. The US Trade Representative was impressed and suggested that we increase our effectiveness internationally by joining forces with UNICE, the principal pan-European business group, and its counterpart in Japan, Keidanren.[4]

Yeutter in all probability thought that, short of a consensus among the most globally important corporations in the world, the kind of intellectual property agreement that the IPC wanted would probably not come to pass. Failure on intellectual property would endanger the entire Uruguay Round process. Congress would probably not agree to the necessary implementing legislation if it believed US business was unhappy with the deal. Years of negotiation might be wasted, hardly the kind of achievement a USTR would want to be linked with in the annals of trade history. The next step for the IPC was to develop the detail of an agreement that would serve to guide the Uruguay Round negotiating group on intellectual property to the right agreement, no easy task given the vast thickets of intellectual property laws around the world. This detail would have to be developed in partnership with the European and Japanese business communities.

Immediately after Punta del Este another cycle of persuasion began. The IPC moved to a systematic activation of international business networks. Groups of European and Japanese businessmen gathered to meet with IPC delegates in cities they all knew: Brussels (November 1986, May 1988), New York (March 1987) and Tokyo (January 1988). The message from US business to their European and Japanese colleagues was that international business had to provide states with leadership on the intellectual property issue in the Uruguay Round negotiations. This message also appealed to a common identity shared by some of the larger US, European and Japanese corporations, that of genuinely global, high-technology-based companies with core intangible assets, global brands and distribution networks to protect. Working on and reinforcing this common identity was important to the IPC. Ultimately it wanted to present states with a model GATT intellectual property agreement in the name of the international business community. Opposing a model bearing the approval of international business would be hard for any state.

The IPC was not attempting to harmonize the rules of intellectual property in the US, Europe and Japan. That would have been an impossibility. At the level of rules, there were just too many sharp differences between the domestic laws of the three to make it feasible to aim for harmonization (an example being the debate over the merits of "first to file" versus "first to discover" in patent administration). Rather the IPC wanted an agreement on a set of fundamental principles of intellectual property protection. Rule harmonization, if it was needed, was a long-run game that could safely be left to WIPO to pursue once an agreement on principles was in place.

On 14 June 1988 a text that was to have a decisive influence on the course of the negotiations on intellectual property was released in Washington, Brussels and Tokyo. Bearing the title *Basic Framework of GATT Provisions on Intellectual Property: Statement of Views of the European, Japanese and United States Business Communities* (the Basic Framework), it represented, in the words of Edmund Pratt, a "multilateral blueprint" for trade negotiators. The report, almost a hundred pages long, was the culmination of almost two years' hard work by the IPC on raising cooperation on global regulatory policy issues among key players in the US, European and Japanese business communities to new levels. The CEOs on the IPC who had pushed for its production described it as an action of the "international business community."[5]

"Community" was probably the right choice of word. The senior members of three distinct corporate cultures had agreed to the globalization of what the report itself described as "fundamental principles" of intellectual property. It was not just a statement of goals or objectives, but the prescription of a set of basic principles that would pattern the domestic regulation of knowledge and information by states. Implicit in the Basic Framework was also a morality of investment in information that states would have to foster if they wished to see the benefits of a high-technology entrepreneurialism within their borders. Piracy would have to be eliminated, infringement of intellectual property would have to be criminalized, states would have to set severe limits on public interest exceptions to intellectual property protection and finally states themselves would have to agree to become the subjects of meaningful enforcement procedures if they did not comply with their obligations to spread the fundamentals of intellectual property. It was a morality that placed corporate private property interests in knowledge at the very center of societally protectible interests.

STANDING ON PRINCIPLE: THE "BASIC FRAMEWORK"

The function of the fundamental principles in the Basic Framework was, in the words of Friedrich Kretschmer, one of the drafters, to provide states with "reference points" or a "yardstick" by which countries could judge the adequacy or efficiency of their intellectual property laws.[6] The selection of "fundamental principles" by the IPC, UNICE and the Keidanren was hardly an exercise in juridical objectivity or comparative law scholarship. Their chosen fundamental principle of patentability, for example, stated that a "patent shall be granted for … products and processes without discrimination as to subject matter."[7] Yet a study undertaken by WIPO in 1988 for the GATT negotiating group on intellectual property revealed that of the 98 members of the Paris Convention, 49 excluded pharmaceutical products from protection, 45 excluded animal varieties, 44 excluded methods of treatment, 44 excluded plant varieties, 42 excluded biological processes for producing animal or plant varieties, 35 excluded food products, 32 excluded computer programs and 22 excluded chemical products.[8] The IPC, UNICE and Keidanren's fundamental principle for the subject matter and scope of copyright simply stated that copyright shall subsist in computer programs. Yet the same WIPO study pointed out that only 20 countries protected computer software through copyright legislation. It did not point out that about half these countries had enacted copyright legislation to this effect because of US trade pressure and bilateralism (for example, Brazil, Dominican Republic, Indonesia, Malaysia, Singapore and Trinidad and Tobago).[9] There were cases where the WIPO study did manage to identify internationally accepted standards, but the US did not accept them.[10] Finally, there were examples where there were no international norms, such as in the case of integrated circuits. (Here the US was operating bilaterally, extending the benefits of its domestic law to nationals of other countries on a reciprocal basis.)

The WIPO survey of the intellectual property world revealed a world of different legal traditions and a variety of approaches in the regulation of knowledge. From the IPC's point of view, however, the link between trade and intellectual property was not about variety and maximizing welfare gains for citizens. It was about doing business. The IPC realized early on that the Uruguay Round of negotiations on intellectual property would be a contest of principles. No trade negotiation over intellectual property could be conducted with negotiators having to wade through, let alone argue about, thousands of sections and cases on intellectual property law. The negotiating game would be about broad principle, principle that did not necessarily square with existing laws. Negotiators who arrived at the table thinking that they could appeal to the rules of their domestic systems in order to block an argument found themselves in for a surprise. The chair of the TRIPS negotiating group made sure that negotiators stuck to the game at the level of principles:

> I said: "This argument that we can't do that because our law does not allow it should be an argument you cannot use." And it was after that not used again (1994 interview).

The Basic Framework was in many ways the seminal document of the TRIPS negotiations. It was a declaration of principles of property wanted by big business for the coming global information economy. A member of the IPC claimed that it established the US negotiating position (1994 interview). There is little exaggeration in this claim. The USTR had called on US business to deliver a set of negotiating objectives. After the release of the Basic Framework it was circulated widely within US policy circles, as well as to US diplomatic missions. The textual impact of the Basic Framework on the US position was there for all to see. The Basic Framework came out between two official communications to the GATT by the USTR, one dated 19 October 1987, the other 13 October 1988.[11] Each communication dealt with suggestions for achieving the negotiating objective on intellectual property. The former document was sparse on the detail of the different aspects of intellectual property and on the detail of what the US wanted. The latter borrowed from the Basic Framework, echoing its structure, drawing on it to fill in the detail of the internal procedures that states would have to adopt for the enforcement of intellectual property, the kinds of border measures that states would have to implement, as well as the shape of the consultation and dispute settlement mechanism that the US wanted. In places the echoes stopped, to be replaced by the same language.[12] All in all, there were enough similarities between the texts for a reader to ask whether the same pen had been at work in both.

The principles of the Basic Framework were drafted to match the business goals of the companies that had been enrolled to support it. Different forms of intellectual property mattered to different industries. The US semiconductor chip industry, for example, was feeling the strain of competing with the Japanese. By 1986 it was Japan and not the US that was the world's biggest producer of chips and by 1989 its trade surplus with the US in semiconductors was past US$1.5 billion.[13] The howls of pain could be heard in Washington, along with dark foreboding of the impact of this on US defense interests. Companies like Texas Instruments saw in intellectual property rights a means to recover their market share. Ironically, the US semiconductor chip industry had achieved its preeminence based on a liberal licensing of patent rights, something that Bell Laboratories had been pushed into by the terms of the AT&T consent decree.[14] In the IPC's GATT initiative the US semiconductor chip industry saw a chance to move away from this open door policy and take out some insurance against the new entrants like Korea. It pushed, for example, for restrictions on compulsory licensing and the option of multiple protection for semiconductor chips (patents, copyright, trade secrets and semiconductor chip law modeled on US legislation). European and Japanese industry went along with this because ultimately their access to the US market was at stake.

Hollywood's agenda was to obtain strong copyright and trademark protection for its global film and merchandising interests. But there were also changes to copyright it did not want. Europe did not have copyright (a term used to describe Anglo-American law) but rather an authors' rights system based on a philosophical conception of the work as the "spiritual child" of the author. Under this system authors had certain very strong moral rights to control the release and use of their work, rights in addition to the economic rights recognized by the Anglo-American tradition of copyright law. Hollywood producers had long been accustomed to wielding absolute power over production. The idea of authors and artists acquiring some power in the Hollywood factory, based on a Continental doctrine of moral rights, seemed akin to giving rights to the battery hen. It was simply out of the question. "We don't want to end up like the French film industry" was the view. Moral rights never made it into the Basic Framework or TRIPS.[15] Hollywood was equally uninterested in using the trade regime to improve the standards of intellectual property protection for performers. Standards protecting the use of live performances were part of the Rome Convention for the Protection of Performers, Producers of Phonograms and Broadcasting Organizations, 1961 (Rome Convention). As one interviewee wryly remarked, the "world needs protection from Madonna, rather than for her." The real point, however, lay in the nature of the Hollywood system. The genuine superstars, those who were whisked away in a Lear jet to the next important meeting, had more than enough bargaining power to protect their interests. Strengthening the rights of those lower down in the system of production might prove inconvenient in unpredictable ways. The intellectual property rights that Hollywood wanted globalized were those relating to its distinctive superstar-based system of production and global marketing, not those rights that protected the intimate relationship between author and work or performer and performance. Thus the Basic Framework stood silent on the protection of performers' rights.[16]

The large players in the US software industry, IBM and Microsoft, wanted to use copyright to protect their software. Copyright and computer experts had lots of doubts about this proposal because, for example, the long term of copyright protection (life of the author plus 50 years) did not seem suitable for software and computer code, which was itself closer to a technological device than a literary work. The large software firms saw the problem differently. They had a mass market to protect. Piracy was a problem. So was competition. Microsoft had the industry standard in DOS and later Windows. The way to maximize its hold over the standard (and therefore the markets in application programs) was through copyright protection. That meant ramming protection for computer software into copyright. The GATT offered the first entrants in the US software industry a perfect platform to this end. Not much more than a decade later Justice Thomas Jackson, a United States District Court judge, would tell Microsoft in his judgment in the antitrust action against it that its claim to absolute rights over licensees based on copyright was ill-founded. By then the worldwide copyright protection of Windows had helped to make Bill Gates the richest man in the world.

The Basic Framework, as one who had been involved in its production pointed out, united companies that under "normal circumstances ... are competitors, and this competition also extends to the legal systems of our countries or continents."[17] Representatives from big business had spent:

> two years' intensive work, with meetings in three continents, a steady stream of mail within several working groups and a final reunion that lasted into the early hours of the morning.[18]

They had united around a set of principles. Whether it would be possible to keep together such a large coalition with its considerable internal tensions over the course of a lengthy multilateral trade negotiation was another matter.

Even within the US business community there were quite marked differences of opinion about the worthiness of a multilateral initiative on intellectual property. The US semiconductor chip industry, for instance, was not particularly supportive of the IPC's multilateral effort (1994 interview). It agreed to back TRIPS if its provisions on enforcement were strong and if, outside of TRIPS, it got the deal it wanted on tariffs and anti-dumping[19] (both means to keep cheap foreign chips out of the US market). Europe also had its problems with the US. Although Europe had been free-riding on the use of the US 301 by engaging in bilateral negotiations with states like South Korea after the US had softened them up (see Chapter 6), ultimately European officials wanted to see some constraints placed on its use. In a press release in 1989 concerning the recently enacted Special 301, the USTR pointed out that "no foreign country currently meets every standard for adequate and effective intellectual property protection as set forth in the US proposal on intellectual property tabled in the Uruguay Round."[20] Europe was just as much a target as every other state.[21] European industry was not happy with aspects of US patent law. Section 104 of the US Patent Act was a case in point. Under its terms someone applying for a patent in the US could not establish the date of invention relying on use of knowledge of the invention that had taken place in a country outside the US. European firms saw this as discriminatory, forcing them to move into US patenting sooner than they might want. TRIPS might give them the opportunity to fix the problem.[22] Europe, along with the other two Quad members, Japan and Canada, also objected to Section 337 of the US Tariff Act of 1930. This section allowed owners of US intellectual property rights to obtain from the US International Trade Commission orders barring the import into the US of allegedly infringing products. The problem with the section from the point of view of GATT trade law lay with its procedures. They gave the US owner advantages over imported products that he or she did not have in relation to domestic products.[23]

The danger for the IPC was that these kinds of detailed North–North disputes might induce a kind of negotiating myopia in which the big agenda of globalizing the institutions of intellectual property became obscured by a lot of smaller agendas about reforming some of the existing rules of intellectual property.

THE COALITIONIST

The two years following Punta del Este in 1986 were critical years of coali-tion- building for the IPC. In this period it built group by group the network that would ultimately make TRIPS a reality. The key was to persuade groups, which would in turn persuade other important groups, with every group regularly interacting with and reinforcing some other part of the net-work. Over time each individual group that was part of this circle of per-suasion became by virtue of being in the circle more and more persuaded of the possibility and desirability of TRIPS.

Enrolling European business in the network was the essential first step for the IPC. A problem for the IPC in early 1987 was that the EC was indicating support for a weaker agreement on intellectual property. In a working docu-ment of February 1987 entitled "Trade Related Aspects of Intellectual Property Rights in the Uruguay Round," the EC made dealing with counter-feiting and piracy its main priorities, leaving a broader agreement for anoth-er time. It was the EC that would negotiate on behalf of the European Community in the Uruguay Round. The IPC had established a line of dia-logue with the Union of Industrial and Employers' Confederations of Europe (UNICE) in November 1986. It proved vital. In Europe's more hier-archically ordered world of business lobbying, UNICE was the key portal of European business influence on the EC. During 1986 and 1987 close cooper-ation developed between UNICE representatives and EC officials; UNICE was given the opportunity to comment on the EC's negotiating position and drafts. In May 1987 UNICE produced its own position paper on GATT and intellectual property arguing that the EC's approach was "deemed too nar-row by European industry" and that the "scope of the negotiations must be broadened" to include other areas of intellectual property where European industry was making heavy R&D investments.[24] In the following months this became the position of European Community negotiators.[25]

Bringing the EC into an inner circle of consensus with the USTR was itself crucial to obtaining the support of the most important group of all within the actual negotiations, the Quad (the US, European Community, Japan and Canada). Of all the groups within the Uruguay Round it was the most pow-erful, having the capacity to move an agenda forward and being the place where the most difficult and important issues were decided. Once the US and European Community came together on intellectual property, the other two Quad members would follow.

The IPC itself established a regular interaction with European officials, because in its own words this provided it with "an opportunity to shape the views of these key officials, who at the time were only beginning to focus on the issue."[26] It kept in touch with representatives from the "Friends of Intellectual Property," a group of states that had been formed around the time of Punta del Este to help prosecute the trade–intellectual property agenda, hosting a dinner for a weeklong meeting of the Friends Group in Washington, DC, in March 1988.[27] Sitting down with members of the IPC at a Washington hotel for dinner would, no doubt, have invested negotiators with a sense of the importance of their negotiating mission. Amidst the tinkle of cutlery and wineglasses they learned more about the kind of agreement on intellectual property rights that was desired by the world's most powerful high-technology corporations.

In that meeting of the Friends Group, a meeting that included the Quad members, 23 delegations from developed countries and the EC sat down to an informal discussion of a US proposal on standards of intellectual property and their enforcement.[28] The interaction between groups such as the Quad and Friends Group allowed negotiators to begin the process of developing a sense of the expectations of other negotiators about what was possible in a negotiation over intellectual property. At the same time as negotiators were getting a lock on the expectations of their counterparts, they were also building a developed country consensus on intellectual property that could be used to overcome developing country resistance. Once the Quad had achieved consensus on an issue, the Friends Group would become the vehicle to take that consensus forward.

Finally, the IPC did not just work on building inner circles of consensus. It also worked on the outer circle—developing countries. The strategy outlined in the Basic Framework assumed that initially a GATT code on intellectual property, "similar in form to the Standards or Subsidies Codes," would be negotiated and adhered to by only those states interested in higher standards of intellectual property.[29] It would not, in other words, be a condition of GATT membership. Once the code was in place, developing countries could be given incentives to join. Bearing in mind the need to get at least some developing countries thinking about supporting and perhaps joining the code, IPC delegations traveled in 1988 to newly industrializing countries such as Korea, Hong Kong and Singapore to begin a dialogue with them. The IPC drew these countries' attention to the fact that their interests were not the same as India's and Brazil's interests: "The Committee went to the ASEANS and said these guys should not be representing you because they don't care about investment climate" (1994 interview). It was a dialogue designed to divide.

SWEEPING HOUSE

If TRIPS came to pass, all states would have to change their domestic laws to some extent in order to comply with it, or risk being subject to the proposed WTO dispute resolution process. Oddly enough, the US was in some significant ways on shaky ground when it came to comparing its domestic intellectual property regime with internationally accepted standards. As we saw in Chapter 2, the US commitment to the international copyright system had been anything but exemplary. A former register of copyrights, Barbara Ringer, had argued that until World War II, the US approach to international copyright "was marked by intellectual shortsightedness, political isolationism, and narrow economic self-interest."[30] After World War II, the principal criticism of the US became its lack of membership of the higher-standard Berne Convention. It had joined the Universal Copyright Convention in 1955, a convention it had played a major role in creating. The Berne Convention was, as we saw in Chapter 5, very much a copyright owners' club. The criticisms of the US for failing to join it were thus based on owners' values. In fact, from a social welfare point of view one could easily construct a good defense of US copyright law. For example, US law was more or less distinctive in its insistence that as a condition of copyright protection a work carry a copyright notice. Under the Berne system states were obliged not to make copyright protection depend on such formalities.[31] Copyright notices and registration requirements are useful because they alert third parties to the presence of a property right, help users to determine who are the owners of the copyright and provide clarity about what is and is not in the public domain. The notice requirement in US copyright law, along with other formalities, remained the principal stumbling blocks to Berne membership by the US.[32]

Once US corporations such as IBM decided on copyright for the protection of software, membership of the Berne Convention became a must. In the papers that Jacques Gorlin wrote for IBM and the Advisory Committee on Trade Negotiations (ACTN) he pointed out that it "is becoming increasingly difficult for the United States to be the leading proponent of higher levels of international copyright protection and still not be a party to the Berne Convention."[33] The US, as Barbara Ringer had observed, was regarded as a "hypocrite on the international copyright scene."[34] It was not, however, hypocrisy bothering US corporations, but cost. The Berne Convention did allow a nonmember like the US to take advantage of its provisions, but this so-called back door method was expensive for large US corporations. A vice president of IBM, in a statement in 1987 to a House of Representatives committee, pointed out that this method cost IBM US$10 million a year.[35]

It had been clear early on to the ACTN that the US had to join the Berne Convention. The process of joining would have to be "orchestrated and managed" if Berne implementing legislation was to find its way through various congressional shoals.[36] The process of management became one of the IPC's domestic tasks. It had to get US policy makers and US law "Berne ready." It also had to remove any obstacles to the US being able to comply with a trade agreement on intellectual property. An example of its domestic machinations to these ends was its opposition to the extension of the manufacturing clause in US copyright law.

A manufacturing clause had been part of US copyright law since 1891, its purpose being to protect the US printing industry by making copyright protection of foreign and domestic works conditional on typesetting in the US.[37] By the early 1980s the manufacturing clause had been reduced in scope, applying to American authors of largely nondramatic literary material seeking copyright in the US. Over the years the American printing industry had proved itself a highly effective lobbyist. In 1982 it had been successful in obtaining an extension to the manufacturing clause to 1 July 1986. President Reagan had vetoed legislation extending the clause, but the Senate had overridden his veto by 84 to 9. The winning argument then had been that the loss of the manufacturing clause would lead to many thousands of US workers in the print industries losing their jobs. This jobs-loss argument looked certain to win another extension of the manufacturing clause in 1986 when a very different kind of opponent loomed before the American printers and unions. A lobby in the form of the Coalition against the Manufacturing Clause, comprising some 56 firms and associations, opposed its extension of the manufacturing clause.[38] The Computer and Business Equipment Manufacturers Association was a key player in this coalition. It argued that the manufacturing clause stood in the way of better intellectual property protection abroad for the US computer industry. A 1984 GATT panel had already found that the manufacturing clause and its extension was inconsistent with the GATT. The GATT panel's report had been adopted by the GATT Council[39] and Europe had announced that it would impose trade sanctions on a number of US industries (paper, tobacco, chemical and textiles) if the clause was extended.

Going into a GATT trade negotiation on intellectual property with a GATT-inconsistent copyright law put a question mark over the US commitment to high standards of intellectual property. It also set potential problems for the US being able to comply with an eventual GATT agreement on intellectual property. Moreover, continuing to use copyright in this narrowly protectionist way was sending a message about intellectual property rules to developing countries,which an increasingly global US computer industry, with a watchful eye on China's market especially, did not want sent, much less acted upon.

The networks that ACTN and the IPC had built around the intellectual property issue paid dividends. All those industries wanting better intellectual property protection campaigned against renewing the manufacturing clause. The USTR, Clayton Yeutter, who had worked in close collaboration with ACTN, appeared before a House Judiciary Subcommittee opposing the extension of the manufacturing clause.[40] Testimony from the most senior trade official in the US carried real weight. Those US industries that would have suffered as a result of Europe's threatened retaliation, if the extension of the clause went ahead, delivered the coup de grâce to the American printing industry's jobs-loss argument by pointing out that losses in their industries would be much greater once Europe retaliated. By the end of 1986 it was clear that the manufacturing clause was not going to be extended by Congress. It became legislative history.[41]

The IPC worked on creating the same impregnable coalition and consensus on intellectual property at the domestic level that it had created at the international level. Supported by the National Association of Manufacturers, the US Council for International Business and the Emergency Committee for American Trade, it pushed for and obtained the widest possible negotiating authority from Congress on intellectual property in the 1988

Omnibus Trade and Competitiveness Act. The US did join the Berne Convention in 1989, and for the first time in the history of its copyright law the presence of a copyright notice was no longer a condition of copyright protection.

A key question was whether the US domestic coalition would hold together. Hollywood, as we saw earlier, under no circumstances wanted TRIPS to strengthen the moral rights of authors, something that the Berne Convention did do. At the same time the US computing industry did want the standards in the Berne Convention to be globalized. The copyright industries and semiconductor chip industry were worried that a new multilateral dispute resolution process might neuter the 301 process that had brought the US such bilateral success. Holding the coalition together for the duration of the negotiations would prove to be a complicated matter. Having managed to get a diverse group of information industries around a set of principles, US negotiators would have to negotiate a text of an agreement that would deliver a payoff to each of those industries. It was also a big trade round. Intellectual property was just one of 14 negotiating groups within the Group of Negotiation on Goods in the Uruguay Round. The fate of TRIPS was in part dependent on what happened in these other groups. No one expected the negotiations on agriculture to go smoothly.

CHAPTER 9

At the Negotiating Table

KICKOFF AND FINAL SIREN

After Punta del Este, a group of ten developing countries led by India and Brazil (the others being Argentina, Cuba, Egypt, Nicaragua, Nigeria, Peru, Tanzania and Yugoslavia) continued to insist that a comprehensive code on intellectual property could not be negotiated within the General Agreement on Tariffs and Trade (GATT).[1] Breaking the resistance of these "hard-liners" was fundamental to achieving the outcome the US wanted. These hard-liners were holding out even though the developing country bloc in the form of the G-77, which had been effective in other fora such as the World Intellectual Property Organization (WIPO) and the United Nations Conference on Trade and Development (UNCTAD), was slowly crumbling within the GATT.

Following Punta del Este, the formal structure for the Uruguay Round negotiations began to be rolled out. The Ministerial Declaration had organized the negotiations into two broad groups: a Group of Negotiations on Goods (GNG) and a Group of Negotiations on Services (GNS). Both had to report to the Trade Negotiations Committee (TNC), the committee that was to monitor the conduct of the entire Uruguay Round. The TNC was chaired by Arthur Dunkel, the director-general of the GATT. At a meeting in Geneva in January 1987 more groups were set up to allow the cogs of the trade bureaucracies of more than 100 states to begin to mesh.[2] The GNG became 14 negotiating groups. Group 11 was the Trade-Related Aspects of Intellectual Property Rights including Trade in Counterfeit Goods. Each group was to have its own chair and "operate as a separate entity."[3] Deadlines, timetables and negotiating plans were imposed. Group 11 had to have its first meeting in the week beginning 23 March 1987 and the initial phase of its negotiating plan completed "by the end of 1987 at latest."[4] It was a tight timetable, especially given the complexity of the subject matter.

For the next couple of years the negotiation on intellectual property became a game of paper flows. Developed countries easily won. In October 1987 the US and the Swiss each submitted a proposal followed by submissions from Japan and the European Community in November.[5] 1988 kicked off with a submission from the Nordic states in February and so it went on. Between 1987 and 1990, 97 working documents were submitted to the TRIPS negotiating group by countries, the GATT secretariat and international organizations. Of these, only 19 came from developing countries.[6] In a 1993 interview a member of the GATT secretariat was to tell us that all developing countries did in the TRIPS negotiations was "to complain to the bitter end."

Actually, there was quite a lot to complain about. Developed countries were taking the opportunity to flood the negotiating process with the most far-reaching proposals on intellectual property. There were paper flows from the secretariat itself providing information on the relationship between GATT norms and intellectual property, and membership of intellectual property conventions, as well as papers from WIPO relating to intellectual property treaties and international standards. The idea that the negotiation would be confined to border control issues and the problem of counterfeits was being swept away. Developing country negotiators making the long journey from Geneva back to home found US negotiators waiting on their doorstep. Bilateral negotiations on intellectual property had been started with Taiwan in 1983 and Singapore in 1984. After the 1984 amendments to its 301 process the US began to use it. Everybody knew about how it had knocked over South Korea in 1985 using 301 (see Chapter 6). Brazil became the next target (see Chapter 6). By 1989 USTR fact sheets were reporting other successes: copyright agreements with Indonesia and Taiwan, Saudi Arabia's adoption of a patent law, and Colombia including computer software in its copyright law. Special 301 was swung into action at the beginning of 1989. When the USTR announced the targets of Special 301, five of the ten developing country "hard-liners" in the GATT found themselves listed for bilateral attention. Brazil and India, the two leaders, were placed in the more serious category of priority watch list, while Argentina, Egypt and Yugoslavia were put on the watch list. Under "Action Plans" formulated by the USTR those countries that had been major opponents of the US at the GATT or WIPO on intellectual property found that their position on the priority watch list was linked to, among other things, their "constructive participation in multilateral intellectual property negotiations."[7] One did not have to be a chess grandmaster to figure out that the gambit of opposing the US on intellectual property at the GATT would provoke a crushing reply.

In truth, it was less a negotiation and more a "convergence of processes" in the words of someone who was a US trade negotiator at the time. Opposition to the US GATT agenda was being diluted through the bilaterals. Each bilateral the US concluded with a developing country brought the country that much closer to TRIPS, "so that accepting TRIPS was no big deal" (1994 interview).

Probably because it was all they could do, some developing states continued to complain and put up resistance. India and Brazil in particular persisted in their objections. Minimum standards of intellectual property protection, they claimed, were a matter of sovereign state law making to be decided according to the different developmental needs of a state. Yet despite this opposition, the midterm review of the Uruguay Round talks by trade ministers on the TNC in December 1988 in Montreal and April 1989 in Geneva produced a short framework agreement in which the ministers agreed that negotiations would encompass "adequate standards and principles" of intellectual property protection and "settlement of disputes between governments, including the applicability of GATT procedures."[8] The flood of paper from developed countries had done its job.

The Ministerial statement that came out of the April meeting of the midterm review was significant for the TRIPS negotiations. The very things that developing countries had been opposing well before Punta del Este, namely the inclusion of a negotiation on substantive standards and the use of the GATT dispute mechanism in the area of intellectual property, were now well and truly on the table. The April Ministerial meeting had delivered a major body blow to developing country negotiators. India and Brazil together had held the line on a narrow interpretation of the TRIPS negotiating mandate. Other developing countries were behind them. By 1989 there was a certain desperation in the GATT secretariat to move things forward on TRIPS in order to keep the US engaged. The message went out from the secretariat to India that India was isolated on the TRIPS issue.[9] The reverse was in fact true. Developing country negotiators had met in February in the resort of Talloires in France to work out a common line of resistance. Opposition to the TRIPS mandate was solidifying.

In international negotiations, trust among allies is the key to success. Without it, cooperation rapidly dissolves. The seeds of doubt sown by the secretariat grew into rumors among developing country negotiators about India's commitment to the cause. At a time when Indian officials should have been working the lines of communication with the capitals of other developing countries they did not. Cooperation between India and Brazil began to drift as the Brazilians became worried by the strength of Indian support. In early April, India failed to attend a crucial informal Third World Group meeting.[10] It all began to fall apart.

At the same time the GATT secretariat put relentless pressure on developing countries through the Green Room process. Key countries were hauled into small group consultations. The groups grew smaller and the strain of resistance greater, so much so that developing country negotiators began to refer to them as the "Black Room" consultations. In the end, the text of April 1989 delivered to the US and its supporters, in the words of Jayashree Watal, "a significant victory."[11] The lesson from the experience (especially for a leader country like India) is nicely captured by a former Indian official to the GATT:

> The impression went round that the show of firmness that the negotiators were making in the period from Sept 1986 to Dec 1988 was only a facade not backed by a firm political support at the capital. No negotiators can hope to muster support from other countries on difficult issues involving disagreement and even confrontation with major powers, if those countries suspect the inherent strength of the stand or even the sincerity of its propounders.[12]

One last event took place in 1988 that contributed to the eventual victory of the US and European Community. For three decades India and Brazil had been a thorn in the side of the corporations that, as we saw in Chapter 3, were players in the knowledge game. These two countries, especially India, had technical expertise with which to counter the OECD-led analyses that the US was relying upon to achieve its agendas on intellectual property, investment and services. The Brazil–India axis had to be broken. There was a second vital reason to discipline Brazil. It was a regional leader in South America. For the US pharmaceutical and information technology sectors there could be only one voice on intellectual property policy in the Americas. In July 1987, the USTR had begun a 301 investigation of Brazil on the issue of patent protection for pharmaceutical products, an investigation that had led the president to authorize tariff increases on Brazilian goods in October 1988 (see Chapter 6). The tariff penalties came less than two months before the meeting of trade ministers at the December midterm review in Montreal. For the first time the US had followed up its threat under 301 in relation to intellectual property and actually lowered the trade boom. In June 1990, the president of Brazil announced that he would seek the legislation the US wanted. On 2 July 1990 the increased duties were terminated by the USTR. In that same year a Brazilian negotiator in the TRIPS group informed an Indian negotiator that "I am only here to observe" (interview 2000). Now India really was on her own.

The US retaliation against Brazil also sent a message about the level of the US private sector's commitment to the intellectual property cause. The Brazilian economy of the 1980s was one in which US multinationals, among others, had a strong presence. By imposing trade sanctions on a wide range of Brazilian goods there was a risk of the US hitting goods made in Brazil by US multinationals. The internationalized nature of production set some limits on the use of 301: "When we retaliate, we will find we have no clothes" (1994 interview). In the case of Brazil, however, the stakes were so high that US business was prepared to wear the possible costs of a 301 action in order to project the steely will of earlier conquistadores.

The negotiations on TRIPS are often said to have begun properly in the second half of 1989 when a number of countries made proposals, or the first part of 1990 when five draft texts of an agreement were submitted to the negotiating group.[13] A more skeptical view is that the negotiations were by then largely over. Developing countries had simply run out of alternatives and options. If they did not negotiate multilaterally they would each have to face the US alone. If they resisted the US multilaterally they could expect to be on the receiving end of a 301 action. This was anything but a veiled threat by the US. Its 1988 Trade Act made, among other things, the failure to make significant progress on intellectual property in a multilateral negotiation a condition of identifying a state as a priority foreign country and therefore the subject of a Special 301 investigation.[14] There could be no clearer articulation of a threat than to enact it as law. At least if developing countries negotiated multilaterally there was the possibility of being able to obtain some limits on the use of 301 actions. At any rate, this was what they were being told by developed country negotiators and the GATT secretariat.

From 1990 onward the main issue to be decided was how far an agreement on intellectual property would deviate from the blueprint that had been provided to negotiators in 1988 by Pfizer, IBM, DuPont and other members of the international business community.

CIRCLES OF CONSENSUS

Negotiating a comprehensive agreement on intellectual property was something of a high-wire act for US and European Community negotiators. An agreement could not in any way weaken the position of international business. The high degree of involvement of international business in the negotiations themselves set limits on what they could concede. Moreover, the sheer scope of the agreement would inevitably give rise to North–North differences. These differences would have to be dealt with in a discreet way. Signaling disunity to the likes of India and Brazil had to be avoided. All this would require high levels of cooperation between developed countries.

In his report on the Tokyo Round of the GATT, the then director-general Oliver Long had observed that it was in "practical terms necessary and realistic for the Big Three [US, European Economic Community, Japan] through the process of prenegotiation, first to attempt to reconcile their own differences before joining in negotiations with other countries."[15] This prenegotiation, however, grounded another kind of strategy in which an inner-circle consensus was expanded to create larger circles of consensus until the goals of those in the inner circle had been met. Developing countries for the most part found themselves in outer circles, if they made it into a circle at all. In the Tokyo Round on 13 July 1978, the EEC, US, Japan, Switzerland, New Zealand, Canada, the Nordic countries and Austria released a "Framework of Understanding" setting out what they believed to be the principal elements of a deal. Developing countries reacted angrily because they had been left out of a process that was laying the foundations for a final agreement.[16] In the TRIPS negotiations the use of circles of consensus would reach new heights.

GATT negotiations had developed a traditional pattern, known as the "Green Room" process:

> In the "Green Room" process, negotiators from all engaged countries face each other across the table (traditionally in the Green Room on the main floor of the WTO Building) and negotiate. Drafts are exchanged and progress is noted as differences are narrowed and brackets are removed in successive drafts.[17]

This Green Room process had, in the case of TRIPS, been profoundly shaped by the consensus-building exercise carried out by international business outside the Green Room. The EC was brought around to the US view on the importance of securing a code on intellectual property. The Quad states were all enrolled in support of the US business agenda, as were the business communities of the other Quad states. Then there were the meetings of the

Friends of Intellectual Property Group in places like Washington where draft texts were worked through by negotiators. After the negotiations on the detail of TRIPS began in 1990 and especially after the breakdown of the talks in Brussels in 1991, further groups were created to move the process toward a final deal. The "10+10" Group, which consisted of a mix of developed and developing countries, was the most representative of these. As the TRIPS negotiations descended into higher levels of informality the "10+10" was contracted or expanded to "3+3" or "5+5" or a group of 25 depending on the issue (GATT, 1993 interview). These informal groups became the real places of action. A list of them roughly in their order of importance would be:

1 US and European Community;
2 US, European Community, Japan;
3 US, European Community, Japan, Canada (Quad);
4 Quad "plus" (membership depended on issue, but Switzerland and Australia were regulars in this group);
5 Friends of Intellectual Property (a larger group that included the Quad, Australia, Switzerland, the Nordic countries and some developing countries like Mexico);
6 10+10 (and the variants thereof such as 5+5, 3+3). The US and the European Community were always part of any such group if the issue was important. Other active developed country members were the Nordic states, Japan, Canada, Australia, New Zealand and Switzerland. Developing country members present in these groups included Argentina, Brazil, India, Hong Kong, Malaysia, Thailand, Chile, Colombia, Egypt, Indonesia, Korea, Mexico, Peru and Singapore.[18]
7 Developing country groups (for example, the Andean Group: Bolivia, Colombia, Peru and Venezuela). In 1990 Argentina, Brazil, Chile, China, Colombia, Cuba, Egypt, India, Nigeria, Peru, Tanzania and Uruguay combined to submit a draft. Developing countries would also meet as a larger informal group.
8 Group 11 (the entire TRIPS negotiating group; about 40 countries were active in this group).

The US and European Community had membership in almost all of these groups. This allowed them to soak up more information than anyone else about the overall negotiations. Whenever they needed higher levels of secrecy they could re-form into a smaller negotiating globule. The transparency of the TRIPS negotiations was in some ways like the transparency of a one-way mirror. This arrangement of groups also allowed the US and the EC the fluidity to build a consensus when and where it was required. For certain issues, such as how royalties from collective licensing were to be divided or the scope of exclusions from patentability, they negotiated privately. Even though they were not always able to secure an agreement between themselves, their disagreement did not derail the TRIPS process itself. Developing country negotiators knew about these "bilaterals" and that in a sense they were wasting their time in the TRIPS negotiations: "We lost interest" (developing country negotiator).

THE JOY OF TEXT

For those who like subterfuge, manipulation, dissembling, hypocrisy and power plays, there can be few better places to ply these skills than a multilateral trade negotiation. Within the culture of trade negotiation these skills serve a greater purpose, that of deal making: "Good negotiators close the deal" (former US trade negotiator). The hot pursuit of a deal produces a paradox of rule irrelevance. The fine legal details of the rules and standards that govern trade relations among sovereign states and are seemingly at stake in a trade negotiation recede into the background:

> Which option will sell at the end of the day? In the GATT context [we] didn't care about specific standards (former USTR negotiator).
> What can you give? What can you get? (former developing country negotiator describing the mind-set of negotiators).
> The reality is that we do not spend a lot of time thinking about legal issues when we negotiate agreements in the GATT...[T]he concerns that we have are with the commercial results of what a negotiated agreement is, rather than with the legal niceties of it (Emory Simon, the then director for Intellectual Property at the Office of the United States Trade Representative).[19]

Ultimately the many deals of the TRIPS negotiation had to end up in the form of treaty language. Negotiators did care about the detail of the text describing their own particular deals. The basic rule for negotiators was to find very clear language to describe the deals favorable to them, while striving to set in ambiguous language those deals in which they had made concessions. The negotiations were a search for clarity and "constructive ambiguity" at the same time. It is in the nature of language that two negotiators can walk away from a piece of text, the one believing that it locks up gains for his country, while the other believes that it unlocks a backdoor exit for her country. It is for this reason that some of those who were involved in the negotiation have gone into print to provide the "correct" interpretation of what the provisions of TRIPS mean.[20]

Negotiating over the text became important in TRIPS after the chairman of the TRIPS Group, Lars Anell, produced a "Chairman's Draft." He had to. By May 1990 there were five draft versions of an agreement on TRIPS, four emanating from developed countries and one from a group of developing countries. The developed country drafts bore all the marks of prenegotiation coordination. Anell amalgamated developed and developing country proposals into a draft that eventually became the formal text of the chairman's report to the Group of Negotiation on Goods.[21] This text of 23 July 1990 bracketed various developed and developing country proposals.

The bracketing and unbracketing of text were part of a status game individual negotiators played with each other. Getting bracketed text into a draft was a sign of success for a negotiator. It meant that an option had been put on the dealing table. The aim then became to get that text unbracketed in the form in which it had been submitted. Such text stood a strong chance of securing passage into the final treaty. For individual negotiators, the unbracketing of text became a measure of negotiating prowess. For the chair, getting a draft agreement in final form was a measure of his or her success as a chair. No chair wanted to be in the position of being responsible for a negotiating group that was unable to reach agreement, thereby holding up the successful conclusion of the entire round. Finally, no secretary-general of the GATT wanted to preside over the failure of a trade round, especially not one as big and important as the Uruguay Round. Each and every negotiator was caught up in a complex web of relationships involving groups in which he or she was an insider or an outsider and individual relationships with other negotiators, as well as with the chair of the group. These webs stretched beyond the group itself. South Korea, for example, was seeking membership in the OECD and so South Korean negotiators did not lend India and Brazil the support they might otherwise have done (Korea became a member in 1996). The individual success of every negotiator depended on other negotiators being able to read what were fundamental sticking points for him or her and finding ways to accommodate them. Without giving, there would not be the possibility of taking. Deals, the stepping-stones of promotion for negotiators within trade ministries, would not be made. The incentives for all negotiators to find an agreement were massive.

THE GREAT HERO

From the US perspective at least, Lars Anell turned out to be the right chairman for the TRIPS negotiating group. "He was the great hero of TRIPS," said one member of the Intellectual Property Committee (IPC). "Lars injected confidence into the whole process. He was a great message carrier. He interpreted messages" (1994, former USTR negotiator).

Building the confidence of developing countries was vital to the success and legitimacy of TRIPS. It was a task to which both Anell and members of the GATT secretariat were highly sensitive. More than one developed country negotiator told us that small countries resent the GATT because they feel left out and think big players simply cut a deal. This is quite a good characterization of what happened to developing countries in the Tokyo Round of the GATT. Developed countries wanted to be able to say at the end of the Uruguay Round that the negotiations had delivered wins for all countries without fear of too much contradiction from developing countries. Creating confidence in the process of negotiation was vital to allaying suspicions about the nature of the deals developing countries would get at the end.

Intellectual property was a new subject for most trade negotiators. Indeed it was new to members of the GATT secretariat and Anell. For this reason the US sent delegations brimming with experts in the various areas of intellectual property such as patents, copyright and trademarks. Moreover, the US had private sector experts waiting in the corridors who had command of the details that mattered to their industries. Sometimes private sector people were in the negotiating room:

> US negotiators were physically accompanied by US business representatives. They sat with members of the US negotiating team and passed messages to them at crucial stages. We [European Commission] don't work that way, that's not our political system (European negotiator, 2001).

Few countries had the resources to match these US tag teams. Other countries would occasionally send an intellectual property expert to accompany their trade negotiator. A lot depended on the resources and the expertise available. The Indian pharmaceutical industry, we were told in one of our Indian interviews, did remarkably little given what was at stake. It became much more active once the agreement had been signed: "The generic drug manufacturers never made a phone call. Now they say they were excluded" (US lobbyist, 1994). There is truth in this observation. Of course, a top Washington lobbyist can phone the CEOs of some of the most powerful corporations on earth: "Expertise and the ability to get one of my CEOs on the telephone is the basis of my influence" (1994 interview).

The inequalities of resources and expertise, not to mention US unilateralism on intellectual property, would make it easy for anyone wishing to do so to depict TRIPS as an unconscionable bargain. Anell and members of the GATT secretariat spent many hours with developing country negotiators talking over the intricacies of the negotiations on intellectual property. They wanted to be able to say that TRIPS was an object of transparency. It was never really that. Multiple levels of circles of consensus, which could be closed when needed, turned developing countries into outsiders when it mattered. Exclusion and lack of transparency had simply assumed subtler forms, the way they always do when the members of an established club have to deal with new arrivals they are obliged to admit.

Anell's aim was to have as strong an agreement on intellectual property as possible. He encouraged the negotiating group to think beyond a code on intellectual property with optional membership and instead suggested that they work toward a multilateral agreement binding on all. The strategy of US business was to develop a GATT agreement largely without the assistance of WIPO. Anell pointed out the flaw in this. He said to them: "They will act as a secretariat for a hostile group of developing countries if you freeze them out" (1994 interview).[22] WIPO was allowed in as an observer. "Then WIPO were helpful and saw it as an opportunity."[23] Anell talked to Bogsch, the director-general of WIPO, after each meeting. This was, as Anell said in an interview, good politics and helpful to Anell who was not an intellectual property expert. More importantly, a potential ally for developing countries had been neutralized.

As the negotiations progressed, Anell and the secretariat made some light but vital touches to the tiller. During the latter part of 1990, Anell began to convene informal meetings of key negotiators in order to speed up the process of obtaining agreement. Smaller groups such as the 10+10 (10 developed + 10 developing), 5+5 and 3+3, along with chats with individual negotiators, were used to discuss various parts of the Chairman's Draft. The GATT secretariat engaged in the "delicate business" of selecting those it thought would be appropriate to attend these small group sessions. Some of the drafting was done in the smallest groups. Suitability for these groups was judged on the basis of the expertise of delegates (interview, GATT secretariat, 1993). African states, the states in which AIDS would cast the longest shadow, the states with populations most in need of access to cheap drugs and therefore affected by the patents regime on drugs, never made it into these groups. Most signed a death warrant for citizens of their country, who desperately needed cheaper drugs, without knowing what was said during the trial of the condemned.

After meetings, the chairman and members of the secretariat would have their own meetings, and revisions to the Chairman's Draft would be made. A consolidated text would be circulated and the process repeated. The closer to a finalized text the chairman and secretariat came, the bolder they became in terms of proposing and drafting solutions (GATT secretariat, 1993). Through this process a draft TRIPS agreement began to emerge. But as the chairman of the Trade Negotiations Committee made clear in his report to an informal TNC meeting on 12 November there was still a long way to go in many negotiating groups, including the TRIPS group:

> Keeping the highly political question of the relationship of a TRIPS agreement to the GATT aside for the time being, there are others on which the negotiators need Ministerial political guidance *now*. I will mention only a few:
>
> - the issue of moral rights under copyright;
> - the protection of computer programs, performers and broadcasters under copyright;
> - the term of protection for sound recordings;
> - the term of protection for patents;
> - whether plant varieties should be protected, whether under patents or otherwise.
>
> These are merely examples, and I could cite many more.[24]

Perhaps these issues in TRIPS could have been finalized through a political process at the meeting of ministers in Brussels on 3–7 December 1990. At least there was an advanced text in the case of TRIPS. But the breakdown of the Brussels Ministerial over agriculture put paid to this hope.

There is little doubt that Anell's diplomatic and negotiating skills exercised a profound influence on the evolution of TRIPS. In large measure he satisfied his ambition to deliver a strong agreement on intellectual property.

"DDT"

For those negotiators working long into the night at Brussels in early December 1990 trying to stitch together the compromises needed to bring the entire Uruguay Round to its conclusion, the news that the talks had broken down was dramatic. Over the next few days Brussels restaurants bore witness to hastily organized dinners as negotiators bid farewell to each other. But the Brussels breakdown turned out to be an intermission rather than the final act. By February 1991 Arthur Dunkel, the director-general of the GATT, was announcing plans to restart the round, and in June 1991 the TRIPS group met again to pick up where they had left off.

The Brussels draft became the basis of further negotiation. Lars Anell remained chair and small group negotiations remained the order of the day. The Brussels text signaled through its brackets the various options that negotiators were now standing by, either as bargaining chips or fundamental sticking points. Progress was slow because the choice of options in TRIPS was in part dependent on gains or losses made by countries in other areas such as agriculture and textiles.[25] The final set of trade-offs could only be decided at the highest political level. The negotiator for India, for example, was not in a position to give up the text that preserved India's option to exclude products from patentability (most importantly pharmaceutical products) on the grounds of public interest, public health or nutrition.[26]

There was another problem. Increasingly the states from the North were fighting among themselves over various issues. US business had managed to unite the key developed states to gain victory over developing states at Punta del Este in 1986. As TRIPS began to be made concrete in terms of draft regulatory standards its potentially far-reaching effects on the laws of even developed states like the US and the member states of the European Community became clear. There was an understanding among developed countries that TRIPS would be drafted in such a way as not to require these countries to make massive changes to their laws.[27] In fact, for the key players (the US and the European Community), TRIPS offered the opportunity to globalize their own domestic models of regulation. Inevitably, when negotiators began to haggle over the drafting of TRIPS it was with a view to using language and standards drawn from their own jurisdiction because it would minimize the sovereignty cost of TRIPS to their state. So, for example, the drafting of the patents parts of TRIPS created not only a North–South division, but also a North–North one in the form of a split between the US and European Community. Patent law harmonization had been and remains one of WIPO's long-running and intricate sagas. There was no way in which TRIPS could be expected to be the vehicle of patent harmonization. Even if, for instance, some US corporations might have preferred the efficiency and certainty of a first-to-file system, a highly influential US patent bar would have trumpeted the virtues of the more costly and complex first-to-invent US system. In the name of the inventor (especially the small inventor) and his or her natural right to what he or she invented first, the US patent profession would have opposed TRIPS to the bitter end. Realizing the risks, international business had definite targets that they wanted TRIPS to meet in the area of patents, targets that included a 20-year patent term, patent protection for products including pharmaceuticals and agrochemicals, the weakening of compulsory licensing, as well as an expanded view of patentable subject matter, including the patentability of animals, plants, micro-organisms, genes and plant varieties.[28]

Once it came to the detail of drafting patent standards a difference of view occurred between the US and the European Community. The US wanted the draft to reflect the philosophy endorsed by its US Supreme Court that "everything under the sun made by man" is patentable.[29] The large players in European industry and the European Patent Office (EPO) were also perfectly happy with this philosophy. At an interview with the EPO in 1993 we were told that "everything would be patentable; it's just a question of time." TRIPS, however, turned out not to be the time. The member states of the European Community, which were also members of the European Patent Convention, were bound by provisions expressly prohibiting the grant of patents on plant and animal varieties, as well as a provision prohibiting the grant of patents on inventions in contravention of morality.[30] There was also disquiet among some member states on the reach of the patent system over living organisms. The EC was encountering considerable resistance from citizen groups to its proposed biotechnology directive. Canada, one of the Quad members, also began to question the extent to which TRIPS should oblige countries to allow the patentability of living organisms. At a December 1991 meeting of the Quad, Canada announced its opposition to plant and animal patents.[31] The European Community, because of the European Patent Convention, wanted a provision that would not create tricky problems of TRIPS implementation. Japan followed its usual practice in such conflicts of not saying much. Without an inner-circle consensus, the US was unable to achieve the outcome it wanted on patents within the broader negotiating group. What ultimately became Article 27 of TRIPS is a more flexible provision than it might otherwise have been. The real problem for the US was not so much Canadian opposition, but the fact that it had been unable to secure an agreement with the EC on the patenting and biotechnology issue. As a US negotiator explained, in those areas where Europe and the US were unable to agree, the provisions of TRIPS are at their weakest (from a US perspective) (1994 interview).

Patent standards were not the only area of North–North disagreement. The US film and recording industries were unhappy, not for the first time, with French producers and performers. The French had set up a video levy scheme and an audio levy scheme (the Germans had established a similar national scheme).[32] Basically, these schemes added a small levy to the cost of tapes, videotapes, tape recorders and VCRs. The collected levies were placed into a number of funds including a videogram producers' fund, a phonogram producers' fund and a performers' fund and then distributed to French producers and performers to compensate them for the copying of their works. Had TRIPS fully extended the principle of national treatment to foreign producers and performers, US producers and performers would have stood to collect from these levies to the tune of at least US$6.2 million in France in 1990 and US$4 million in Germany for the same year.[33] TRIPS, however, did not extend the national treatment principle in this way. US film companies had asked the French for a share of the producers' levy. National treatment, the French replied, would be extended only if the original images of the film had been first fixed in France. The International Intellectual Property Alliance continued to campaign on this issue right up to the end of the Uruguay negotiations, arguing before Congress that "no agreement is preferable to a bad agreement."[34] This particular bluff aimed at securing total victory did not work.

The US was also unhappy with Japan because it had managed to obtain a form of words in the draft of TRIPS allowing Japanese shops to continue the practice of renting sound recordings. The European Community along with Switzerland was pushing for a strong system of protection for geographical indications and appellations of origin (for example, Champagne, Bordeaux) while the US, not blessed with an abundance of globally recognized appellations, resisted the European Community's proposals. Developing countries stayed on the sidelines in these debates. These North–North negotiating issues were very much about how global industries could make further gains in developed country markets. For developing countries the TRIPS negotiations were essentially about trying to minimize their losses.

The cooperation between the US and European Community on intellectual property from time to time frayed at the edges. One of the key objectives of the US pharmaceutical industry was to set the strongest possible limits on the use of compulsory licenses. The US proposal flowed from a principle of prohibiting compulsory licensing subject to some exceptions.[35] Other countries started from the position that such licenses could be granted subject to certain conditions being met. Ultimately, the more liberal approach to compulsory licenses prevailed. India in particular, realizing the importance of a compulsory license provision to the pharmaceutical sector in developing countries and sensing a loss in the battle over the patenting of pharmaceuticals, was able to draft and table reasonably permissive language for a compulsory license provision. That language made it into TRIPS because it gained the support of the European Community. European support was, in part, a "tit-for-tat" response to the pressure tactics the US was putting on Europe over the negotiations in agriculture.

In order to push the Uruguay Round negotiations toward a conclusion and under pressure from the then USTR Carla Hills, the director-general of the GATT, Arthur Dunkel, tabled on 20 December 1991 a compromise document, the "Draft Final Act Embodying the Results of the Uruguay Round of Multilateral Trade Negotiations."[36] The understanding made clear in the text was that no part of the Draft Final Act was considered agreed until the entire package was agreed. On the outstanding TRIPS issues the Dunkel draft of TRIPS (the draft having been prepared by Anell and the GATT secretariat) gave every major state a win of some kind. So, for example, the European Community lost on moral rights, but gained on appellations of origin for wines and spirits; the Japanese were able to preserve their practice of CD rental even though rental rights were recognized; the US won on moral rights and in the extension of patents to all fields, but had to tolerate the fact that countries had the option of excluding some things from patentability. Developing countries received the benefit of transitional periods before they had to comply with TRIPS (four years for developing countries and ten years for least-developed countries). Given the magnitude of the institution-building task they faced in intellectual property this was not seen by them as very much of a win. It wasn't.

In India, the Dunkel draft text was labelled "DDT" and thought to be just as dangerous as the chemical of that name for the health of the country. For those bureaucrats in the Indian Patent Office who had seen the Indian-designed patent system produce a flourishing pharmaceuticals sector capable of competing in global markets, DDT was very hard to swallow: "All our efforts were wiped out in one second by Dunkel" (former Commissioner of Patents, India, 1996). India held out the longest of any developing country on the Uruguay Round, reserving its position on the acceptability of the entire Dunkel Draft Final Act.[37] When it came to the signing of the Final Act at Marrakesh in April 1994, India did sign, thereby assuming the obligations of TRIPS. If any country could have mustered the willpower to resist the US agenda on TRIPS to the end it would have been India. It had, after all, not so many decades earlier thrown out the British Empire. Some Indian parliamentarians and members of the judiciary delivered eloquent speeches about TRIPS as the beginning of the recolonization of India. Hundreds of thousands of Indian farmers protested in the streets about the patenting of seeds, but this time there was no Mahatma Gandhi to lead them. In any case, there were no negotiations in which the mass unrest could have been utilized to support a position. Seeing the shift of geopolitical sands that followed the fall of the Berlin Wall, the Indian government decided to send India into the WTO regime, the most far-reaching trade regime ever negotiated by states. It was time for India to enter in a more significant way the world of merchandise trade, trade in services and intangibles. Indian industry, the pharmaceutical industry included, would have to learn to play by the rules set in Washington and New York.

In 1993 the GATT council, under its Trade Policy Review Mechanism, reviewed for the first time the performance of India. At the end of the review the chairman, Ambassador András Szepesi, stated that the "Council warmly welcomed the fundamental policy changes in India since 1991."[38] India had at last embraced the neoliberal agenda of market globalization.

WHEN THE CHIPS ARE DOWN

India was not the only place where the DDT was causing misery. There were signs of unhappiness from the US pharmaceutical industry:

> The GATT is beginning to smell like the United Nations. This is an unfortunate consequence of the Dunkel leadership. Dunkel has had a particular affinity of making concessions to developing countries. It is philosophical, not pragmatic and is an enormous break for the biggest pirates (Harvey Bale, senior vice president, Pharmaceutical Manufacturers Association).[39]

Jack Valenti, the president of the Motion Picture Association of America, said the text was "fatally flawed," and Jason Berman, the president of the Recording Industry Association of America, said it was "seriously flawed."[40] The two key intellectual property lobbying organizations, the IPC and International Intellectual Property Alliance, also criticized aspects of the Dunkel draft.

All the critics were annoyed by the time given to developing countries to bring their laws into line with TRIPS. One or two years to implement TRIPS was more than enough, figured the US pharmaceutical industry. The one or two years the US pharmaceutical industry was prepared to concede in the way of a transitional period was hardly generous, given that developed countries had evolved their own systems of intellectual property protection over hundreds of years. Giving the states of sub-Saharan Africa ten years in which to be TRIPS compliant did not seem, at least on the face of it, "overly long and discriminatory," to borrow the IPC's description.[41] There was also the issue of cost. Developing countries would have to find tens of millions of dollars to set up the infrastructure of intellectual property protection (patent offices, copyright offices, courts, judges etc.), an infrastructure that would largely service the needs of foreign rights holders. This in countries where the legal system could not afford its citizens even the most basic protections against violence.

US lobbyists kept up the pressure on the issue of the transitional periods. Their problem, as one of them explained to us, was that the CEOs who had helped to make TRIPS a reality wanted to see some immediate return for their companies. Ten years is a long, long time in the life of a CEO. Moreover, it was these CEOs that paid the fees that kept the lobbyists in business. So the transitional periods were routinely denounced by all in Washington. When in 1994 we interviewed major US corporations about their views on TRIPS not one of them failed to point out the unfairness to US industry of the transitional periods.

When Dunkel had submitted his draft to the TNC on 20 December 1991 he had pointed out that it still required schedules of commitments in the market access negotiations relating to goods, commitments in the services negotiations and in the agricultural negotiations. Negotiations in these areas would drag out the Uruguay Round for another two years. But until these matters were settled no part of the draft was final, for Dunkel held firm:

"These negotiations are governed by the principle that nothing is final until everything is agreed."[42] He also went on to say that all the negotiating groups under the GNG would cease to exist (with the exception of the market access group). The negotiations from January 1992 would have to be based on a "global approach." With much of the technical drafting done and many issues resolved, the Uruguay Round had now become a matter of hard bargaining among the key players, especially the US and European Community.

Most countries accepted the Dunkel draft as more or less the final deal on intellectual property. In the US, the motion picture industry and the pharmaceutical industry continued their complaints about the draft text, publicly suggesting that ultimately the US was better off staying out of any final agreement and using its 301 process to open markets. Privately, a strong lobbying effort was under way to get the USTR to obtain changes to the text. By 1993 time was running short. The Uruguay Round had been going since 1986. The US administration had fast-track authority from Congress to negotiate an agreement, authority that carried an expiry date of 15 December 1993. Under fast-track procedures Congress would have a simple decision to make—it could either reject or accept the total package. US industries wanted to see changes in about 15 or so Dunkel texts dealing with matters such as anti-dumping, audiovisual services in the services agreement and tariff issues in a number of areas including textiles and steel. It was a long list of demands.

The US administration wanted the draft of TRIPS changed so that US industry got a share of copyright levies being collected in Europe, full "pipeline" protection on filed pharmaceutical patents and the transitional provisions limited to two years.[43] When Peter Sutherland, the director-general who had succeeded Dunkel, brought down his gavel to close the Uruguay Round negotiations on 15 December 1993, these changes were not there. One change, however, did appear.

Intel Corporation and other members of the Semiconductor Industry Association (SIA) had for a long time been worried about the draft compulsory licensing provisions of TRIPS. The CEOs of these companies had first been alerted to the implications of the early drafts of TRIPS by the patent attorneys who worked for them. Pentium, the heart of Intel, was there for the taking by the Koreans who, apparently, were "licking their chops" when they saw the early versions of the compulsory licensing provision (SIA interview, 1994).

In the dying days of the round, the members of the SIA lobbied hard to secure a change to the compulsory license provision. The industry decided to go it alone because the IPC took the view that enough had been done on this particular issue. Perhaps because most of the industry's members were located in California, and California mattered to any president, the SIA had excellent access to the administration. The SIA went to Congress and then to the president directly to state its case. Intel led the charge. On 8 December 1993 the CEO of Intel, Andy Grove, stated the industry's concerns to Micky Kantor, the then USTR. The bottom line, sent by fax the next day to the USTR's office, was that unless there were changes to the compulsory licensing provision Intel would oppose a GATT agreement. Lying behind this statement was the influence of the semiconductor chip industry in Congress, influence that could make trouble for an administration wishing to sell Congress a GATT package. A letter of 10 December was then faxed to the USTR's office explaining in detail the problems Intel attorneys had with the compulsory licensing provision. There were five days to go before fast-track authority ran out. The SIA had turned compulsory licensing into a "make or break issue" (SIA interview, 1994). In case there were doubts about the industry's intentions, articles appeared in the papers not so much signaling as shouting the message:

> "The entire industry will come down hard against GATT," Mr. Craig Barrett, chief operating officer of Intel, the world's biggest chipmaker, said (Chipmakers Try to Scuttle Push for GATT, *Financial Times*, Tuesday 14 December 1993).
> "Such a deal [the Dunkel draft on compulsory licensing] would destroy the American semiconductor industry," said Michael Maibach, director of government relations for Intel Corp. Nothing less than the "future vitality of our industry" is resting on the GATT talks, Maibach said. "If it's a time of war and they need a chip for a missile, that's one thing. But what the GATT provides is they (demand the license) and they simply have to send us a royalty check." (Last-Minute GATT Bargaining May Set Future for Many Firms, *Investor's Business Daily*, 2 December 1993).

Intel's message must have clarified for US trade negotiators the last-minute changes they absolutely had to have in the draft TRIPS text and those they could give up. A few days later an early morning phone call to a representative of SIA from Michael Kirk, the US negotiator, confirmed that the necessary changes had been obtained (SIA interview, 1994).[44] It was probably fitting for the US that of all the areas of technological knowledge that TRIPS locked up, chip making, which lay at the heart of so many military and civilian technologies, was locked the tightest.

After the conclusion of the Uruguay Round on 15 December 1993, the Final Act Embodying the Results of the Uruguay Round of Multilateral Trade Negotiations was signed on 15 April 1994. The decision was also made to bring the World Trade Organization Agreement into force by 1 January 1995. TRIPS entered into force on the same date. A year later the US began an action against Japan arguing that Japan had breached its obligations under TRIPS in relation to sound recordings.[45] The time had come for the US to begin collecting rents from the rest of the world.

CHAPTER 10

Biogopolies

PATENT PRIVATIZATION

The changes in patent law in the 20th century were massive. Most of them attracted very little public discussion. Yet the foundations of patent law were relaid to accommodate inventions/discoveries in three fields: chemistry, biology and computing science. Patent law, as we shall see, has become one of the main mechanisms by which public knowledge assets have been privatized. TRIPS itself is an outcome of this process of privatization of the intellectual commons. Unlike in the case of the privatization of utilities such as gas, water and the railways, broader public discussion of the costs and benefits of patent-based privatization has not taken place. Although these changes were carried out in the name of the individual inventor they were linked to the private purposes of the corporate players in the knowledge game that we described in Chapter 3.

Much of the tedious detail of patent law and administration becomes readily understandable when it is read in the light of three private purposes:

1 to obtain monopoly control of any knowledge in any field that is likely to prove important to commerce in some way;
2 to enable the formation of cartels;
3 to reduce the costs to industry of obtaining patents.

The instruments of change have been the legislatures, the judiciary, patent offices and the patent profession. The drivers of change have been the large companies and policy entrepreneurs like Prindle (see Chapter 3), Edmund Pratt and Jacques Gorlin (see Chapter 4). The legislature, judiciary and patent office are, as in the case of any other area of law making and reform, meant to act in the public interest, but in the case of patent reform public interest has become a leaf swept away by the winds of private gain.

PATENT ADDICTION

Cartels of all kinds were simply a fact of international economic life in the first part of the 20th century (see Chapter 3).[1] They were present in most commodity markets including cocoa (in 1937 a buyers' cartel involving

Unilever led to West African growers burning cocoa supplies in protest), coffee, corn, sugar and tea. There were cartels in strategically important metal industries such as steel, aluminium, beryllium, cobalt, copper, lead, magnesium, mercury, tin and zinc. Generally speaking, the more technologically sophisticated the process of production, the more use was made of patent and know-how agreements among competitors. Other forms of intellectual property such as trademarks were also involved. Through these agreements members of the cartel "networked" their territorially based patents in order to coordinate their actions in world markets. The details of these arrangements varied as did their legality in different jurisdictions.

The patent monopoly by its nature gave its owner strong rights over the making of the invention, including the terms on which it could be licensed. An arrangement between two producers dividing market territories and setting limits on production, which would have been illegal in the absence of a patent monopoly, could be legal as a patent licensing arrangement. For international producers the national monopoly privilege of patents became the privilege of international cartelism. Two or more international players would come together and negotiate an agreement on the intellectual property rights relating to the products and technologies in the industries in which the players were involved. Typically, the agreement would divide the world into areas (e.g., the British Empire, the US, Central America, each of these being more precisely defined, sometimes in terms of latitude). The agreement might specify that some areas were to be the exclusive territory of party A and others the exclusive territory of party B. Some territories might be shared. Party A would agree to grant party B "sole and exclusive licenses" to patents and trade secrets owned by party A and of interest to party B in its exclusive markets. Party B would return the favor. There would also be obligations on the sharing of information relating to the patents and know-how. Once this framework of cooperation on intellectual property rights and technology was in place all sorts of games could be hidden by a dense cloud of licensing arrangements. Party A might, for example, license a patent to party B in order to help it fight off a competitor threatening party B's market. The contractual "networking" of intellectual property portfolios belonging to two large players gave those players legal tools with which to explore the possibilities of fixing price, production and markets. Not every agreement on patents hid a cartel. But many did.

Patent-based cartels were most strongly present in the chemical and pharmaceutical fields. Some of the most complex were to be found in the coal tar industry (important in dyes, explosives and medicines). Over two or three decades the cartels involved German companies (I. G. Farben, Bayer, Badische, Kalle and Höchst), Swiss companies (Ciba, Sandoz and Geigy), the British company ICI and the American companies DuPont and the National Aniline Chemical company.

For some chemical companies the move into pharmaceuticals made sense. Drugs could be synthesized through chemical processes and chemicals were a source of raw materials in the pharmaceutical sector. I. G. Farben was a prominent player in the pharmaceutical cartels of the 1930s, forming agreements with other European companies such as Ciba and Hoffmann La Roche, as well as US companies such as Sterling Products. Perhaps it was because cartels brought peace from competition for their members that they occasionally bore the word "treaty" in their title. Merck, then the largest pharmaceutical manufacturer in the US, signed in 1932 a "Treaty Agreement" with the German company E. Merck of Darmstadt, in which the parties agreed to cooperate on more or less everything, thereby earning itself an antitrust action in 1943.[2]

Cooperation among chemical companies was not always the rule. National industries would sometimes push states into a protectionist use of patents. A good example was the UK's change to its patent law in 1919 preventing the patentability of chemical compounds. Chemical processes remained patentable. Fearing the might of I. G. Farben, UK industry pursued a strategy of free-riding by concentrating on inventing better processes that duplicated German dyestuffs. This was to be precisely the strategy that the Indian government adopted in its Patent Act of 1970 for its pharmaceutical manufacturers: grant process patents for pharmaceuticals, but not product patents, thereby providing an incentive for national producers to patent cheaper processes for making pharmaceutical products. By the time India and other developing states had begun to use the patent system to serve national goals, the game in the West had changed.

The changes in the US pharmaceutical sector were especially dramatic.[3] Prior to World War II, the US pharmaceutical industry was similar to other manufacturing industries. The number of drugs of high therapeutic value under patent were few. There was also a competitive generics industry. Companies wishing to protect their proprietary medicines found that trademarks and advertising were in fact more important than patents, which in any case were hard to obtain when it came to chemical compounds. In most European states, including Germany, it was not possible to get a patent on a chemical compound (but it was possible to obtain protection for chemical processes, which was enough for companies like I. G. Farben to be able to run their cartels). The discovery prior to World War II of penicillin and sulphanilamide led to an era of wonder drugs after the war. Companies like Pfizer, Bristol, Parke Davis and Merck rushed toward patents over antibiotics. Obtaining patent protection was absolutely vital. These companies had seen what a competitive market could do to the price of a drug like penicillin. Penicillin, which had not been patented, had gone from being US$3,955 a pound in 1945 to US$282 a pound in 1950.[4]

One obstacle stood in the way of companies obtaining a patent hold on antibiotics. The discovery of new antibiotics like streptomycin depended on the discovery of naturally occurring substances in soil samples that killed harmful microorganisms. An obvious objection to patentability was that these substances occurred in nature and so they were really unpatentable discoveries. Here the patent profession rode to the rescue. For decades the profession had been successfully pushing the principle that substances that occurred in nature, but had been isolated and purified by the discoverer, were in fact patentable. Technically they no longer existed in nature. Progressively the principle of purification/isolation came to have a wider and wider application in the case of chemical patents.[5] In the case of the patents for broad-spectrum antibiotics, the US Patent and Trademark Office (PTO) accepted the application of the principle and granted the patents. In fact, it granted too many of them. Companies found that each one of them could make life difficult for the other. Rather than live in a world of mutually assured patent litigation, these companies swapped patents in order to form a producers' cartel. The prices of antibiotics like tetracycline were held constant by Lederle, Pfizer, Bristol, Upjohn and Squibb between 1951 and 1961.

During this time these companies experienced a period of enormous expansion based on the supranormal profits they obtained by means of the patent system. However, the profits of each individual company tended to come from only one or two drugs. For example, in 1960 Terramycin and tetracycline accounted for 33 percent of Pfizer's sales; chloramphenicol accounted for 45 percent of Parke Davis's sales and Merck saw Divril account for 39 percent of its sales.[6] When these patents ran out, the companies would be cast back into competitive markets. For these companies there was now a massive incentive to strengthen the patent system. The patent system had played a crucial role in globalizing these firms and now they had an overwhelming interest in globalizing the patent system. They would need longer and stronger patents to protect the blockbuster drugs on which they had become financially dependent. They would need every country in the world to recognize product and process patents[7] for pharmaceuticals so that it would be possible to become a monopoly supplier in every market of their choice. They would need standards of patent protection that would make it difficult for the generics industry to compete with them in these national markets. They would need stronger trademark laws to protect their global marketing strategies, trademark laws that could not be tampered with by developing countries. They would need something like TRIPS.

Chemical companies became the biggest users of the patent system. The patent profession supplied the necessary technical distinctions that enabled patents offices to conclude that a given chemical discovery really was an invention after all. Naturally, to begin with, the companies did not have it all their own way. The US PTO was from time to time criticized by the patent profession for not being sufficiently cooperative in the grant of patents. The courts also proved less than helpful at times. The US Supreme Court in particular was a source of irritation to the patent faithful. In 1930 an editorial of the *Journal of the Patent Office Society* complained that the "permissible monopoly under a patent has been shorn to the extent that it is subject to the existing anti-trust laws and it cannot be used for restraining commerce."[8] Other courts would on occasion also remind the profession and the US PTO that the patent system was there to serve the public rather than industry. The District Court of Columbia, for instance, observed in 1957 that:

the Patent Office should be very careful and perhaps even reluctant to grant a patent on a new medical formula until it has been thoroughly tested and successfully tried by more than one physician.[9]

In truth, however, the history of chemical patenting turned into one of relentless expansion. Whatever judicial reservations were expressed from time to time about this became as pebbles against a giant rising tide.

MOTHER NATURE'S SOFTWARE

The explanation by Watson and Crick in 1951 of the structure of the DNA molecule revealed the code on the basis of which Mother Nature operated. An organism's physical expression begins with DNA code. This code is itself made up of pairs of bases in a sequence. There are only four bases involved in the code; A always binds with T, and C with G. The entire sequence of linked pairs for an organism (the genome) is a very long set of instructions for the chemical assembly of the organism. This long set of instructions is broken up into a large number of discrete parts that describe different tasks or functions to be carried out. The instructions come in packages. Three bases are required for an amino acid and up to 20 amino acids are required for a protein. Each complete package of instructions for a protein is a gene. Roughly speaking, the DNA instructional sequence is translated into amino acids, and those amino acids are assembled into different kinds of protein molecules. It is the bounded interaction of many functionally different protein molecules that constitutes a living cellular system, whether simple or complex.

In the early 1970s techniques for directly cutting and splicing DNA code were found. Just like software, Mother Nature's code could be rewritten. Multinationals in the chemical, agricultural and pharmaceutical sectors became interested in genetic engineering for a variety of reasons. By the 1960s and 1970s the rate of chemical innovation had hit a real plateau. In the US, for example, the number of new chemical entities introduced to the market fell from 233 in 1957–1961 to 76 in 1967–1971.[10] Nature was imposing the law of diminishing gains on the industry. The chemical industry was also facing a lot of criticism from the environmental movement for the high levels of environmental damage it had caused. Genetic engineering seemed a much cleaner technology and would therefore be easier to sell to an increasingly environmentally conscious public. It appeared to offer the possibility of an almost endless range of products in the global markets of agriculture, food, medicines, medical therapy and chemicals. DNA code was a standard common to all organisms. The new techniques allowed segments of it to be moved from one species to another quickly and with seemingly predictable effects, at least from an engineering point of view. The issue for companies was how to turn the valuable parts of it into a proprietary standard.

The breakthroughs in molecular biology led to technologies and products for which there was a demand. The patent system was not particularly significant to the basic research in molecular biology. Much of this research had in fact been carried out over the decades by scientists working in public universities and institutes as members of an international community, driven by curiosity and the need for recognition in that community. Nor was the patent system important to the existence of markets. Markets need willing buyers as well as sellers, and patents do not create willing buyers. The patent system was, however, important in the decision of who would take up a commercial opportunity that existed in the marketplace. The experience with penicillin and streptomycin was highly instructive in this respect. If a company allowed research to remain in the public sector or it licensed the technology widely, its rates of return would be comparatively low.[11] Patents, on the other hand, could deliver to it a very high rate of return. Once the breakthroughs in molecular biology had occurred the multinational companies with markets in areas affected by the breakthroughs began to plan how to exploit the new opportunities of the technology. Their planning took into account the need to change the patent system. They wanted the patent system to deliver the kind of returns in biotechnology that it had in chemical technology.

The changes to the patent system that occurred in relation to biotechnology patenting were not the causes of the bio-industrial revolution, but rather an outcome. The patent system was there to be used, and use it the companies did. Plants, animals, microorganisms and genes as well as the tools and processes for the production of these things became targets of patenting. By the late 1980s the use of the patent system in the fields of genetic engineering and molecular biology was well under way. For genetic engineering the number of patents granted by the US PTO had risen from below 20 in 1978 to almost 200 in 1987.[12] For molecular biology and microbiology the number of patents granted increased from approximately 400 in 1978 to over 1,000 in 1987. The bulk of patents went to US corporations. Compared with what was to come in the 1990s these numbers now seem pathetically small.

PATENT ENGINEERING

The breakthroughs in genetic engineering provided companies with four broad patent targets. There were units of life (cells, microorganisms, plants, animals), the molecules and other elements of those units (proteins, amino acids), the instructions for the assembly of those molecules (the DNA sequences) and the methods and processes for the analysis and manipulation of the DNA instructions and molecules. Patenting in biotechnology had been going on for decades in areas such as fermentation technology. Genetic engineering presented new vistas of product and process patents. Animal breeding based on selection of animals, for example, could never result in a patented animal, but a genetically engineered mouse would turn out to be patentable.

For the pharmaceutical and chemical industries genetic engineering had opened up a biological Eden filled with overwhelming temptation. A patent could be used to claim a DNA sequence and the protein that it encoded. The search was on for blockbuster proteins like Genentech's tPA, a protein drug for dissolving blood clots, which in the first five months of 1987 had brought the company US$100 million in sales. An obvious strategy was to patent as many DNA instructions as possible even if a company could not be sure what they were instructions for or exactly what tasks the relevant proteins performed. The main thing was to get exclusivity in the instructions themselves and then figure out the functionalities and product implications later. Of course, all firms large and small were making the same calculation, thus triggering a herd-like rush to the patent office. In the US, human partial gene sequences were a favored target. In 1991 the US PTO had applications covering 4,000 such sequences. By September 1998 the number of sequences being applied for had climbed to more than 500,000.[13] During the 1990s the major patent offices around the world found themselves doing much more business in the biotech field.

From the point of view of the larger players in the industry this rush to patent was, ironically, alarming. Many small, start-up firms were also filing patent applications. The US public sector, for reasons we shall explain in the next section, was also heavily involved. In 1992, for example, the National Institutes of Health (NIH) had applied for patents on more than 2,750 partial gene sequences and in 1993 it filed for a US patent claiming 2,421 partial gene sequences.[14] The universities had also joined the queues at the patent office. Two US academics, Stanley Cohen and Herbert Boyer, obtained a patent in 1980 for a method of introducing "genetic capability into micro-organisms for the production of nucleic acids and proteins," a method that the patent abstract went on to point out would be useful in areas such as the production of drugs, fixation of nitrogen and fermentation.[15] The Cohen–Boyer technology turned out to be foundational to genetic engineering. The patent on it made millions for its owner, Stanford University. But the patent sent something of a chill down the backs of the large private sector players. In truth, a lot of the foundational work in genetic engineering was being done in the university sector, as well as other public sector organizations, most notably the NIH. There was no guarantee that the major breakthroughs in genetics and genetic engineering and therefore the major patents would come out of corporate laboratories. This posed potentially serious problems for the tradition of patent cartelism in the chemical and pharmaceutical industries. With so many players in the biotech field all holding patents, forming a cartel, let alone enforcing one, was almost impossible, especially if government entities were holding some of the vital patents. The Pharmaceutical Manufacturers Association in 1992 sounded a cautionary note on the patenting of gene sequences, arguing that government ownership of gene sequences was undesirable. Similarly, the Industrial Biotechnology

Association, a trade association that represented most of biotech in the US, also urged the NIH not to pursue the patents and to put the sequences into the public domain.[16]

A dilemma had emerged for the large players. If these players were to secure high returns from the technology of genetic engineering, patent law had to be adapted to enable the appropriation of the technology and its products. At the same time, if patent standards were liberalized too much, with so many new players in the game, the ownership of the knowledge would be diffused among many. That would force all players into licensing, and only ordinary profit levels. Similarly, if the US government owned such basic information, it might in a trustee capacity impose licensing conditions designed to encourage the emergence of competition or keep prices of the products based on the genes down in some other way. As one representative from a large life sciences company mentioned to us, "You don't make much on royalty deals" (1999). It was the voice of a collective corporate experience with the patent system in chemicals and pharmaceuticals over ~~decades~~ speaking.

~~four~~ categories of biotechnology that we described earlier ~~problems~~ of principle and application. The foundations of patent ~~been~~ laid in an era of mechanical invention. Drawing a distinction ~~between~~ invention and discovery and applying it in the case of a steam engine was comparatively easy. As companies moved into the patenting of chemical compounds the invention/discovery distinction started to get fuzzier. Drawing on the metaphor of engineering, one could liken the synthesis of new compounds to invention in mechanical engineering. The use of the metaphor becomes more problematic in the case of organic chemistry where the chemist finds molecules that exist in nature and have useful properties. In the case of patent claims over DNA instructions and their corresponding proteins, the metaphor seems even weaker. It is hard to claim an entitlement to the DNA code on the basis that it had been engineered. It, after all, had been in existence for thousands of years before the genetic engineer and corporate laboratories. It had been uncovered or found rather than designed and built.

Chemical companies in particular had been rehearsing technical arguments about the patentability of chemical inventions before patent offices and courts for almost a hundred years. These companies also had experience with biotechnology going back that far. They knew how to overcome problems of patentability in order to make patent principle serve their strategic needs. As we mentioned earlier, the problem of patenting products had been met by the principle that one could, through an act of isolation and purification, transform a naturally existing product into an invention. For the principle to apply the invented product had to be different in kind from the naturally existing product.[17] By the 1990s this rider to the principle was being largely ignored by patentees and patent offices. Patent offices continued to grant patents on DNA codes purified by the removal of redundant segments of code even though the purified DNA coded for the same protein as the naturally occurring sequence.

There were other fundamental problems of patentability in the case of DNA. Before an invention can be patented it must be shown to be useful. The idea behind the requirement is to force the inventor to move beyond discovering information that might or might not be useful and into products and processes that are part of the "useful arts." If applied strictly in the case of DNA code, the requirement of utility might defeat many patent applications since often the applicant has little idea of what the function of the DNA is and what it might be useful for in product terms. The utility requirement had also been the subject of analysis in the chemical field. In the mid-1960s the US Supreme Court reversed a trend toward a weakening of the utility requirement for chemical patents, pointing out that the "basic quid pro quo" for the grant of the patent monopoly was an invention possessing a specific and defined benefit to the public.[18] If an inventor could not specify a concrete and practical use for the invention, and a patent was granted, the effect of the patent might be "to confer power to block off whole areas of scientific development."[19] The Supreme Court's approach, however, did not stick. During the 1990s utility turned out not to be a high hurdle in biotech filings with the US PTO: "You get it
it" (US patent attorney, 1999). Patents were granted on DN
practical utility of which the patent office, the inventor and the p
very little idea. Patents had become hunting licenses, the very thing
Supreme Court had said 30 or so years earlier that they were not.[20]

The patenting of genes, which through the 1990s increasingly drew more public attention, was the culmination of a business approach that had been evolving in the chemical, agricultural, seed and pharmaceutical sectors for all of the 20th century. Genetic engineering was only a part of biotechnology, albeit a significant one. As biotechnological production had become more and more industrialized, so the patent system's shadow over it had lengthened. Of course, this dynamic was different in each country but, in general, developments in US patent law have turned out to be the most influential, even if they were not always the first. The conclusion of the US Supreme Court in Diamond v. Chakrabarty in 1980 made it clear that a microorganism that had been modified by the application of genetic engineering techniques could be the subject of patent. The fact that it was living was not a bar to patentability. Similar decisions had already been reached in 1969 by the Supreme Court of the Federal Republic of Germany and by the Australian Patent Office.[21] Nevertheless, the Chakrabarty decision had a catalyzing and global effect on biotech patenting simply because of the sheer size of the US market. For all its totemic status, well before Diamond v. Chakrabarty, US patent attorneys were claiming microorganisms, but claiming them in a solution or inert matter so as to minimize objections based on discovery or living matter. These claims were being let through by the US PTO. Not for the first time the reach of the patent system was being extended through some clever drafting of patent claims.

Step by step during the course of the 20th century, living systems and their parts were absorbed into the patent system. In some cases the developments go back to the 19th century. Louis Pasteur was granted a patent in relation to a process for fermenting beer in 1873; the US PTO allowed a claim for "yeast free from organic germs or disease, as an article of manufacture." Process patents involving microorganisms were routinely granted by patent offices (the patent, however, not protecting the microorganism per se). Plants and animals also became objects of patenting. Genetic engineering, argued patent applicants, resulted in new structures not previously found in nature. In 1987 the US PTO announced that as a matter of patent policy "nonnaturally occurring nonhuman multicellular living organisms, including animals" were patentable subject matter. The following year, two Harvard professors were granted a patent that claimed, among other things, a mouse into which activated human cancer genes had been inserted. It was DuPont that ended up with the exclusive rights, however, because it had sponsored the research.

In the US the spread of patents into the plant kingdom began in 1930 when Congress passed the Plant Patents Act. The US initiative was the first significant legislative move in the world to extend patents to plants.[22] The patenting of plants was restricted to asexually reproduced plants. Tuber-propagated plants were excluded from this category because in the case of tubers like potatoes the part of plant involved in reproduction was also sold as food (unlike in the case of a fruit tree, for example). Sexually reproduced plants were not included in the Plant Patents Act. The effect was to keep large grain crops like wheat and corn out of the reach of plant patents. Congress was not yet ready to open the door that led to a monopoly-based commerce in seeds. In any case, plant breeding in the US since the middle of the 19th century had been characterized by a strong public sector research program and the provision of seed to farmers for free first by the US PTO and then by the US Department of Agriculture.[23] There was no obvious failure of US agriculture that one could use to justify the creation of intellectual property rights over the big item crops of US agriculture.

The other major congressional excursion into intellectual property rights for plants was the Plant Variety Protection Act of 1970. Fear of competition from European plant breeders explains much of the motivation for legislation. After meeting in Paris in 1956 for the first time to discuss plant protection, in 1961 a small group of European countries signed the International Convention for the Protection of New Varieties of Plants (the signatories were Belgium, France, Federal Republic of Germany, Italy and the Netherlands). UPOV (the widely used French acronym for the convention) meant that European plant breeders would be receiving protection specially designed for plants, including sexually reproducing plants. The large markets in the grain crops were now open to this kind of right. What European plant breeders had, US plant breeders also had to have. UPOV came into operation in 1968, and in 1970 US plant breeders had, in the shape of the Plant Variety Protection Act, a similar form of protection.

A significant feature of the US intellectual property system for plants was that it evolved in a way that gave individuals a menu of options when it came to plant protection. A plant breeder could apply for a standard patent (referred to as a utility patent) for a plant. In the case of some plants this patent protection might be combined with plant patent or plant variety protection. The options for protection in other words were not necessarily mutually exclusive.[24] The same information could be locked up in more than one way. Utility patents could be used to protect parts of plants, including genes inserted into the plant as well as to protect traits across different varieties of plants. Utility patents had another huge advantage. They limited the ability of the farmer to operate independently of the seed companies. Under plant variety law, the farmer had the right to save seed for the purposes of replanting it or selling to other farmers for the purpose of crop production. US farmers took advantage of their right to save seed. In 1986 the *purchases* of soybean seed and wheat seed amounted to 54 percent and 60 percent respectively.[25] A lot of seed, in other words, was being saved and exchanged by US farmers, as it had been for hundreds of years by farmers everywhere. The utility patent in contrast provided the farmer with no such seed-saving exemption. It could be used to lock up the use of seeds where plant variety law could not. Using patent law, seed companies could turn farmers into repeat customers.

In many ways that are beyond the scope of this chapter to detail the patent system in the US and other countries was adapted to meet the needs of those in the biotech business. Living systems like plants and micro-organisms posed fundamental problems for patent law and its administration. There was the problem of how to describe a "plant invention" satisfactorily so that others could reproduce it. Plants and microorganisms could not be described as easily as mechanical inventions and they did not necessarily follow the dictates of a patent description when they reproduced. This made it hard for inventors to disclose their invention to the public (sufficient disclosure being a basic requirement of patentability) and hard for others to repeat the invention. In truth, those applying for patents over living systems, unlike the inventor of a mechanical device, had only a partial understanding of how their "inventions" worked. The response to these kinds of problems was the evolution of a patent system of ever deepening complexity that became increasingly disconnected from its duty of serving the public welfare. The Plant Patents Act of 1930, for instance, relaxed the description requirement for plants. Systems of deposit for microorganisms evolved in both the US and Europe, but they were mired in complexity, making it difficult for others to gain access to the invention.

Lying at the heart of the reengineering of patent law have been the large chemical and pharmaceutical companies, the biggest users of the patent system. Together they have formed a transnational medium pushing a common message: increasing patent protection will increase the supply of biotech products to the marketplace. As lobbyists and litigators they have been active in all the key patent jurisdictions (US, Europe, Japan). TRIPS, we have seen, provided them with the experience of lobbying for global standards. Making sure that congressional representatives stay focused on the need to protect their patents is so vital to the pharmaceutical industry that it has 297 lobby-ists working for it.[26] Whether it is in the US or Europe the large players in this industry will have an ease of regular, high-level access to senior politi-cians and bureaucrats unmatched by even the best organized NGOs when it comes to discussing issues like the price of patented AIDs drugs.

The large companies have been prepared to absorb the cost of appeals against patent office decisions. Patent offices with their more limited budg-ets have not been in a position to keep up with these kinds of strategic liti-gation games. Courts, too, have noted that companies have persisted in very expensive litigation when the patents have expired and one might have expected a settlement.[27] The deeper game in these kinds of cases has been the pursuit of a precedent. The complexity of chemical science combined with the complexity of patent law has seen companies apply for patents on chem-ical inventions that are the same as inventions on which the patents have expired. Eli Lilly and Co. tried this with their blockbuster drug Prozac. Sometimes this has been picked up by the courts and sometimes not.[28] Patent offices are even less likely to pick up instances of double patenting.

Patent offices over time have undergone a cultural change in which their motto has become one of keeping their multinational customers happy. The motto makes good economic sense because, increasingly, patent offices have to fund their operations from the patent fees they collected from patentees. The larger patent offices lead the smaller ones in a process of quiet harmo-nization. When the Australian Patent Office (IP Australia) wants to know what to do about the patentability of mathematical algorithms it takes its lead from the US PTO. The three large Patent Office players (the US PTO, the European Patent Office and the Japanese Patent Office) have a program of trilateral cooperation.

The policy committees that are tucked away in major patent offices invariably have heavy private sector representation with no or little repre-sentation from consumers, environmentalists, or health and food security movements. Consumers for patent offices are the multinationals that make use of their services. Our interviews in patent offices suggest patent tech-nocrats believe that NGO movements do not understand the patent system and therefore are not in a position to make a contribution to patent policy. Outsiders critical of the patent system's commodification of basic informa-tion are instructed that a patent does not confer the right to commercial exploitation, merely the right to exclude. When critics question the patent system's expansion they are told that patent rights are needed to encourage the commercialization of socially valuable technologies. For the purposes of classifying a living system as an invention its "engineered" nature is emphasized, but for the purpose of relaxing the disclosure standard the "living" nature of the invention is emphasized. The technical density of patent law obscures its basic contradictions. The capacity of patent thinking to accommodate contrary positions allows it to answer any criticism.

A central player in the reinterpretation of patent law principles to serve commercial rather than public interest is the US Court of Appeals for the

Federal Circuit (CAFC). The idea of the CAFC, as Silverman observes, was pushed by "a very small group of large high technology firms and trade associations in the telecommunications, computer and pharmaceutical industries" that were interested in their version of patent justice.[29] Patent appeals from the Court of Federal Claims, the International Trade Commission, the US PTO and the US district courts (in most cases) are all funneled to the CAFC, giving it centralized power over patent law principle. Created in 1982, when the US Court of Customs and Patent Appeals and the US Court of Claims were merged, the CAFC was charged with the task of increasing the doctrinal stability and unity of patent law. Whether it has done this is open to question. Analysts have pointed to the large number of times the court has flatly contradicted itself, as well as its distortion of patent law in the context of biotech patenting in order to better serve the private sector.[30] What it has done is to increase the chances of a patent holder succeeding in litigation. During the 1940s and 1950s, getting a court to find a patent valid was tough. So, for example, one study of patent decisions of circuit courts of appeals found that, for the period 1940–1944, the number of patents held valid was 17.6 percent and for 1945–1949 it was 22.25 percent.[31] When the CAFC arrived on the scene in 1982 the odds changed dramatically in favor of the patent holder. In 1988 in Harmon's first edition of his book dealing with the CAFC's decisions he observed that an "accused infringer who loses below has less than 1 chance in 15 of turning things around on appeal."[32] By the fourth edition (1998) those odds had reduced to 1 in 7.[33] They remained, nevertheless, pretty good odds for the patent holder.

The CAFC has almost single-handedly created a multibillion-dollar patent litigation market in the US. In 1981, just before the CAFC came into existence, 835 patent infringement actions had been filed in the courts. By 1998 the number was 2,218. In the same period the revenues from the licensing and litigation of US patents rose from US$3 billion a year to more than US$100 billion per year.[34] Patenting is a rich company's game. Not many companies can wear the estimated US$100 million bill that Polaroid and Kodak did in their patent dispute in 1989. Not many companies can build patent portfolios that stretch across the jurisdictions of the world. The big money in licensing comes from a vast web of patents. The kind of odds the CAFC hands out to alleged patent infringers increases the bargaining power of owners of large patent portfolios. It is a private bargaining power, used behind the curtain of commercial-in-confidence, making its effects hard to measure. Bargaining can easily stray into bullying when one side has so many intellectual property levers at its disposal.

THE UNIVERSITY-INDUSTRIAL KNOWLEDGE COMPLEX

During the 1970s there were congressional fears that the US was losing its mastery of the knowledge we described in Chapter 3. Senator Birch Bayh, a US senator from Indiana, began to push the idea that the stronger the patent system became, the better the US would do against its competitors (at that time West Germany and Japan) and in regaining lost markets. Speaking to the Patent Law Association of Chicago in 1979 he observed that the "mood of Congress has changed in its sensitivity to the patent system" and that there would be much more activity in this area.[35] He helped to fulfill this prediction by introducing, with Robert Dole, the Bayh-Dole Act, which took effect in 1981.[36] Essentially the Bayh-Dole Act allowed universities and small businesses to own patents in inventions that they had developed with federal funds. Prior to Bayh-Dole, patents in such inventions ended up with the relevant federal funding agency or the inventions were put straight into the public domain by means of publication. Bayh-Dole saw US universities and hospitals hurrying to the patent office. In the five years following Bayh-Dole these organizations increased their patent applications in the human biological area by 300 percent.[37] The fate of publicly funded technology was now in the hands of university offices of technology transfer.

Bayh-Dole was generally hailed as a success. The university sector saw its income from the licensing of intellectual property in technology soar, but that income was unequally distributed. In 1992, of the top 31 royalty leaders in the US, six universities earned between US$12 and $26 million, while the other 25 earned between US$500,000 and $6 million.[38] That left a lot of other universities earning a lot less. Only so many universities were at the leading edge of biotech. The chances of any one of them developing a truly foundational technology of the Cohen and Boyer kind were slim. It was the Cohen and Boyer patents that had put the University of California and Stanford at the top of the royalty tree. The universities clustered in and around Boston and San Francisco gained enormously from the patent-based commercialization of biotechnology. For most other universities it brought complications because their researchers now had to navigate their way through the patents owned by others on the research tools of biotechnology.

Bayh-Dole and other legislation that Congress passed in the 1980s, making it easier for universities as well as businesses both large and small to obtain patents on federally funded inventions, did one important structural thing.[39] It integrated universities much more deeply into the corporate knowledge game. Many entrepreneurially minded academic scientists in the 1980s left their universities to set up small biotech companies, knowing that they could draw on federal funds for the development of their technology and still retain a patent position. This migration followed a distinct geographical pattern, with most start-up companies being established in the Boston and San Francisco areas. Today these areas account for more than one-third of public biotechnology companies.[40] Most of the knowledge patented by the public sector flowed to the private sector via the conduit of licensing. In most cases a university did best by having a technology licensed as widely as possible rather than by hanging on to the technological knowledge and doing the product development. University patenting thus assisted rather than hindered the private sector. The same was true of patenting by biotech start-ups. For the most part, start-ups followed a licensing strategy, could be bought by a large player or were seeking a strategic alliance with a large player.

Universities also turned out to be key to genomic decoding exercises. In the 1980s the technology of working out the sequence of a genome cost around US$100 per base pair. It was also slow. Laboratories in the 1970s, for instance, could do only 150 base pairs a day compared with the several million a day that it is possible to do today at under a dollar a pair. Given the high costs and speed of sequencing technology, the sequencing of the human genome with its 3 billion base pairs would happen only if governments were prepared to foot the bill and the public sector was prepared to do the work. The Human Genome Project, which was launched in 1990, was conceived of as primarily an international public sector project that would see data about human genes and nucleotide sequences put in the public domain. James Watson, the codiscoverer of the DNA structure, became the first director of the Human Genome Organization, the international organization set up to coordinate the worldwide decoding and mapping effort. The development of fast automated sequencing machines and different strategies of sequencing changed the costs of sequencing. By the late 1990s it had become feasible for a single firm to sequence the human genome. The Human Genome Project now found itself in competition with rivals that had commercial purposes in mind. Craig Venter, one of the original players in the Human Genome Project, went into partnership with Perkin-Elmer Corporation, and in May 1998 created a new company, Celera. Based on Perkin-Elmer's state-of-the-art sequencers, capable of pumping out 100 million base pairs a day, Venter predicted that the race to sequence the genome would go to Celera. Other players such as Incyte Pharmaceuticals also entered the game.

Through the public debates over the patenting of DNA, companies small and large have relentlessly pursued patents over DNA sequences, genes and proteins of human, plant and animal origin. Of the 1,175 patents granted worldwide on human DNA sequences between 1981 and 1995, 76 percent went to companies, mostly of Japanese or US origin.[41] Scientists working in the public sector have continued to place sequences in the public domain. But this practice does not, because of the purification/isolation principle that we discussed earlier, necessarily prevent companies from obtaining patents on purified versions of the same genetic information. In any case, universities, with one eye on the possibility of licensing income, have begun to manage the intellectual property generated by their academics along private sector lines. Universities and scientists know that if they are to get millions in research grants from the DuPonts and Monsantos they must not jeopardize the possibility of taking a patent position.

At the same time, companies have been anxious to forge links with universities because for all their private R&D dollars they are profoundly dependent on public science in all fields of technology. In biotechnology the dependence is striking; for example, more than 70 percent of scientific papers cited in biotechnology patents originated in solely public science institutions compared with 16.5 percent that originated in the private sector.[42] The US private sector needs the funding of basic public science to continue. The challenge for it has been to find ways in which to uplift this basic research from the public domain and utilize it in commercial strategies. Patent offices, the patent profession and the courts have all played a role in reinterpreting patent law to allow this uplift from the public domain to take place. Patents, instead of being a reward for inventors who place private information into the public domain, have become a means of recycling public information as private monopolies. The US legislature has played its part by enacting laws that have brought patent culture into the very corners of public research. In a meeting of two research tribes, the public and the private, it is the public that has adopted the patent mores of the private. Public institutions have learned to turn public goods into private ones, something we discuss further in Chapter 14.

HARD-CORE CARTELS

The chemical cartels of the 20th century were some of the most powerful ever to colonize the world economy. The companies participating in them were among the first to become genuinely global. Early on in the 20th century they learned to use patents, trade secrets and trademarks to bind themselves together into tight dominant groups that could operate across borders according to agreed production and marketing plans. Obtaining patents in new technological processes was a basic strategy of insurance even if the product pipeline coming from these new processes was uncertain. No large player could risk not following another into the systematic patenting of emerging technologies.

The fast move into biotechnology patenting is an old practice in a new technological context. The practice of cartelism based on intellectual property rights among the corporate players in the knowledge game is also an old custom that is not likely to change. A good example is the private antitrust action that has been brought by US and international farmers against Monsanto and its coconspirators alleging the use of patents to fix prices and restrain trade in the GM corn and soybean seed markets.[43] The complaint alleges that, beginning in 1996, Monsanto, DuPont, Dow Chemical, Novartis, AstraZeneca and others entered into licensing arrangements to build a cartel in which Monsanto would be the "hub" of the GM industry, and the coconspirators the "spokes."

What has varied is the attitude of governments toward knowledge cartels and their use of intellectual property rights. Under President Reagan the policy of the US became one of the supply of stronger and stronger intellectual property standards to the US market, as well as the globalization of those standards. At the same time, William F. Baxter, a Reagan appointee to the Antitrust Division in 1981, introduced a hands-off policy when it came to the policing of the use of intellectual property rights by corporate America. By adopting a regulatory policy of raising intellectual property standards and rejecting the deregulatory tool of competition law it was thought that US companies would do better in terms of innovation and trade. The antitrust action against Microsoft notwithstanding, the US state continues to push its global regulatory strategy for intellectual property in the belief this will increase the gains to its knowledge-based economy. At least in the short term this is likely to prove to be true.

In the longer run, however, US support for big business's regulatory agenda of ever longer, broader and stronger intellectual property rights for the global information economy risks a deepening of cartelism. The chemical and pharmaceutical oligopolies of the 20th century will, using intellectual property rights over biotechnological processes and products, progressively transform themselves into the biogopolies of the 21st. The biotech market in the US is characterized by the presence of large numbers of small start-up companies. Entry into the market by smaller players remains relatively open because of strong venture capital markets in the US.

Aggressive patenting of biotechnology has been a feature of the US biotech market by both public and private players. Patents over biotechnological information enhance the tradeability of that information. For most small biotech firms and universities the market for their patents is constituted by multinationals with interests in chemicals, pharmaceuticals and agriculture. For many biotech start-ups their preferred destiny is to be swallowed in one way or another by the very large fish, most of them US fish in gene technology. Patents act as a signal that they are worth swallowing. They also offer the purchaser of the patented information some security of title. The incentives for multinationals to form strategic alliances with smaller players in the biotech industry or to take them over are strong since the internal R&D effort of even a multinational cannot be guaranteed to fill its product pipeline. The fact that small firms and the university sector have adopted a patenting culture is an advantage for multinationals, since it opens the way to the exclusive acquisition of promising new technologies. If, for example, a small biotech firm has patented a gene that looks promising in the drug field it will have to enter into an alliance with a big pharmaceutical company. Only such a company can wear the development, regulatory, distribution and marketing costs of any resulting drug. In short, the competitiveness of the market in biotech information really extends only to the discovery phase rather than to the development and marketing phase. The tradeability of biotech information from the discovery phase means that much of it will eventually end up in the hands of the large players in the pharmaceutical, chemical and agricultural sectors.

Accompanying these information flows of propertized information are changes in market structure that will also have consequences for the competitiveness of markets. During the last century, nationally strong companies began to grow globally, through a process of international market expansion, mergers and acquisitions, transforming themselves into vertically integrated multinationals with interests in chemicals, pharmaceuticals, agriculture and food. In recent times this process has produced some of the biggest companies the world has ever seen (witness the recent mergers between Pfizer and Warner-Lambert and between Glaxo Wellcome and SmithKline Beecham). From time to time warnings have been sounded about the growing concentration of important technological information in smaller groups. The Nuffield Council observed in its report that there were "six major industrial groups who between them control most of the technology which gives freedom to undertake commercial R&D in the area of GM crops."[44] In its report on *EC Regulation of Genetic Modification in Agriculture* (1998) the Select Committee of the House of Lords also warned of the problem of cartels and monopolies in the agrochemical/seed sector.[45]

Biotechnology is a fundamental technology that reaches into all aspects of four very basic areas: food, health, reproduction and environment. This time around the reach of multinational intellectual property webs over biotechnology will be much greater than it was over chemical technology. Multinationals may now register product patents in developing countries such as India, thereby giving themselves options in those markets that they previously did not have. Patents over seeds have cost implications for agricultural economies. All states will find the gossamer threads of intangible property growing ever tighter around their economies.

The dangers of biogopolies are not simply those that relate to prices and consumer welfare, although they are real enough. They run deeper. The globalization of intellectual property rights will rob much knowledge of its public good qualities. When knowledge becomes a private good to be traded in markets the demands of many, paradoxically, go unmet. Patent-based R&D is not responsive to demand, but to ability to pay. The blockbuster mentality of the large pharmas takes them to those markets where there is the ability to pay. Drugs for mental illness, hypertension and erectile dysfunction are where the blockbusters are, not tropical diseases.

The promise of genomic-based technologies to liberate "us" from disease refers to a largely Western industrialized "us." Even in Western markets there will be a wide variability in who has access to biotech health products and services. The argument that but for intellectual property rights these drugs would not exist does not wash. As we have seen, the private sector is profoundly dependent on the public for the foundational research. Knowledge assets that are generated with public money are uplifted and recycled as private goods by means of the patent system. The price we pay in the form of patents to biogopolists is not the price of the discovery as they would have us believe, but the price of development and distribution. Through trademarks and other means they exercise a tight grip on distribution. Global intellectual property rights are a high price to pay for a delivery service. Citizens pay and pay again for patented information. Taxes are used to fund public research. That public research often ends up as a private monopoly. The costs of patenting are generally a tax deduction, as are many of the research and development costs. In turn, the profits of multinationals from patents become the subject of transfer pricing games that minimize the tax they pay by shifting profits to the lowest tax jurisdiction. Transfer pricing has been a chronic problem in the pharmaceutical industry; developing countries sometimes experience overpricing of active ingredients thousands of percent higher than the lowest available price elsewhere.[46]

In many ways that we cannot document here biogopolies will bring costs. An OECD report in 1989 warned that biotechnology in the short run would bring few trade benefits to developing countries.[47] A biotechnology that operates under a private property regime may intensify the trade problems of developing countries. Access to seeds, the traits of which farmers need, will depend on the ability to pay. Public sector plant breeders in developing countries may find it difficult to deliver seeds to their farmers if the tools of molecular biology needed to do the job are in the hands of a few global private sector players. Much of what happens in the agriculture and health sectors of developed and developing countries will end up depending on the bidding or charity of biogopolists as they make strategic commercial decisions on how to use their intellectual property rights.

CHAPTER 11

Infogopolies

PRIVATE COPYRIGHT

Copyright protection matters to the publishing, recording and motion picture industries. During the 1980s it also came to matter to the software industry. When these industries came together for the purposes of the TRIPS campaign they publicly argued that:

> lack of effective enforcement of copyright threatens industries, such as the motion picture and publishing industries, manufacturers of computers, computer programs and communication systems, and the broadcasting and music and recording industries.[1]

As we shall see, the threat was not so much to entire industries as to individual players who did not want to lose their position of dominance. These players turned to copyright law in the hope of finding immunity from competition and the uncertainties of technological change. Copyright law became a battleground as copyright users began to find their rights being whittled away. Giant technology companies such as IBM, Microsoft, EMI, Polygram, Sony and Disney pushed what might be termed the "private interest perspective" of copyright law. The public interest perspective was put forward by public libraries, educational institutions and the consumer movement. The outcome of these unequal struggles is a copyright law that probably has never been more distant from its true goal of serving the public welfare.

SOFTWARE BLUES

During the 1980s IBM came to rely on copyright to protect its library of software. This was a dramatic change of policy. IBM had built up its almost total dominance of the international computing industry by giving away its software. Why did it change strategy? Explaining this about-face takes us back to the 1960s when the computing game was about selling mainframes to corporate customers like banks and insurance companies with data processing needs. Each manufacturer would set up the interaction between the hardware elements and software elements of a computer in different ways. As a result an IBM program could not be run on a Rand or Burroughs machine or in some cases on an IBM machine of a different series. Interoperability was missing from the computing world of the 1950s and 1960s.

Beginning in 1964 with its release of the System/360 series, IBM developed a computing architecture that allowed application software written for the System/360 to be run on successive series of IBM machines.[2] In order to help the spread of its operating system IBM gave it away. It made the source code for its operating system available so that other programmers could easily understand the way in which IBM's operating system worked and to modify it if need be. Not only was IBM giving away its software, it was also actively campaigning against proprietary control over software. In 1966 the vice president of IBM, sitting on a President's Commission on the Patent System, proposed that patents should not be granted on software.[3] IBM at this stage was doing exactly what Richard Stallman, the founder of the Free Software Foundation, recommends to all software developers. It was providing the source code of its operating system to those who requested it and allowing others to copy and modify it if they wished. Furthermore, it and other computer manufacturers encouraged their customers to form free software sharing organizations.[4] And through this sharing of software knowledge and techniques IBM was helping to create a bigger community of software developers, a community that would in a few decades give (not sell) the world the Internet.

IBM's approach to software changed in the late 1970s. By this time the demand for software had grown dramatically. Despite its dominance on the hardware side IBM was facing competition from other manufacturers of IBM-compatible hardware, these manufacturers being able to take advantages of patent licenses that IBM had to provide under antitrust law. In 1978 IBM began attaching copyright notices to its software and in 1983 it began to restrict the flow of technical information about its software to other software companies.[5] Significantly, it began to withhold source code from other programmers.

Source code is the computer language in which the instructions of the program are expressed. Like spoken languages, computer languages are distinguished by different vocabularies and rules of syntax that, for instance, make some more suitable than others for programming in the field of mathematics. Without the source code it is very difficult to understand how a program works and to write another program that might work in connection with it. Reading the source code is the most complete source of information concerning the interface specifications in much the same way that reading a book is the best source of information about it, if one is planning to write a sequel. Techniques do exist to get at interface information in the absence of the source code. These techniques, broadly referred to as reverse engineering, involve using the object code of the program (the zeros and ones that the computer translates into electronic impulses, thereby allowing it to execute the program).

In order to reverse-engineer IBM software other programmers had to make copies of it. IBM's claim that copyright applied to computer software was designed to prevent competitors being able to obtain interface information that would allow them to develop IBM-compatible programs. Having set the industry standard through its dominance, IBM now wanted to use copyright to exclude others from competing under the standard. Its strategy was based on hiding the copyright work (the source code) and then extending copyright to block access to the source code via the object code. In this way it was also undermining copyright's purpose of encouraging the publication of works so that others might have immediate access to the ideas in those works (copyright does not protect ideas).

During the 1980s IBM led a global campaign pushing for the recognition of copyright over software, arguing against any meaningful reverse engineering exception. It could not have foreseen, of course, that in so doing it would enable Microsoft to use copyright to exercise a proprietary hold over a standard on which most of the PC world would come to depend. Japanese companies were a major target of this campaign. In the early 1980s Japan's Ministry of International Trade and Industry (MITI) was throwing its weight behind a draft Japanese software law that would have provided for a shorter term of protection for software than copyright (only 15 years), as well as allowing for the compulsory licensing of software.[6] The World Intellectual Property Organization (WIPO) was also in the midst of drafting a special treaty for the protection of software. Fearing the consequences of such an open-access regime IBM threw its weight behind copyright as the proper vehicle of protection for software. In 1984, the year in which the US had linked its 301 trade enforcement mechanism to intellectual property (see Chapter 6), US trade officials with the support of the European Community pressured MITI to drop the draft law. MITI complied. In 1985 Japan changed its copyright law to explicitly protect computer software. WIPO, seeing the way the trade winds were blowing, stopped work on its draft treaty. The effect on the software industry was that copyright became the legal platform for the protection of software around the world.

The extent of IBM's campaign has yet to be fully documented. It was IBM that, as one of the key players on the Advisory Committee on Trade Negotiations (see Chapter 4), hired Jacques Gorlin to write a strategy paper on folding protection for computer software into the multilateral trade regime. Whenever a copyright policy committee somewhere in the world was considering the issue of copyright protection for computer software, IBM would fly in North American experts to present the case against reverse engineering. As one member of an Australian policy committee who had witnessed one of these performances remarked to us, it all seemed "very persuasive." (Australia was important strategically because it could serve as a model in the Asian region.) At every significant conference on copyright and software an IBM executive would present the arguments for why reverse engineering was a bad thing. After a while, second-generation computer software companies like Sun would send a representative to present the alternative view. After Japan, Europe became an intense theater of activity.

In 1989 the EC, as part of its goal of harmonizing copyright law, released a draft Software Directive. The draft said nothing directly about the techniques of reverse engineering, primarily because "it was drafted under the influence of those companies who controlled or owned the proprietary standards" (Brussels lobbyist, 1993). Companies such as Bull, Fujitsu, Olivetti, NCR and Sun Microsystems depended on gaining access to interface information contained in the proprietary standards of IBM and Microsoft. The absence in the draft Software Directive of any guarantee of access meant that they would be forced to bargain with IBM and Microsoft for access or take their chances in the courts. Bull and the other companies responded in 1989 by forming a lobbying organization, the European Committee for Interoperable Systems (ECIS). IBM countered by establishing the Software Action Group for Europe (SAGE), other group members including Microsoft, Apple and Lotus. Over the next couple of years a tide of copyright specialists and computer experts washed through the EC's corridors in one of the biggest lobbying efforts the commission had ever experienced.

The lobbying went well beyond erudite exchanges on copyright principle. The core of the ECIS argument was that the inability to reverse-analyze (ECIS preferred this term to "reverse engineering" since it better described the process of trying to understand how a program worked) would virtually eliminate competition in the software industry. Those parts of the commission concerned with competition policy (DG IV and DG XIII) understood this, for in 1980 they had brought an action against IBM requiring it to provide interface specifications to competitors, something that IBM agreed to in 1984. SAGE countered this competition argument by playing the piracy card and relying on industrial xenophobia:

> They linked reverse analysis to piracy. They also said it was part of a Japanese conspiracy to get the upper hand in the computing industry. [Fujitsu's membership of ECIS was used to support this line.] They managed to achieve in people's eyes an amalgamation between piracy and reinforcing intellectual property. Naturally, they never explained that reinforcing intellectual property reduces competition (Brussels lobbyist, 1993).

Attempts by ECIS to build a coalition with lead developing countries on this issue began promisingly, but then foundered as countries like Argentina began to worry about getting into trouble with the US at the bilateral trade level.

When on 14 May 1991 the Software Directive was adopted its provisions allowed for the reverse analysis of a program. ECIS had managed to secure some compromises through a lobbying effort aimed at the European Parliament. From the point of view of ECIS the scope of reverse analysis was far from ideal, but it was something that members of ECIS could live with (Brussels lobbyist, 1993).

Having left the software community with the legacy of copyright protection, IBM once more changed its approach. Copyright did not turn out to be the strategic tool it had hoped for. Although it took more than a decade of confusing litigation, courts around the world eventually found doctrinal ways in which to make interface information available to software innovators. IBM also faced another problem. It did not dominate the world of personal computing. There Microsoft and Intel ruled. Microsoft controlled access to the PC operating system using copyright. Intel provided the microprocessors that formed the heart of PC hardware. During the 1990s IBM went back to what it knew best—patents. In 2000 it received 2,886 patents from the US Patent and Trademark Office (PTO), thereby topping for the eighth year in a row the US PTO's league table of private sector patent recipients.[7] Included in its already huge portfolio of patents were patents on software. Allowed by the US PTO, the effect of such patent claims is to shift the patent system from the protection of information that is embodied in a useful product or process to the protection of useful information outside a specific industrial context. A software patent allows IBM to claim the production of a curve on a screen without the need to relate the production of that curve to any other process or product. The potential blocking effect of these patents on other software developers is obvious.

A company like IBM, which holds a large number of software patents, can generate millions of dollars of royalty flows in relation to information, as well as shaping the future of the software industry and the Internet. One consequence of IBM's strategy of linking software to copyright and patents is that it has led the Internet into an era of public–private regulation. It is a form of regulation in which patent and copyright offices grant privileges to companies over the essential software tools or methods of business needed to carry on commerce over the Internet. The companies in possession of the privilege use it to order the markets to which the Internet relates. Internet markets were characterized by low barriers to entry, something that helped dot.com companies to proliferate. Public–private regulation threatens to raise those barriers. An example is the 1-Click patent that Amazon obtained in September of 1999. This patent covered a method of single-action ordering based on a single mouse click. Potentially many more customers end up placing orders rather than dropping off through a trail of tedious form filling. Other Internet businesses wishing to use the 1-Click method will have to pay a royalty or, if they are unable to secure permission to use it, have to find an ordering system that does not infringe the patent (the 2-Click, 3-Click etc.). How fundamental this particular patent turns out to be, time will tell. More broadly, the companies that colonize the Internet with these kinds of patents and are able to enforce them using a combination of software tracking tools and the threat of litigation are in a position to become, in effect, the Internet's private regulators. Through the mechanism of licensing they create the conditions that shape the evolution of e-commerce.[8]

HOLLYWOOD TRADE BALLYHOO

Cartelism and protectionism in the US motion picture industry have run longer than any of its shows. Right from the industry's beginnings, when Thomas Edison used his camera and film patents to cartelize the industry, intellectual property rights have been an important tool of domination. Edison, unable to conquer his competitors in the courts using patents, formed a patent pool with them in 1908.[9] The Motion Picture Patents Company (MPPC) was formed to control all aspects of the industry, from the production of raw film to the exhibition of pictures. Patents over film and the manufacture of projectors knitted cartel members together. The MPPC struck a deal with Eastman Kodak Company for exclusive purchase of raw film. After that, all aspects of the business were controlled through licenses given by the MPPC to make use of film, to manufacture projectors, use the projectors to show movies and so on. The MPPC functioned as the private regulator of the industry, collecting royalties, preventing patent infringement and making sure that licensees stuck to the terms of the deal.[10] To gain greater control over distribution, members of the MPPC established in 1910 the General Film Company. With the exception of a company run by William Fox in New York, the General Film Company became the only source of films for exhibitors in the US. Fox brought an antitrust action against the MPPC in 1913 that brought about its demise.

By the 1930s, Twentieth Century Fox, Loews (the owners of Metro-Goldwyn-Mayer), Paramount, RKO and Warner Brothers had become the "Big Five" in the US and international movie business. Their power was based on the control of film production, distribution and ownership of "first-run theaters" (lucrative outlets where the public paid a premium to see new releases). It was the ownership of a network of theaters that enabled the Big Five to exploit their intangible assets (the copyright in films) to the maximum via various licensing practices such as block booking. This empire of the moguls ran into an antitrust suit that saw in the 1950s each member of the Big Five agree to pull out of theater-pooling arrangements and divest themselves of specific theaters. The antitrust action did little to threaten the preeminence of the Big Five, for they retained their hold over production and distribution. Exhibitors still depended on them. Moreover, the antitrust action did nothing to disturb the domination of US film companies in overseas markets.

Hollywood's global supremacy had been achieved surprisingly early. By 1925, US films had 95 percent of the UK market, 66 percent of the Italian market and 77 percent of the French market, primarily because US producers, having made a profit in their large domestic market, were able to set cheap prices for overseas markets.[11] At the same time the US market remained closed to foreign producers because of the tight control exerted by US companies over distribution and exhibition in the US. During the 1920s European states, worried by the Americanization effect of US films, began to impose import, distributor and screen quotas.

The conquest of foreign film markets was achieved with the close cooperation of the US government acting through US trade commissioners. The US government realized that the export of a film was not just the export of an inert good. US films communicated many cultural and moral messages. The saying that trade follows the film turned out to be true, at least for the US.

Also important in Hollywood's ascendancy was its trade association, the Motion Picture Producers and Distributors of America (MPPDA). Formed in 1922 by key players in the industry, its immediate purpose was to persuade an increasingly outraged middle America that Hollywood could be counted on to clean up its drug- and sex-crazed image both on- and off-screen without regulatory assistance. The MPPDA became occupied with much more than just the projection of moral decency. Its real work became the formulation of policy, especially trade policy for the US film industry. It took on the responsibility of gaining and maintaining market access for large US film producers. The US government, realizing the strategic value of the film industry, gave it maximum cooperation, allowing, for example, the Motion Picture Export Association (MPEA) (in 1945 the MPPDA split into the Motion Picture Association of America and the MPEA) to become a legal export cartel under the Webb-Pomerene Export Trade Act of 1918. Through the MPEA, the US film industry was able to operate in international markets as a single entity, setting prices, terms of distribution and overcoming restrictions on the import of US films. The MPEA's (renamed the Motion Picture Association [MPA] in 1994) position meant that foreign governments negotiated with it directly, a practice that continues today. As the MPA's website points out, it is referred to as "a little State Department." Jack Valenti, the current head of the MPA, confirmed this for us in an interview when he described negotiations with South Korean officials over intellectual property and market access the results of which "we mailed off to the USTR" (1994 interview). Probably, in matters of intellectual property, trade and culture, the MPA becomes "the State Department."

Over decades the influence of large US film companies and the MPA on the evolution of US copyright law as well as international copyright standards has been profound. The MPA was one of the earliest petitioners under Section 301 of the Trade Act, bringing an action against South Korea in 1985. It has been one of the drivers of US bilateralism on intellectual property rights, insisting that the US in no way compromise its capacity to move bilaterally against countries if the need arises. Enrolling the heaviest of political heavyweights in its cause has not been a problem for the MPA. Presidents Reagan, Bush and Clinton, as well as successive US Trade Representatives, have all supported the MPA's agenda on intellectual property. Most US presidents have wanted a sprinkling of Hollywood's glitter. US political parties have been models of bipartisan cooperation when it has come to working with the MPA (1994 interview). It has been one of the key actors in the global demonization of piracy and the resulting process of criminalization of copyright infringement.

The US film industry has been a prime mover in fashioning a distinct conception of copyright that we might label "financier's copyright." When discussing copyright a contrast is normally drawn between the Anglo-American system of copyright and the European authors' rights system (see Chapter 8). The former is a conception of copyright as a set of economic rights while the latter is based on the idea of an indissoluble personal link between the creator of art and his or her artistic output. This link gives rise to certain rights such as the right of paternity and the right to integrity, rights that exist above the usual economic rights to be found in systems of copyright. Economic copyright with its public welfare goals hardly suits a US film industry that wants total private control over a product it distributes globally. This is even more true of an authors' rights system. Financier's copyright is a third distinct view of copyright. It rests on the view that copyright must serve the financier of copyright works by guaranteeing rights of exploitation in whichever markets the financier chooses to operate. If new technologies like the Internet come along to threaten existing investments or make new forms of exploitation possible then the financier is entitled to new rights that allow him or her to manage the contingencies of the technology. Copyright becomes the servant of the financier rather than the author or the public welfare.

The US film industry's desire for a financier's version of copyright arose because it was among the first US industries to become an exporter and investor in overseas markets. Benefiting from the disruption to Europe's film industry caused by World War I, the US industry by 1925 had a global grip on export markets, a grip it has never lost. The film industry's belief in financier's copyright has resulted in an implacable opposition to the system of authors' rights both nationally and internationally. The right of integrity, for example, gives authors, potentially at least, some rights over how their works might be used in a film. Directors may also use the right to exercise some control over the commercial fate of their films (for example, preventing the colorization of a film shot in black and white). More broadly, one could argue that in a world where works can be digitized, seamlessly integrated with others and communicated instantaneously to millions, the principles of paternity and integrity become more important to authors rather than less. For Hollywood these rights represent a threat. They are potential interferences in its worldwide systems of production, marketing, distribution and exhibition. The right of integrity might give an author rights in the film editing process. Control over commercial exploitation is no longer total. Thus when it came to moral rights in TRIPS, the MPA successfully opposed their recognition. Similarly, the major producers have not been supporters of rights of property being granted to performers (a right, for example, that goes to a person who plays the music as opposed to the person who composed it). Rights in audiovisual performances were kept out of the International Convention for the Protection of Performers, Producers of Phonograms and Broadcasting Organizations of 1961 (Rome Convention) and again in the WIPO Performances and Phonograms Treaty (WPPT) of 1996. TRIPS also offers very little to performers. As one performers' organization we spoke to put it: "No promotion there [TRIPS] of performers' interests" (1993 interview).

Under financier's copyright all other interests, those of authors, performers and states in supporting their own cultural industries, are subordinated to the producer's interest in maintaining a global system of production and distribution. Crucial to Hollywood's global distribution system are rights of copyright, such as the right of importation, which allow major producers to make decisions about the timing and sequence of the release of films in various country markets (for example, a release sequence might be theater, video, cable and then free-to-air television). Whenever an important commercial asset such as Mickey Mouse or A. A. Milne's Winnie-the-Pooh threatens to fall into the public domain, because copyright protection is about to expire, ferocious lobbying takes place to extend the term of copyright protecting these assets.[12] Here the difference between an economic conception of copyright and financier's copyright comes sharply into focus. Under an economic conception of copyright, which seeks to minimize the social cost of copyright monopolies, there can be no justification for extending the term of copyright protection to works already in existence. Under financier's copyright private informational assets must never enter the public domain where they can be the subject of market competition. The fact that, as in the case of Mickey Mouse, Disney would have still had the benefit of trademark protection is irrelevant. Control over commercial exploitation, as we explained earlier, must be total. Ideally in this world corporations would be globally recognized as the actual authors of copyright works (a position that obtains in the US by virtue of the work-for-hire doctrine). For the time being the MPA has been unsuccessful in obtaining recognition of such a position in TRIPS. In today's world of financier's copyright, authors and performers are largely left to protect their interests under the principle of the freedom of contract. This works well if they have the bargaining power of a Madonna.

Financier's copyright is, without a trace of irony, defended using free trade and free speech arguments: "Ideas and art ought to be able to flow freely in the world" (MPA, 1994 interview). Here free flow refers to a free flow of licensing and royalty deals, broadcasting rights, theater releases and so on, all based on images that have been tightly locked up by intellectual property rights. It is an easy argument for Hollywood to make. Its position of being able to supply most of the needs of the audiovisual sector of countries around the world was achieved through protectionism based on a domestic monopoly over distribution and export cartelism.

Another factor in Hollywood's success has been its persistent copying of others. Films from other countries, such as Kurosawa's *Seven Samurai*, turn up recycled in a different genre (the cowboy movie *The Magnificent Seven*) and are pumped through Hollywood's distribution network to become worldwide hits. American directors routinely steal action scenes from Eastern martial arts movies. This appropriation of ideas, plots and scenes by Hollywood is turned into products, the copyright in which is vigilantly policed by a corps of entertainment and intellectual property lawyers. In the name of free trade, US trade officials fiercely resist efforts by countries to write in a cultural exemption in free trade agreements that deal with trade in the audiovisual sector (something that Europe tried to do in the case of the General Agreement on Trade in Services). Instead they urge countries to liberalize trade in their audiovisual sector, ignoring the reality of a globalized US film industry that can price for overseas markets at rates that would bring an anti-dumping action if the commodity were different. Where states resist with television and film quotas on foreign programming in an effort to protect their already marginal national industries, they find themselves in a trade dispute with the US. The pressure to remove quotas is relentlessly applied. No quota is too low to be ignored. When Indonesia imposed a screen quota requiring its first-run theaters to show at least two Indonesian films each month for a minimum of two days, both the MPA and the International Intellectual Property Alliance raised the matter with the USTR as part of their recommendation in 1993 to list Indonesia under the 301 process (Indonesia was placed on the watch list). The endgame for Hollywood is no restriction on its capacity to reach any type of screen in the world at any time and place.

Arguments about the effects of Hollywood's global production system on national cultures and identity can become like a maze without an exit. Even if, however, one believes that claims about US cultural hegemony are overstated, there is at least a plausible case to be made that the output of the US film and TV industry serves to dilute national cultures. It may also be a mistake to cast the problem in terms of US cultural imperialism. The real issue may lie in the relationship of a global system of cultural production to many national ones. For reasons we are about to develop, intellectual property rights play a critical role in providing incentives to participate in the former and not the latter.

Hollywood these days does not represent so much a place as a distinctive business approach to cultural production that makes entertainment its lodestar. If entertainment requires the audience to be diverted from the truth or a compromise in integrity, then so be it. The reactions of test audiences to prerelease screenings shape the spectacle of film more often than does historical truth. The film studios that grew to prominence in the US in the 1920s have become part of media, merchandising, music and electronics conglomerates. US film studios and their film libraries have ended up in conglomerates of non-US origin.[13] Columbia Pictures in 1989 became part of Sony's corporate structures, which range over music (for example, Sony Music Nashville, Sony Classical), television (Cinemax Latin America, Showtime-Australia, Carlton Production [UK]), games (Sony PlayStation) and theaters (Sony/Loews, Sony-IMAX Theater). Matsushita Electrical Industrial Co. bought MCA, Inc., in 1991, a purchase that included MCA movies and Universal Studios. Paramount Pictures, which became the first national distributor of movies in the US in 1914, was acquired in 1994 by

Viacom, Inc., a giant in broadcast and television (e.g., CBS Television and MTV), video (Blockbuster), publishing (Simon & Schuster), theaters and distribution (United International Pictures and United Cinemas International). Part of the package was also the Paramount theme parks. News Corporation also has one of the oldest US film producers and distributors, Twentieth Century Fox, as part of its media interests. Warner Brothers, one of the original Big Five of Hollywood, has traveled a journey that has seen it, as Warner Communications, Inc., merge with Time, Inc., to become Time Warner in 1990 and then become part of AOL Time Warner in 2000. Walt Disney Company has become a publishing, broadcasting, cable, music, movie, theater, merchandising and theme park conglomerate.

These conglomerates operate a genuinely global system of cultural production. For all of them, images, sounds and text are assets to be used over and over again around the world in theaters, on cable, in magazines or even as three-dimensional dress-up characters in theme parks. The whole purpose of intellectual property rights is to maintain an iron grip on informational assets capable of being deployed and transformed in many ways for exploitation in different kinds of markets. For individuals with a hunger for global stardom this global business of cultural production is the only game in town. For those who are successful, intellectual property rights bring massive rewards. Michael Jackson can strike a deal with Sony that brings him a 25 percent royalty rate and a share of the profits from Sony's record operation.[14] But few can travel to such stardom since a world in which everyone is a superstar is a world in which no one is. Global stardom is based on the increased supply of a restricted number of faces. At the same time as this system of cultural production uses intellectual property rights to reward performers, it increasingly creates disincentives to participate in systems of cultural production outside it. These disincentives take the form of a hierarchy of cultural production processes consisting of the local, regional, national, international and finally global. The hierarchy is in part constituted by intellectual property rights because it is the commercial exploitation of these rights that brings with it the riches of international stardom, riches that signal to the rest of the world that one has really made it. The local, regional and national come to be seen as the lower steps of a pyramid, steps that become a means of ascending to a global apex.

The media conglomerates of today have distribution companies within their structures giving them worldwide control over the release, marketing, exhibition and licensing of their informational assets. Worldwide distribution systems had been put in place by the Big Five film producers of Hollywood decades before these producers became part of the megamedia merger and acquisition process of the last two decades of the 20th century. The effect of a global hold on distribution is described by one industry insider:

> As a producer, I can make the most thrilling or challenging movie imaginable, with the best crew and the most talented cast, but unless I have a well-thought-out arrangement with an effective worldwide distribution resource, one which

understands how to market a film in different countries and when necessary to different audiences, I am, to a great extent, wasting my time.[15]

In short, intellectual property rights deliver rewards to a comparatively small number of star artists whose works are pumped through the distribution networks commanded by the likes of News Corporation, Sony, Viacom or AOL Time Warner. For the rest (the majority) they remain largely an empty promise. They deliver little to artists involved in systems of national cultural production.

"MARY HAD A LITTLE LAMB"

When in 1877 Thomas Edison wanted to test the device he had made for recording sound, he sang the words to "Mary Had a Little Lamb" and then played them back.[16] Much as in the case of other technologies with which Edison was involved the technology of the phonograph or sound recording went through a series of patent battles. Two other rivals emerged, Alexander Bell's Graphophone and Emile Berliner's Gramophone.

In the US, the business structure of the sound recording industry began to develop at the beginning of the 20th century. Similar to the film industry a division between majors and minors soon developed. The Victor Talking Machine, formed in 1901, became part of the Radio Corporation of America (RCA) in 1929. Columbia Phonograph, which had begun before 1900, became in the early 1930s part of the Columbia Broadcasting System. The major companies in the sound recording business were born of or increased their size through a complex process of mergers and acquisitions. The forces behind this shifting corporate landscape were industrial giants like Philips, AT&T and General Electric, which were themselves struggling for control over new technologies such as radio, electrical sound recording and sound in movies. By the 1930s, RCA (its major shareholders included General Electric and AT&T) dominated the US market, Decca and EMI had the British Empire market, Pathé-Marconi had control over the French market, including the colonial market, and Philips presided over northern and central European markets.[17]

Throughout the 20th century, sound recording companies continued to be strategic pieces in a larger game as corporations tried to fit together interests in information with different kinds of hardware (for example, books, record players, telephones, radio sets, televisions, tape recorders, computers) and media (publishing, radio broadcasting, TV broadcasting, cable television, Internet broadcasting) against a background of changing technology. Just as with film companies, recording companies have become part of media knowledge/entertainment conglomerates.[18] So, for example, BMG (Bertelsmann Music Group), a subsidiary of the Bertelsmann Media Group, acquired RCA Records in 1986. The Warner Music Group, initially part of Warner Brothers Pictures, acquired the labels Atlantic, Elektra and Asylum in the 1960s and created the label WEA. These labels became part of Time-Warner,

Inc., in 1988, Time-Warner itself merging with AOL in 2000. Sony Corporation acquired CBS Records in 1988. Similar kinds of merger and acquisition trails characterize EMI and Universal/Polygram.

The recording industry grew in the first half of the 20th century, its growth apparently not hindered by the absence in most states of a separate form of intellectual property in sound recordings.[19] Since the fixing of sounds in a device is essentially an engineering skill, one can see why many people argued that no separate intellectual property right should be granted to sound recording producers. Once copyright opened its doors to mediums of technological distribution of artistic, dramatic, literary and musical works there was no obvious way in which to draw the line on copyright protection for technologies. In the second half of the 20th century copyright increasingly took on the industrial character of the patent system applying to subject matter such as software. Authors and composers became increasingly worried by copyright's technological turn. They saw it as compromising the artistic purity of copyright. At a more practical level, authors were worried that the recognition of a "neighboring right" in the form of a sound recording would undermine their control over the use of works as well as add to users' costs. Users would now have to pay additional license fees to producers of sound recordings.[20] It was the resistance of key author associations that helps to explain why it took more than 30 years for an international standard for the protection of sound recordings to emerge in the form of the Rome Convention of 1961.

The US did not join the Rome Convention. Aside from some constitutional issues, powerful broadcasting organizations in the US did not want to endanger a status quo in which they received records from the recording industry for free or at a discount. Domestically, the US did not recognize a separate copyright in sound recordings until 1971. This had not stopped the development of a recording industry in the US because, of course, there were many incentives for record producers to produce records even in the absence of a separate copyright in their sound recordings. In any case, it was clear that record manufacturers in the US could rely on the doctrine of misappropriation to protect their interests. The real issue for the majors in the recording industry was piracy. As we saw in Chapter 2, piracy is rarely used in a legally precise sense. The line between a pirate and a smaller but legitimate competitor becomes, at times, blurred. Once tape cassettes arrived in 1963 the industry concluded that everyone could be a pirate at home. Rather than tarring their millions of customers in the West with the label of pirate, the sound recording industry began to refer to the problem of home taping. Use of the piracy label was reserved for larger-scale copying, especially by those in developing countries. By the 1960s the major players in the US had come to the view that piracy would have to be halted using the tools of criminal law.[21] It was also clear that all states would have to accept responsibility for eliminating the scourge of record piracy.

The key actor in coordinating the industry's piracy strategy became its international trade association, the International Federation of the

Phonographic Industry (IFPI). Formed in 1933, its mission was to represent "the interests of the recording industry worldwide in all fora" (IFPI interview, 1993). After its major lobbying effort on the Rome Convention, IFPI began a campaign against piracy. It pushed for and obtained in 1971 the Convention for the Protection of Producers of Phonograms against Unauthorized Duplication of their Phonograms. It then proposed a three-stage plan for dealing with piracy, described by one of its director-generals as follows:

> Stage I was protecting the major markets; Stage II protecting minor markets in the record-producing countries and thus throwing a cordon sanitaire around 90 percent of the world's production. Stage III was clearing the countries which were very largely piratical and are mainly, but not entirely, situated in the developing world.[22]

For the major players in the sound recording industry TRIPS was part of Stage III. At our interview with IFPI officials in 1993 we were told that the "GATT initiative is an attempt to deal with backsliding countries [on the issue of record piracy]." Developing countries, we were told, had to do two things: they had to criminalize "all activities involved in piracy" with the penalties being "truly deterrent" and then "governments must accept responsibility for seeing that criminal provisions are utilized." The imprint of this objective on TRIPS is there for all to see. Article 61 obliges members to provide for criminal procedures and penalties in the cases of trademark counterfeiting or copyright piracy as well as requiring "imprisonment and/or monetary fines sufficient to provide a deterrent."

TRIPS itself is part of IFPI's ongoing global strategy for dealing with pirate countries. It develops a morality tale about the evils of piracy and the need for strong copyright protection to support a nation's indigenous recording industry. The tale is told over and over again to various officials in problem countries such as Poland. At the practical level, IFPI sets up an antipiracy unit to stir local officialdom into action. It suggests model laws that Poland could adopt and begins to urge the formation of a national recording industry association. The national association is important. It is a permanent local presence in Poland, reminding Polish law enforcement officials to make it a priority to carry out surveillance of the recording habits of Polish citizens. Moving into a post-communist society, Polish citizens find that they have not quite left surveillance behind.

IFPI's morality tale, which depicts copyright protection as crucial to the livelihood of artists, does not sit comfortably with the history of the majors in the recording business. It is a history, as Schilling observes, in which "the majors either disavowed black music entirely, shunted it onto less-supported subsidiary labels, or recorded black artists like Nat King Cole who were closer to the white mainstream."[23] It was black musicians who with "hot jazz" led the US and then the rest of world into the "swing" era and then with rhythm and blues laid the musical base from which rock and roll developed. The black innovators of these styles were not dependent upon the intellectual property rights system to stimulate or preserve their creativity. For the most part this system, which was devised and managed by whites, delivered the rewards from their music to others. Billie Holiday, when told by fans she should be rich, said: "I made over 270 songs between 1933 and 1944 but didn't get a cent of royalties in any of them."[24] It was a near-universal experience. A white business culture that understood the power of intellectual property rights became the free-rider on a musically innovative black subculture that did not. It is a story not dissimilar to the pharmaceutical industry's pattern of behavior of taking genetic resources created by indigenous groups.

Record piracy is also fought using technological tools. Beginning with the audiocassette, each new recording technology that hardware manufacturers like Philips and Sony delivered to the marketplace also became for the recording industry copying machines. Innovations such as the twin cassette deck saw the recording industry argue that the mere placing of such a technology on the market was an invitation to unauthorized copying. These arguments did not win the day legally. The division between the hardware manufacturers and the recording industry grew in the 1970s, partly along nationalistic lines since the innovators in the consumer electronics field were Japanese firms like Sony and the record companies experiencing piracy were US-based. The two industries clashed in 1986 over how to limit the copying capabilities of the digital audiotape (DAT). The majors in the recording industry, unhappy with the no-restrictions approach of the Japanese, denied the Japanese electronics industry access to their catalogues of music. The lack of a huge market in prerecorded cassettes meant that consumers were unlikely to support the new technology. As a result the Japanese abandoned attempts to introduce the standard in consumer markets. After this experience two Japanese companies decided to become copyright owners of music and sound recordings.[25] Sony acquired CBS records in 1988 and Matsushita purchased MCA in 1991 (this included the MCA record division, which in 1988 had acquired the Motown label).

The processes of integration that have seen the majors of the sound recording industry (as well as the independents that have distribution deals with them) nested within media/knowledge conglomerates have also brought with them a gradual consensus on the need to lock up music by technological means. The first sign of this was when 12 Japanese consumer electronics companies (including Fujitsu, Matsushita, NEC, Sony, TDK and Toshiba), European consumer electronics companies (Philips, Thomson and Grundig) and the international recording industry represented by IFPI and the Recording Industry Association of America signed in 1989 a Memorandum of Understanding known as the Athens Agreement. In it all sides agreed to incorporate the "serial copy management system" (SCMS) developed by Philips into DAT recorders. An approach to managing the introduction of new technologies like recordable CDs to consumer markets by means of a joint working group was also decided. The European and Japanese electronics companies also agreed to accept "the principle of royalties" when it came to tapes and recording equipment and not to oppose the recording industry's pursuit of such legislation. Such legislation followed in the US in the form of the Audio Home Recording Act of 1992, legislation that imposed royalties on digital tape recorders and tapes. This legislation also required manufacturers and importers to adopt the SCMS standard and prohibited the selling of technical ways around the standard. The Athens Agreement, a private understanding among the big players, had become public law. The European Union also gave this understanding the force of law through a directive on private copying.

Technologies of encryption and scrambling, which are used by media/knowledge conglomerates, are not a replacement for copyright norms, but rather a complement. The basic commercial objective is to maintain control over the times and places in which information is distributed (whether the information is music or movies). Copyright, we have seen, has routinely been used by publishing cartels to divide world markets. Copyright is a social lock. Electronic locks can achieve precisely the same division. So, for example, the movie industry has invested heavily in an encryption technology for DVDs known as CSS. CSS encryption works so that a DVD from the US will not play on a DVD player bought in Europe. European consumers are locked in to purchasing European DVDs at a time and price set by an export cartel—the motion picture industry.

The community of computer programmers has shown in a Houdini-like way that it is possible to escape from any electronic lock. So, for example, CSS can be decrypted using a program called DeCSS, which is available on the Internet. Realizing the likelihood of such successful electronic escape artistry, media/knowledge conglomerates during the 1990s pushed for anti-circumvention measures to be enacted into law. Such measures in essence make it illegal to manufacture or distribute circumvention devices such as DeCSS. Social and electronic locks become part of a circle that enforces and reinforces private control over information. Anyone wishing to enter this circle has to do so on terms dictated by those with power over the locks. A potential manufacturer of DVD players has to license the CSS encryption so that encrypted DVDs will play on the recorder. The film industry sets the conditions of manufacture, including the region in which the DVD player will operate.

The strategy of the sound recording and film industries on anti-circumvention law was to set a global standard and then work on bringing states into line with it. The first stage of this top-down global regulatory sequence was completed with the adoption of the WIPO Copyright Treaty (WCT) (1996). This treaty recognized an anti-circumvention principle at a time when very few nations had it as part of domestic law. The US inserted this anti-circumvention principle into its domestic law through the Digital Millennium Copyright Act of 1998 (DMCA). In the words of the Recording Industry Association of America:

The greatest gains from the DMCA will be realized internationally. This law is a model for ratification and implementation of the WIPO treaties in other countries, where protection of sound recordings online is not sufficient.[26]

US law in the eyes of the industry is also a model for how other countries should punish sound recording infringements. The No Electronic Theft Act imposes up to three years in prison and/or US$250,000 in fines. Criminal prosecution is no longer confined to cases of infringement for commercial gain. The act also allows for punishment in the case of digital trading in MPEG-3 files, the digital format that compresses otherwise bulky audio CD files, thereby easing their transfer from one computer to another.

Exactly where the private understandings and recommendations of media/knowledge conglomerates will leave the global digital economy is a matter of conjecture. While the sound recording and film industries have been successful in their long-term strategy of expanding ownership rights and criminalizing the infringing use of information, it will not be possible to put everyone in jail. The number of Internet users is large and US jails crowded. Moreover, a generation of Napster users who have experienced the power of being able to gather in cyberspace and swap music files directly may be reluctant to accept and, more importantly, internalize the music industry's global moral narrative about the evils of piracy. They are also less likely to accept a moral code that is so transparently self-serving. As a number of government studies have shown, the majors in the recording industry operate complex monopolies in national markets.[27] Monopolists rarely earn moral respect and they create incentives to piracy. When the rock band Metallica sued Napster, they lost rather than gained fans. Street credibility becomes vanishingly small when you join those who wish to squeeze copyright royalties out of every sound byte. Those on the outside of the industry will come to know a truth everyone in the industry already knows: only very few artists can expect a sizable income from royalties. The chief beneficiaries of the emerging global system are a few investors and a few stars. The huge hits, points out Burnett, come from a "small group of international pop stars (who total less than 100), all of whom receive massive industry support and promotion."[28] Genuine innovation in the industry is left to smaller companies to support. If successful their fate is to become part of the stable of labels that belong to a media/knowledge conglomerate.

Even if, however, the music and film industries fail to persuade us of their moral message they may nevertheless be successful in redefining intellectual property norms in ways that give them a powerful hold over the business models of the digital economy. The Napster litigation, which at the time of writing still continues, is an example of this. Napster allowed users visiting its website and using its software to swap music files located on the hard drives of their own computers. It meant that users were reproducing and distributing music and sound recordings the copyright in which belonged to the majors. Rather than suing millions of Napster users for direct copyright infringement, the recording companies successfully sued Napster for contributory copyright infringement.

Napster was, as far as the recording industry was concerned, a piratical business model. But it was a business model. It showed what could be done in the distribution of music using the Internet as a tool. Much of the market power of the majors in the recording industry is based on the distribution side of their businesses. It is this capacity to deal with the complexities of distribution to retailers that explains why so many independent recording companies sign distribution deals with the majors.[29] The expensive distribution infrastructure that the majors in film and music own and run is a barrier to entry that the Internet threatens to topple. Once there is an alternative way to reach millions of consumers, individual artists might decide there is no reason to bargain away their intellectual property rights in exchange for access to a distribution system that rewards only the few. The reasoning that all recording executives fear from musicians is the following: "In the digital era, it costs nothing to ship your music over the Internet to a fan. So the biggest reason for labels just went away."[30]

The response of the recording and film industries has been to lobby and litigate for ever longer, broader and deeper copyright standards, standards that will give them a hold on content and make it harder for others to develop their own. So, for example, the WCT 1996 recognizes a right of communication for copyright owners. This right is free of any reference to a technological context and is so general that limits on its extension become hard to see. The same treaty protects the integrity of the electronic rights management information that forms part of the copyright user surveillance systems being put in place by media/knowledge conglomerates. An older model of copyright law, which served the public domain by defining copyright ownership in terms of narrow privileges, is being replaced by a model that serves global corporate investors in digital technologies by defining copyright ownership in terms of "gapless" rights. The major copyright owners argue that even temporary reproductions within computer memory amount to reproduction for the purposes of copyright law. Even the most fleeting cascade of electrons is being claimed by them as part of their income stream. Access routes to digital content whether through fair dealing or compulsory licensing have been bitterly opposed. The authority and coercive apparatus of the criminal law is brought in to legitimate a morality of ownership that completely ignores the communal origins and value of knowledge. Instead of encouraging entrepreneurship the risk is that copyright and other intellectual property rights will promote fealty to the corporate business models of a few.

CHAPTER 12

Democratic Property Rights

GOOD AND BAD PROPERTY

In this book we have seen that property rights have important effects on innovation. They can be positive, as with patents motivating pharmaceutical innovation. Equally, we have found they can be negative. Feudalism was a system of property rights that discouraged innovation by denying property rights to most of the population (serfs and slaves) who were chattels of a smaller property-owning class. Owners of large numbers of people do not need to innovate to create wealth. The ancient Egyptians invented the steam engine (as a toy) without using it to fuel an industrial revolution. Why bother with labor-saving technology when you have access to a limitless supply of slave labor? Feudalism was also a system that rewarded courtiers who pleased the king with monopoly rights to control whole industries. These were what were originally called patents. These patent monopolies were precisely what had to be dismantled for feudalism to be transformed into capitalism.

The negative effects of information feudalism have involved intellectual property rights being deployed to lock up knowledge from competitors who might use it. In Chapter 3 we saw how earlier industrializers such as DuPont and IBM played the knowledge game to secure a wall of patents that would guarantee monopoly profits against innovators who might take market share by improving on their product design. The laboratories of knowledge that firms like these developed—General Electric, AT&T, among them—were great engines of innovation. However, their patent attorneys also turned the patents generated into weapons of monopoly. When companies had a strong portfolio of patents, trade secrets and trademarks they could negotiate licensing deals with potential competitors for the use of technology from a position of strength. Competition could be eliminated by networking territorially based patents in order to control production, fix prices and divide markets.

The use of patent license agreements to form cartels was often approved by courts as a proper exercise of a proprietary right. This new legal technology for creating monopolies frustrated the legislative intent of antitrust laws. From 1890, as the work of Alfred Chandler shows, US antitrust laws had a large impact in deterring cartels. This contributed to the dominance of the US over formerly stronger economies such as the UK.[1] It was not that antitrust prevented mergers, it encouraged them as an alternative path to cartels for controlling markets. The new megacorporations had the scale and scope to exploit the potential of emerging technologies. The knowledge laboratory was one of the ways they used scale and scope to advantage. The irony is that these knowledge laboratories became the basis of a new kind of cartel—the knowledge cartel. Networked patents solved the twin problems of the illegality of commodity cartels and the difficulty of enforcing cartels when firms had a strong incentive to cheat (building market share by undercutting the cartel on price). Patents were legal monopolies and licensed patents that prescribed price and division of markets were legal cartels that could be enforced by the law of contract (as applied to the license agreement). Licensing agreements were complex, hybrid creatures made up of territorial deals on patents, know-how, trade secrets and trademarks.

In Chapter 11 we saw how Microsoft used copyright licensing to play essentially the same game of creating a knowledge cartel. Once Bill Gates had shown how it was possible to use DOS to lock up computer operating systems to influence the selection and development of other software, we saw in Chapter 10 how the patenting of life allowed biogopolies to play a similar game. In this case, DNA was a standard that had already been created as Mother Nature's operating system. What was being patented were DNA instructions or slight modifications of them. As with the cartels of old industrial knowledge, the objective was to confront competitors with a thicket of patents stretching over a chemical domain that would deter them from entering that terrain. This is why you see, for example, the antitrust suit against Monsanto for the way it is alleged to deter entry to competitors for its seed market and fix prices with patents in seeds on which farmers are hooked. Monsanto's strategy, which it now seems to be moderating, was that just as feudal lords could dictate the economic terms on which serfs farmed through control of property in land, Monsanto could dictate farmers' terms by control of property in seeds.

If we are right that for centuries universities have been the great incubators of innovation (see Chapter 14), then there is a profound risk in rewarding universities, as governments are increasingly doing, for securing patents and other intellectual property rights. To the extent that patents lock up knowledge rather than open it up as a platform from which further advances spring, promoting university staff because they have secured patents corrupts the historic mission of the university. Like most universities, our own, the Australian National University, is as guilty as any in specifying that securing patents is a promotion criterion, without qualification as to whether the patent opens up or closes off the intellectual commons. Similarly, bringing in outside grants is unqualified as a promotion criterion, when of course outside funding that distracts the university's research effort away from work on the intellectual commons in favor of secret research to benefit only the private funder should be grounds for demotion.

Structurally, tying the funding of public universities to their success in securing private patents accelerates the privatization of the intellectual commons. The university ideal is that knowledge should be the common heritage of humankind. In this regard the decision of MIT to put their course materials on the Internet, free of charge, is a step to reverse the erosion of that heritage. Universities do not need to collude in the fatuous notion that men and women of ideas need generous royalties to write great books and give brilliant lectures.

Another troubling structural effect of rewarding scholars for securing intellectual property rights is that it makes their work progressively more subservient to the priorities of the rich. For most of their history, medical schools in universities gave the greatest plaudits to the fundamental scientific breakthroughs that promised the greatest long-term benefits to human health. This was an ethos with egalitarian effects because the greatest unsolved health problems happened to be concentrated among the poor, particularly among those who live in the tropics. The commercialization of university medical research had a reverse effect. Only 13 of the 1,223 new drugs marketed between 1975 and 1997 were specifically developed to treat tropical diseases (and only four of these were a direct result of pharmaceutical industry R&D). "Only ten percent of health research targets the illnesses that make up 90 percent of the global disease burden."[2] Universities should cease valorizing medical research according to the commercialization it enables. Selling patents is a good thing only in so far as it succeeds in creating research resources that place important new knowledge in the public domain. Universities selling patents is, in itself, a bad thing.

DEMOCRATIZING INTELLECTUAL PROPERTY

If intellectual property rights are contingently a force for good or ill, how do we secure the good? The answer proffered in Chapter 1 was that the more genuinely democratic the political deliberation for deciding such matters, the more efficient the intellectual property rights are likely to be in securing the public good. We might make the same point about the discussion in the last section about the corruption of the public purposes of universities by the pursuit of property rights. A medical school is more likely to do justice to its public purposes when it rewards its faculty for securing a patent after due deliberation of the existing fruits and future promise of the research enabled by the patent. It is less likely to do so when it rewards patents nondeliberatively — as by an automatic promotion increment or a salary or research funding bonus based on patent revenues.

In Chapter 1 we argued that overly strong intellectual property protection is conducive to excessive monopoly while weak protection results in free-riding and therefore underinvestment in innovation. Further, the argument was that democracies are likely to go closer to getting this balance right. Following the reasoning of Douglass North,[3] it was concluded that more democratic societies are likely to have more efficient property rights than totalitarian ones—like feudal or communist societies. For these economic arguments to apply, however, three conditions were specified: (1) all relevant interests must be represented in the negotiation of the property rights; (2) all involved in the negotiation must have full information about the consequences of various possible outcomes; and (3) one party must not coerce the others. This book can be read as a treatise on why and how these conditions of representation, information and nondomination have not been met in the development of the global intellectual property regime over the past two decades.

Representation

The post-TRIPS intellectual property order is producing staggeringly inefficient consequences for Africa. We have seen that because most of its people cannot afford patented drugs, almost none of the meager purchases its people do make for patented drugs is ploughed back into research to solve the health problems that matter to them. Mostly they can't afford to buy drugs, but when they do their purchases subsidize research on rich people's diseases. They could import generic AIDS drugs from India, but when they do the global intellectual property regime punishes them through well-funded litigation by drug companies, threats from Europe and the US to withdraw foreign aid, USTR watch-listing, and the threat of bilateral sanctions backed by WTO dispute panels. How did they allow themselves to sign up to such an inefficient regime that is so transparently against their interests? One answer is that they were not represented when the deals were done. Egypt and Tanzania were the two most active African states. Neither could be described as a key player. Neither was in the room for the most important or decisive meetings that sentenced millions of African AIDS victims to death for want of drugs that were placed beyond their reach by monopoly profits extended by TRIPS patents. In Chapter 9 we documented how the Green Room process in Geneva built circles of consensus beginning with meetings between the US and Europe, then including Japan, then Canada (the Quad), then Quad "plus," then Friends of Intellectual Property (developed countries like Switzerland, Sweden and Australia), and only then the 10+10 that included 10 selected developing countries. The WTO formally meets the conditions of equal democratic representation for all states, but the informal reality was that most states were not represented until the virtual fait accompli of a chairman's draft was on the table.

Full Information

The African states signed up for 20-year patent terms on pharmaceuticals, for example, without understanding that the effect of this could be millions of preventable AIDS deaths among their people. It was not just that they were not effectively represented by being in the room. Even if they had been in the room, because none of them had intellectual property experts on their

WTO delegations, the implications of TRIPS for the health of their people would not have been clear to them. TRIPS had the transparency of a one-way mirror. The US and EC knew exactly what was going on. Whenever there was a risk of a wider discussion going in a direction that would provide full information to developing states on the implications of TRIPS, they pulled the negotiations back to narrower circles (like the Friends of Intellectual Property). Then the Friends would send their experts out to snow developing countries within their sphere of influence on the implications of what had been settled. In thousands of ways that we cannot document, hundreds of networks were activated to send out a positive message about TRIPS. Lawyers in developing countries, for example, who had multinationals for clients could be counted on to argue that TRIPS would make their developing country economy a truly modern one. All this information created a veil of ignorance in many developing countries. South African trade negotiators simply did not understand that they were signing an agreement that would contribute to a situation by 2001 where, according to Médecins Sans Frontières, a 15-year-old would have greater than a 50 percent chance of dying of HIV-related causes.

Coercion

In Chapter 6 we saw how the US used its coercive 301 and "Special 301" (intellectual-property-specific) powers bilaterally to soften up opposition to TRIPS. As we argued in *Global Business Regulation*,[4] this is a general US strategy. First, use threatened trade sanctions to negotiate strategic bilaterals one by one. Place particular importance on knocking over the most likely opponents to your favored multilateral deal. In the case of TRIPS we saw in Chapter 6 that these were countries like Korea, Brazil and India. Then go into the multilateral negotiations with a sequence of strategic bilaterals already having made certain terms of the favored multilateral deal a fait accompli. The multilateral pulls those not subject to the bilaterals up to the new standard and in some respects also raises the standard a little further (perhaps in exchange for concessions on other matters like agriculture). After the multilateral deal is done, the US then returns to a new round of bilaterals to begin a new cycle of raising the bar. For example, after failing to rule out parallel importing and weaken compulsory licensing in TRIPS, the US is now aiming to accomplish this in the new round of bilaterals. The Free Trade Agreement the US signed with Jordan in 2000 is an illustration of this new wave of bilateralism. The US is also seeking to short-circuit the TRIPS transitional arrangements for developing countries by persuading them bilaterally to implement all the TRIPS obligations earlier than required.

A further point to make about the use of coercion is that it is not a reciprocal possibility in intellectual property negotiations. The US can credibly threaten trade sanctions, foreign aid withdrawal, flight of investment and refusal to transfer technology to an African state. The African state cannot credibly threaten the US with any of these things. We will return to the role of coercion in persuading importers of intellectual property rights to sign an agreement that dramatically increased the costs of intellectual property imports to them. For the moment, the point we are making is simply that nondomination as a condition for democratic deliberation to settle an efficient regime of property rights was absent from the new global intellectual property regime.

In terms of the economic theory of democracy and efficient property rights outlined in Chapter 1, therefore, there is one level of explanation for the settling of an international agreement like TRIPS, which was clearly an economic disaster for nations that were net importers of intellectual property rights, and particularly for those that would be unable to afford the drugs that might save millions of lives from epidemics like AIDS: that is that the TRIPS negotiations were nonrepresentative, based on misinformation and domination. But this is too abstract an explanation to be fully convincing for such a politically counterintuitive outcome. In the next section, we seek to summarize more historically what we have concluded in the book about why it happened. Then in Chapter 13 we return to the theme of how to democratize the intellectual property regime.

THE PUZZLE OF TRIPS

In Chapter 1 we posed the puzzle of why more than a hundred nations that were large net importers of intellectual property rights signed a TRIPS agreement that benefited a tiny number of countries that were net exporters, most particularly the US, which is a huge net exporter. An important part of the explanation, as revealed in the last section, is certainly that most importer nations did not have a clear understanding of their own interests and were not in the room when the important technical details were settled. One delusional belief that existed within the Australian delegation to the Uruguay Round, and that we suspect may have been common in other delegations, was that Australia was in the process of becoming a "clever country" and one day would be a net exporter of intellectual property rights. This delusion was promoted by the lobbying pressures Australian trade negotiators were put under during the round. As in the US, trade negotiators with limited resources had an interest in accepting at face value the exaggerated estimates of Australian business on how much they were losing to pirates. Australian companies that were exporters of intellectual property rights—the Australian film, recording and software industries—were enthusiastic about TRIPS because they wanted the WTO to crack down on pirating of their copyrights in Asia. They lobbied for their concentrated interest in Australia's support for TRIPS.

On the other side of the ledger, Australians who would be paying more for imported intellectual property rights were a diffuse interest. They were individual consumers who would pay more for their CDs, computer software or drugs. Public health agencies, which were more concentrated consumers of patented drugs, simply did not understand the implication of what was being decided in Geneva: that they would be paying more for drugs. Even when those public health agencies understood the game, as in the case of the New Zealand Department of Health, and tried to do something about it, they found that their ministers ended up on the receiving end of a storm of international lobbying by the international pharmaceutical industry and trade threats. New Zealand was "watch-listed" by the USTR in 1991 because of its compulsory license provision and the fact that a New Zealand distributor of generic drugs, Pacific Pharmaceuticals, applied for a compulsory license involving US drug patents. The license was never granted.

Nor was the organized consumer movement in Australia, or anywhere else apart from India, active in lobbying against TRIPS when it counted in the late 1980s and early 1990s. So this was a classic case of Mancur Olson's thesis that diffuse public interests tend to be unrepresented because the costs to individuals of organizing large groups are not matched by the small gains for each individual.[5] Producer interests were decisively more organized than consumer interests even in states that were predominantly consumer states.

In a producer state like the US, these forces were all the more profound. US consumers who are not shareholders in the companies that control most of the world's intellectual property rights are also worse off as a result of TRIPS; in the long run they pay more for their drugs, CDs and so on. One reason a regime was possible that was even of doubtful benefit to the citizens of the US concerns time lines. US politicians get contributions for their next campaign from multinational companies. Reagan and Bush Senior were out of office before any effects of TRIPS came to realization; indeed, most of the effects on developing countries (and the political backlash against it by AIDS activists) fell due after Clinton was out of office. A large campaign contribution and an immediate surge in "business confidence" for the president has a political timeliness that impacts of today's trade negotiations a decade later do not. Once US trade negotiators have their incentive structure set in this way, there are comparable moves they can make to distort the incentives of developing nations. US watch-listing or priority-listing is an immediate threat to a government, as is withdrawal of funding for an aid project. In contrast, any costs associated with agreeing to an intellectual property deal that will not phase in for a developing country until five or ten years after the final round of negotiations are likely to be costs dealt with by a future political leader.

For members of the Cairns group (agricultural exporters), like Australia, there was in the Uruguay Round the immediate promise of greater access to European markets for agricultural products and reduced US subsidies for its competing agricultural exports. Again there were concentrated interests in Australian farm lobbies who wanted this presumed immediate payoff from the Uruguay Round. In a deal where Australia gets agriculture and the US gets intellectual property there were loud voices for the agricultural deal, while those who would lose from intellectual property were silent. Agriculture was seen as a here-and-now priority, intellectual property a long-term matter with uncertain structural effects. As it turned out, the agriculture payoff was itself uncertain as the US did not honor its agriculture commitments to Australia.

In sum, the pro-TRIPS interests were concentrated while the anti-TRIPS interests were so diffuse they generally did not even recognize their interests until after the horse had bolted. The carrots and sticks arranged by intellectual property–owning interests involved short-term incentives, while the costs TRIPS would impose seemed much further into the future (and often they were).

A further very important consideration to intellectual property–importing states arose from the tenacity of Special 301 US bilateralism. Most of these states had serious dread of watch-listing by the US and were attracted to a strategy that would put an end to aggressive bilateralism. TRIPS seemed to them the multilateral approach to accomplishing this. The US encouraged this interpretation. The US line was that it was only the want of a credible multilateral agreement that forced it to throw its weight around bilaterally. In truth, the US never stopped its bilateral program of treaty making on intellectual property, actually intensifying the pressure after TRIPS was concluded.[6] A US strategy of successive waves of bilateralism and multilateralism to raise regulatory standards perhaps suggests that these states were naive to think diplomacy could be stabilized multilaterally. On the other hand, what alternative do these states have? Bilateralism is like cooking an elephant and rabbit stew: however you mix the ingredients, it ends up tasting like elephant. Multilateralism is the only prospect for constraining the elephant by rules under which it agrees to submit to binding arbitration.

All these factors caused a tipping point in trade negotiations. Once a majority of states for the reasons outlined above had decided to jump on the TRIPS bandwagon, a holdout faced a worrying risk. This was that foreign investors would brand them as hostile to innovation-based investment, the most useful kind to have in the new information economy. Some US multinationals gave explicit signals that they were not interested in investing in nations that were not firmly committed to the TRIPS crusade against "piracy" (see Chapter 2). Indeed, pharmaceutical companies began signaling that they were mainly interested in investing in states that supported TRIPS plus —more than the 20 years' patent protection guaranteed by TRIPS. States began to compete with one another to show such companies that they were committed to TRIPS, to TRIPS plus and to extravagant enforcement gestures directed at "pirates." China executed a few. TRIPS was about legitimacy. Strong intellectual property laws became part of the "good governance" reforms the IMF and World Bank were looking for to bring investment to developing countries.

Another element of the successful transformation of the world intellectual property order was technical assistance. The US would follow up its successful bilateral negotiations with offers to comment on (read draft!) the target state's revised intellectual property law. Nations that were not well endowed with intellectual property lawyers would struggle for competent drafting advice if they were resisting the US, but if they were reforming their law to comply with US wishes, the legal advice they needed was always made available, as were trips to Geneva to acquire intellectual property expertise. The World Intellectual Property Organization (WIPO) during the 1990s drafted a lot of intellectual property laws for developing countries that were TRIPS plus in nature just to make sure that those countries would not get into trouble with WTO dispute resolution panels.

The most structural element of US strategy was forum shifting. When UNESCO became a forum where developing countries advanced dangerous visions of knowledge as the common heritage of humankind, it was time for the US to pull out and eliminate funding for UNESCO. Developing country proposals to reform the Paris Convention to suit their own industrial property interests was a reason to pull out of this forum. WIPO was also a forum that gave a platform to advocates from developing countries of lower intellectual property standards. This was the reason that the US shifted the crucial forum for global standard-setting in the 1980s from WIPO to the General Agreement on Tariffs and Trade (GATT). There, as we have seen, developing country troublemakers would not even be in the room when important decisions were taken. The tradition of consensus decision-making at the GATT was that if a draft that had been agreed between the secretariat, the US and the EC was challenged by a developing country, the chairman would rule without discussion that there was no consensus on this issue. Out of session the US and EC would be given an opportunity to sort out their differences with the recalcitrant state. The stew created by *two* elephants and a rabbit would taste even more like elephant than a bilateral stew. In our interviews there was considerable disagreement on whether Chairman Dunkel had any influence at all on the intellectual property draft text or whether it was all Anell; whether the chairman was a cipher of the US/EC in his drafting or a powerful actor. What is clear, though, is that the US found it an advantage to negotiate from "more neutral text." They would say: "We still hold with our submission, but agree to negotiate from this text" (1994 interview).

At this point the story looks like a deeply structural one about what nations need to do to survive and flourish under contemporary capitalism. Yet at the beginning we saw that it is a story of visionary individuals like Jacques Gorlin, Eric Smith, Jack Valenti and Edmund Pratt who imagined the simple idea of linking intellectual property to the trade regime. Individuals like Gorlin and Smith were not powerful men; they were Washington legal and economic entrepreneurs who got things done by getting powerful people like Edmund Pratt of Pfizer and John Opel of IBM interested in their big idea. "Expertise and the ability to get one of my CEOs on the telephone is the basis of my influence" (1994 interview). In some cases that kind of influence reached even higher, for example arranging for Steven Spielberg to give a private preview of *Schindler's List* in the White House so he could ear-bash President Clinton on the importance of TRIPS. During the 1980s almost everyone in the US business community who thought about it at all considered TRIPS a pipe dream. It wasn't just that it was against the interests of almost everyone except a comparatively small number of powerful US and European knowledge firms; TRIPS seemed like a bad idea to most key individuals in the GATT secretariat and the EC. There was no initial interest at all from European and Japanese business, let alone their governments. The implausibility here was about linking an agreement to expand monopoly rights to a regime that was about dismantling trade monopolies and removing barriers to competition.

The visionaries were right. With the counterfeiting code the US backed in the Tokyo Round of the GATT, they thought small and lost; with TRIPS they thought big and won. By taking one step at a time — first getting European business on side, then their governments, then Japanese business, and so on — they finally rendered the implausible plausible. Then the US state was genuinely willing to throw its weight around in the successive waves of bilateral and multilateral coercive trade negotiation we have described. Actually they did not throw it around as much as the business reformers wanted. But this was wise diplomacy; the USTR used minimal necessary force while projecting an enforcement pyramid from watch-listing to priority watch-listing to priority foreign country–listing, to trade and aid sanctions and cancellation of benefits under the Generalized System of Preferences. As regulatory theory prescribes,[7] the pyramid projected an image of invincibility, as articulated by one Australian trade official: "At least on important issues, everyone will comply or face retaliation" (1993 interview).

The first basis of diplomacy was that jumping on the TRIPS bandwagon was in their own interests if they wanted to attract capital and become a knowledge economy. "TRIPS ratification can build confidence...It's a signaling flag—'I'm for foreign investment'" (1993 UNCTAD interview). The combination of the enforcement pyramid mentioned in the previous paragraph and perceptions of what was needed to *become* an investment destination led Tunisia's GATT negotiator to construe signing as inevitable, legitimacy building and common sense:

> It doesn't affect us yet. And eventually we have to develop intellectual property standards. So we might as well commit to it as part of a package that is in our national interest (1997 interview).

The gentle but strategic diplomacy of Lars Anell as chair of the TRIPS negotiating group in Geneva, for example in ruling that existing national legal traditions would not be an argument allowed into the debate, was also a velvet glove over the iron fist of US and European corporate power. Thus the visionary few did realize their long-term strategy for making the US a richer country at the expense of most of the rest of the world by orchestrating shorter-term payoffs for key global actors who lacked the clarity of vision to see longer-term interests. The US axis on TRIPS showed genuine diplomatic wisdom in the way they expanded the circle from US business to the US state to Europe, the Quad, Quad-plus, the Friends Group, 10+10 when they were succeeding in building consensus, then narrowing the circle back to the Quad and back to Washington when they struck divisive issues. All the time they worked on confidence building outside the circle. Even on India, the most powerful holdout, the US worked tirelessly, pointing out to India that its analysis would change when the reforms India was putting in place to become a more open economy were realized, that it had a software and film industry that gave it very different interests from other developing countries such as the ASEANS, and so on. At the same time, "The Committee [the US] went to the ASEANS and said these guys [India and Brazil] should not be representing you because they don't care about investment climate!" (1994 Washington interview).

Hence, the explanation for the globalization of the US intellectual property regime by the trade/IP linkage requires both a structural grasp of economic interests and an understanding of entrepreneurship in ideas by individuals who knew how to harness structural power. There was, as one of them said, "a success breeds success thing" during the long march from the Caribbean Basin Initiative to the GSP to Special 301 to strategic bilateral victories to TRIPS to TRIPS-plus bilaterals. Here it is also important to keep in view an op-ed like "Stealing from the Mind" (Chapter 4). Two decades ago it took a leap of imagination for ordinary citizens to conceive of what they were doing in copying an item of software, music or videotaping a television program, as theft. As a matter of law, these things were never criminal offenses in most nations until TRIPS. The public relations campaign to define information piracy as a crime has reframed popular consciousness of intellectual property. It was important to define TRIPS as a matter of simple justice, because the fact is it is a matter of complex injustice. It pulled off a huge structural shift in the world economy to move monopoly profits from the information-poor to the information-rich. As we go deeper into an information economy, the implications of this for widening inequality in the world system, even within the US and Europe, will become more profound. There will be a digital divide, an access-to-drugs divide and a divide between those who avoid taxes by shifting their intellectual property rights around the world system and those who simply pay them.

CHAPTER 13

Resisting the New Inequality

THE NEW INEQUALITY

At another level, TRIPS was pulled off because it mattered so much to those who lobbied for it. These people understood the new realities of information economies and where wealth came from. In an industrial economy wealth came from controlling capital and labor. Our analysis of information feudalism is that the TRIPS visionaries saw wealth as coming from controlling abstract objects like patents. Their big idea was that if you came to own a patent in a genetically engineered cow that produces twice as much milk as existing cows, you had an asset that was equal in value to all the herds of all the world's dairy farmers. And a more liquid asset than all that milk and all those cows! Here we see the sense in which these visionaries sought to transcend industrial and financial capitalism and move back to the future of a new feudalism. Instead of extracting wealth from cowherds by owning the land, making the cowherders their vassals, the infofeudal aspiration is to propertize things that make cows productive, requiring the cowherder to choose between going out of business and paying you for this knowledge. Similarly with the Internet. The Net evolved as part of the intellectual commons, but the infofeudal strategy is to propertize "Gateskeeping" software so that the choice is either to pay your taxes to Baron Bill or some other infofeudal Sheriff of Nottingham or to choose not to be a serf of the Net. Of course the story is more interesting and complex than that; there are Robin Hoods of infofeudalism—the Free Software Movement and many groups like Napster. Information feudalism is therefore like medieval feudalism in that it is a fragile and partial accomplishment, constantly under threat from competitive capitalism and from the activism of democratic citizens.

Information feudalism, as represented in Table 13.1, is not an accomplishment that is realized; it is a project of some of the visionaries we interviewed for this research, which is under challenge. Later in this chapter we will discuss how it might be challenged more strongly. Yet each of the historical layers in Table 13.1 secured only very partial control that has both an inegalitarian residue today and an oppositional movement, beginning with the primordial hegemony of men over women and the continuing struggle of feminists against it. Information feudalism is a new variant of the transformation of the relations of production about which Karl Marx wrote so eloquently. Marx failed to grasp in a rounded way how partial and variegated these transformations are. There are ways in which they all have liberating effects, lifting some of the tyrannies of the old order, as Marx clearly saw in the transition from feudalism to capitalism. Marx also saw that the new dominion also brings in new inequalities that in some ways build upon persistent inequalities of the old order. This is the way we read Table 13.1.

All of the prior institutional projects of world history, conceived narrowly for our purposes as projects to redistribute property unequally, have important surviving features today. They are never fully supplanted. So with information feudalism. It will certainly not supplant industrial and financial capitalism, or the persistent residues of colonialism, or the king's power to tax centrally, or serfdom and slavery, or patriarchy. Our contention in this book is that information feudalism is an evocative way of describing the contemporary institutional push to redistribute property rights unequally. It contributes another cumulative layer of inequality. The question is how much will we let it contribute. We are not suggesting that infofeudalism's effects on inequality will be deeply institutionalized in anything like the degree of the institutions of medieval feudalism. Indeed one objective in describing the information feudalism project of the visionaries we interviewed is to encourage democracies to stand up against the dangers and prevent information feudalism from ever being fully entrenched into the institutions these visionaries are seeking to make.

Table 13.1 *Inequality and Property Rights in World History*

Era	Emergent property right
Primordial/Ancient	Patriarchal; men over women and children
Feudalism	Lord over land and vassals
Centralized state	King over taxes
Imperialism	Major powers over colonies, slaves
Industrial capitalism	Capitalists over labour and surplus value
Finance capitalism	Bankers and investors over securities, bonds, derivatives, interest
Information feudalism	Infogopolies, biogopolies over abstract objects

RETHINKING PIRACY

Two can play the piracy game. A recent Oxfam publication on "patent injustice" included as one of its policy recommendations: "Stop patent protection on bio-piracy."[1] The pamphlet continued:

> WTO rules should be amended to prevent bio-piracy. As a first step, the TRIPS regime should be harmonized with the Convention on Biodiversity, with patent holders required to disclose the origin of biological materials and to demonstrate prior informed consent of the original holders of knowledge applied in the development of patented products.

This is a strategic countermove from the NGO side. The indigenous justice issues in purloining indigenous knowledge for the financial gain of multi-national corporations is also a human rights issue. More broadly, the UN Economic and Social Council Sub-Commission on Human Rights in August 2000 explicitly suggested that TRIPS implementation may be straying into the violation of basic human rights, including:

> the right of everyone to enjoy the benefits of scientific progress and its applications, the right to health... there are apparent conflicts between the intellectual property rights regime embodied in the TRIPS Agreement, on the one hand, and international human rights law, on the other.

In any principled national legal system, basic human rights to health, education and indigenous rights to their cultures take precedence over (trump) utilitarian considerations. The global expansion of intellectual property rights is justified, spuriously or not, on utilitarian grounds: expanded reach for intellectual property will increase innovation and therefore economic growth. Increasingly it is recognized in international law that, just as in democratic national law, the first claim on our legal institutions is to ensure that basic human rights are honored. Then within that rights constraint, we should seek to design legal systems to optimize other good consequences — like innovation. Strategically, therefore, it does make sense for NGOs concerned about TRIPS injustice to work through the international human rights regime to ensure that the Council for TRIPS guarantees ground rules on compulsory licensing of intellectual property rights that will protect fundamental human rights.

Citizens should have their rights to private property guaranteed. But as was argued in Chapter 2 there is a difference between guaranteeing persons their right to exclude others from using their Cadillac and excluding others from using the times tables. If someone else is allowed to use my Cadillac, that reduces the value of my property, indeed may totally deprive me of its use when I need it. In contrast, if someone else uses the times tables, my use of them is in no way compromised. It would be morally wrong to give someone an intellectual property right in the times tables because that would artificially deprive those who could not afford to pay of something basic to their right to an education.

There is a continuum between a Cadillac, where ownership cannot be shared among many, which involves no knowledge fundamental to the common heritage of humankind, and the times table, access to which can be shared without limit and is part of the shared knowledge fundamental to the educational rights of our children. At some point along that continuum, we allow property rights to swing in so that there might be incentives for invention. Even then, we constrain the number of years we allow the knowledge to be locked up, or we limit the right in some other way (such as making it contingent upon registration or allowing its free use in certain circumstances). Knowledge is forever, but intellectual property rights are not and should never be.

In Chapter 2 we saw that when we grant intellectual property rights in the times tables, in seeds that farmers use in traditional agriculture, in genetically modified parts of the human genome, to appropriate indigenous medicines or art, the worry is that we turn citizens into trespassers in their own cultures. By reproducing the times tables, growing their own seeds, using traditional medicines or selling indigenous art they may be trespassing on an intellectual property right that has been appropriated by a large company. Mrs. McDonald is told that by naming her family fish and chip shop McDonald's, she is in breach of the trademark of an American company. This is what we mean by being a trespasser on your own heritage. Increasingly this worry is real, especially for the most fragile and embattled indigenous cultures of the South.

This is what information feudalism means. When Monsanto contractually imposes obligations on farmers using the lever of its control over intellectual property in seeds, Monsanto does act like the feudal lord who allows serfs to till his land so long as they honor the obligations that are his due. Colonialism was an extension of the feudal notion of the vassal to the level of relations between whole states. We saw in Chapter 5 that the major powers imposed upon their colonies, against the interests of those colonies. They signed treaties at Berne and Paris on their colonies' behalf. The deal was that the vassal state would receive the protection and beneficent knowledge of its colonial master in return for propertizing its cultural commons into the hands of corporations from the colonizing state.

New colonies today are universities. Scientists increasingly are vassals of knowledge corporations. They starve scientifically unless they generate ideas corporations are interested in buying and selling. As scientists sell more of their ideas to multinationals, they enslave themselves as trespassers on their own intellectual commons. Freedom of inquiry is blocked at various turns by patent and copyright obstacles. At a more banal level, they cannot distribute to their students copies of papers written by colleagues; they must get permission from a multinational publisher and pay a small royalty to them. If they are scientists in a poor country, where universities cannot afford the royalties, they are turfed off the intellectual commons. Thanks to the new commons created by public investment in the Internet, they can at least surf the Net in search of noncopyrighted material. Just as in Hollywood Rupert Murdoch reaps larger rewards than the inventive people who write screenplays and direct, so the serfs of science receive meager rewards for creativity compared with the corporations that come to own their ideas. The system is designed that way. Dissembling robber barons are the actual beneficiaries of stealing from the mind.

REFORMING PATENT OFFICE REGULATION

A flourishing area of scholarship in economics, law and across the social sciences is business regulation. Sociolegal scholars who study how regulatory agencies do their job have conducted countless empirical studies of almost every kind of agency except patent offices. Copyright offices have been similarly neglected. The only recent study by Deepak Somaya does reveal real differences in the way patents are administered in different countries.[2] US and Japanese patent administration was found to differ; US administration was more supportive of the exclusive property rights of patentees. In contrast, Japanese patent administration was more demanding of explanations on how inventions worked, giving more priority to facilitating the sharing of new knowledge and to rapid dissemination of innovation: "[T]he Japanese view inventions more as a public and less as a private, good," patents "more as a means to reward inventions and less a right to exclude others from use than in the United States."

Somaya found European patent administration to lie between the US and Japan, with Germany closer to Japan and the UK closer to the US. This is exactly as one would expect from David Soskice's theory of comparative capitalisms.[3] According to Soskice, both German/Japanese and US/UK capitalism are successful models. The German/Japanese model, which they share loosely with Sweden, Switzerland and South Korea, among others, involves substantial intercompany cooperation including sharing of innovation, with the state playing a framework-setting role on matters ranging from labor markets to training to innovation policy. Under the Anglo-Saxon model, the state plays an arm's-length role and intercompany collaboration is discouraged by competition and intellectual property law. This Anglo-Saxon model, according to Soskice, is better for the development of service industries, such as the superior finance sector we see in London and New York, and for tightly coupled production systems (airlines, large software houses, large entertainment systems). The German model is superior for relatively complex production processes and after-sales service, such as sophisticated engineering products, from motor vehicles to washing machines.

What follows from the Soskice analysis is that societies must choose their system for regulating intellectual property with an eye to how it will fit other crucial legal and industry policy institutions, from competition policy to labor market policy. Institutional mismatch, falling between the coherent institutional packages for engendering different kinds of flourishing capitalisms, is the worst choice to make. Put another way, every society must choose how to regulate property rights in the context of the niche in which it seeks to excel in the world system. Again this is a prescription for rich, local, democratic deliberation on how to enforce property rights. It is a prescription against buying any WIPO Anglo-German hybrid regime as "best practice" in getting the best of both worlds.

Peter Grabosky and John Braithwaite have made the only attempt at a systematic study of the enforcement strategies of all the significant regulatory agencies in one country, 101 of them. Only one page was devoted to the patent office compared with 28 pages devoted to environmental regulation. In a hierarchical clustering analysis of enforcement and interview data from 96 of the agencies, the patent office was classified as a "Benign Big Gun," an agency that had enormous enforcement powers in its legislation, but that never or rarely used them. For example, at that time (1986) there had been only two criminal convictions under the Trade Marks Act in Australian history. Grabosky and Braithwaite concluded that:

> The Patents, Trademarks, and Designs Office is the only agency in our study which relies predominantly on controlling corporate malpractice by establishing a framework and an information base which enables aggrieved parties to pursue their own interests in the courts.[4]

Indeed one senior interviewee in this study likened the patent office to a land titles office; his was not a regulatory agency at all. Patent offices in most countries for most of the 20th century seem to have been rather like the Australian office. TRIPS changed this; some of them now have active programs for tracking down intellectual property pirates and prosecuting them, though in most nations this job is delegated to the police. Basically, however, the land titles mentality remains.

Yet for most of the history of the institution there has not been a land titles mentality. We saw that in feudal England and up to its zenith in the Elizabethan era, patents were granted primarily for reasons of state to give monopoly control over an industry to a powerful courtier. The Statute of Monopolies of 1624 changed that by restricting grants of patents to inventions. The grant of a patent, however, continued to be a matter of public interest deliberation, not at all like the simple registration of ownership of the land. The state had to be convinced that the public benefit of encouraging innovation by granting the patent outweighed the harm to commerce of preventing others from exploiting the innovation. English courts approached patents not predisposed to find ways to extend the reach of the patent. This regulatory philosophy was also adopted in the US. It was regarded as particularly important that patent offices ensure in the public interest that an application was not a trivial adaptation of an old patent that had expired (and therefore a ploy to extend the period of monopoly rights), a ploy that was and is all too common. Also it was viewed as important that the patent application demonstrated a specific and defined benefit to the public. A reason for this was the historical experience of how chemical giants, especially the Germans, had deterred competitive entry to a product market early in the 20th century by registering a thicket of patents that covered everything and anything that a potential competitor might find useful.

In Chapter 10 we saw that the US Supreme Court in the mid-1960s reversed a trend toward the weakening of the utility requirement in patent law, but this did not stick; the weakening trajectory returned for the rest of the century. As one US patent attorney practicing in the biotech field put it in a 1999 interview, today "you get utility if you can spell it." The publication of new final guidelines on utility in January 2001 by the US Patent and Trademark Office requiring inventors to show a "specific and substantial utility" is an admission of just how little was being asked of inventors in relation to gene-based technologies. More generally, we saw in Chapter 10 that during the 1940s and 1950s getting a US court to declare a patent valid was tough; by the 1980s the odds had changed dramatically in favor of the patent holder. In this, the US courts have become handmaidens of US corporate interests, which are the big beneficiaries in the world system of thickets of patents in areas like biotechnology. It was these corporate interests that guided the formation of the US Court of Appeals for the Federal Circuit, the court that hears patent appeals (see Chapter 10). More disturbing is why the courts of nations that are net importers of intellectual property rights have succumbed to the hegemony of Anglo-American law in this respect. Perhaps it reflects a wider Anglo-American-Franco-German domination of the intellectual agenda of the epistemic community of intellectual property law coordinated by the World Intellectual Property Organization.[5] The intellectual property exporting nations have grabbed not only the trade agenda but also the jurisprudential agenda to the exclusion of independent thought from legal thinkers in intellectual property importing nations or indeed jurists in exporting nations who have a balanced concern for consumer interests.

Essentially the courts and executive governments in the Western world, though not in India and some other sophisticated developing countries, have rubber-stamped the capture of patent offices by multinationals. The economics of this is straightforward. Under the "new public management" patent offices increasingly have to fund their operations from the fees they collect from patentees. For patent offices everywhere most patentees are US and European companies or their local agents. The other financial fact of life is that as intellectual property rights have become more economically crucial to big business they have bankrolled patent offices out of contesting their strategic litigation games. Multinationals appeal patent office decisions in the courts mainly with an eye to securing precedents that turn the body of law to their structural advantage. Patent offices have had neither the legal resources nor the will to adequately contest these strategic litigation games.

What is to be done then about the progressive capture of the patent offices and courts by multinational corporations? One might also ask the same question in relation to copyright and trademark offices. The work of these offices is just as important to the public welfare and the structural problems much the same as for patent offices. Just as regulatory scholars have neglected the practices of patent offices as an object of study, so NGOs have neglected them as objects of lobbying. The consumer movement, development NGOs and to a lesser extent trade unions have now heard the TRIPS wake-up call. The realization that they were deceived and excluded on the TRIPS debates is one of the reasons they were out on the streets in Seattle and are active on the Internet today resisting a Millennium Round of the WTO. The not insignificant political clout that these NGOs now have, their capability to join arms with developing countries to form a democratic veto coalition against another WTO round, give them the capability to intervene with demands for the reform of patent office administration. At the moment the anti-TRIPS NGOs see reforming patent office policies as a rather less romantic activity than street marches in Seattle. One of our objectives with this book is to persuade them that it is time to shift this perception.

Consumer groups in many countries today do have the clout to demand seats on the policy and consultative committees of patent offices, copyright offices and trademark offices, seats that are currently occupied almost exclusively by business, copyright, patent and trademark attorney interests. It is not enough for NGOs to make submissions to these committees or to have a token representation. Submissions without advocates on decision-taking committees tend to become part of filing history rather than committee action. NGOs can set themselves the objective of campaigning in a classic hard cop–soft cop fashion for reform of patent or other intellectual property offices. The soft cop NGOs can take their seats on policy committees within the walls of the patent office and seek to push for changes in patent administration that: (1) demand resistance to the strategic litigation games of the multinationals; (2) demand effective application of the tests of patentability in the public interest; (3) demand that human rights, such as rights to health and indigenous rights, are taken seriously in patent determinations; and (4) insist on denial of patents to companies that do not adequately document the know-how needed to work the invention properly once the patent has expired. The fourth point is important so that others can exploit the information in the patent that society has received in exchange for the grant of the patent privilege and so new generations of innovators can stand on their shoulders. The hard cop NGOs can attack the patent office (and indeed the soft cop NGOs) from outside the walls, accusing them of regulatory capture. Experience in other domains with combating regulatory capture by big business, for example with environmental regulation, suggests that persistence over a long period with this strategy of hard cop and soft cop NGOs competing for political influence is what produces public-regarding reform.

The objective of such an NGO strategy needs to be much more than demands for critical reforms to patent office regulatory administration on matters such as utility and strategic litigation games. Political lobbying also needs to be directed at regulating intellectual property offices with a new jurisprudence of intellectual property. Preeminent here is the need for indigenous rights groups to lead demands for intellectual property rights law and administration to be constrained by fundamental international human rights obligations. Human rights law must be clarified and made more explicit in its application, to ensure that it precludes actions by intellectual property offices leaving indigenous people as trespassers on their own culture. Compulsory licensing of intellectual property rights, something the US failed to weaken radically through TRIPS, will be one of the weapons here, a matter we will return to below. For the moment we simply make the more abstract point that patentable inventions should: (1) pass meaningful standards of patentability; (2) be linked to a full disclosure of know-how test; and (3) not threaten, through the issuance of the patent, any fundamental human right as defined by the international human rights instruments the state has ratified. The structural reform of patent administration needed to enforce these three tests is a shift from state administration captured by big business to tripartite administration where patent examiners are monitored on one side by business and on the other by NGOs, particularly consumer groups with links to indigenous rights, human rights and development NGOs. Tripartism has been demonstrated in other regulatory arenas to be the key reform for deterring regulatory capture and corruption.[6]

There is a fourth test that must be added to the patent, disclosure and human rights tests. This is the competition policy test. Again NGOs have the key role of blowing the whistle to the national competition regulator when their monitoring of the decisions of patent examiners reveals that competition law has been breached. In short, the competition regulator needs to be positioned as a check and balance on the decisions of intellectual property regulators and NGOs, the whistle-blowers who alert competition regulators to matters of concern. For the reasons outlined in Soskice's theory of comparative capitalisms, it is vital that intellectual property and competition institutions are mutually responsive so as to support an inter-company system that is fertile soil for investment. Furthermore, NGOs in most countries will need to lobby for a more aggressive use of competition law principles in relation to the exercise of intellectual property rights. The hands-off-intellectual-property policy of the Reagan administration meant that competition principles stood silently by as intellectual property monopolies inflicted heavy losses on consumers and the process of innovation around the world.

NGOs could also lend their strength to the cause of globalizing competition policy rules aimed at defeating global knowledge cartels, which are beyond the reach of any one national competition authority. Finally, globally networked NGOs could campaign/lobby for the transplant of good regulatory initiatives aimed at improving tools of competition law for dealing with the ill effects of intellectual property monopolies on innovation. The concept of a dependency license in French law, for example, is aimed at giving rights of access to those who are in a position to improve on the patent holder's original invention.[7] Such licenses recognize the sequential nature of innovation and prevent intellectual property from being used to turn innovation into a winner-take-all game based on legal stratagems.

There is also a need to reform the deliberative quality of intellectual property regulatory administration. This need has become greater as the patent system expands to cover technologies that raise moral issues. As argued above, getting an efficient balance in intellectual property rights requires representation, transparency and nondomination combined with institutionalized opportunities for thoughtful deliberation. Tripartism, which gives a plurality of NGOs a voice alongside government officials, business and representatives of patent attorneys, would be a big step along this path. But the deliberative process also needs attention. Before decisions of patent examiners become final and the subject of formal appeal, those decisions should be tabled for discussion by these parties. Patent examiners may actually find this helpful. Under the European Patent Convention, for example, inventions that are contrary to morality are not patentable. At the moment there is no deliberative process that a patent examiner can participate in to work out what this might mean in relation to a specific invention.

A deliberative process might also help patent examiners to contend with senior patent attorneys representing large corporate clients who threaten to litigate whenever a patent examiner questions one of their patent applications. Patent examiners are expected to push through patent applications and not ask too many questions. Around the table most draft decisions would be straightforward and go through with minimal discussion. The greatest value of such a deliberative process is contestability, patent examiners knowing they might be called upon to defend their draft decisions not only by business critics but by NGOs of various kinds as well. This pressure would improve the quality of reasons given by patent examiners in their written decisions and this in turn would put pressure on patentees to improve the clarity of their patent applications and the care with which they explain its utility, inventiveness and the descriptions of the invention needed to make it work. For intellectual property to be an integral part of a comparative capitalism that buzzes with efficiency and administrative competence, deliberative competence is needed.

DELIBERATION ON THE COUNCIL FOR TRIPS

As we saw in Chapter 6, the TRIPS Council process currently operates as a floor, a platform upon which the US and the EC are building a new bilateralism to further ratchet up intellectual property standards. The economic price of this will be less competitive markets, new and more domineering global knowledge cartels, with no proportionate gains in innovation. In absolute contradiction of the general direction of EU rule making, "We're harmonizing on the highest level possible rather than the lowest [one might add, and rather than mutual recognition] with intellectual property" (1993 EC interview). Now Europe is working through the Council for TRIPS to push this "highest possible level" globally.

Because we think transparency of policy deliberation will lead to the conclusion that further ratcheting up of global intellectual property standards will increase distortion and reduce the efficiency of the world trading system, we should not be afraid of the Council for TRIPS. Or at least we should not be afraid of it so long as it can be rendered a representative, transparent, nondominating forum for policy deliberation. Senior members of the WTO secretariat today have a profound understanding of the way US bullying, with respect to TRIPS more than anything else, has destabilized the WTO as an institution. A delegitimated WTO risks destabilization of the liberal trading order. Responsible trade diplomats realize this is in no one's interests, least of all in the interests of the US and Europe. To put the trade diplomat's dilemma more starkly, is it possible to conceive of another WTO round without the Council for TRIPS making the intellectual property regime work more representatively, transparently and less coercively?

Learning from the new power they found at Seattle and in the scuttling of the Multilateral Agreement on Investment, developing countries should consider forming a veto coalition against further ratcheting up of intellectual property standards. The alliance between NGOs and developing countries on the access to medicines issue and the fact that this alliance managed to obtain the Declaration on the TRIPS Agreement and Public Health at the WTO Ministerial Conference at Doha in November 2001 suggests that this coalition is a realistic possibility.[8] The position of such a veto coalition could be converting the Council for TRIPS from a body that secures a platform to one that polices a ceiling. This bold new agenda for the Council for TRIPS would be standstill and rollback of intellectual property standards in the interests of reducing distortions and increasing competition in the world economy. If developing countries cannot forge a unified veto coalition against further ratcheting up of intellectual property standards, they can be assured that they will be picked off one by one by the growing wave of US bilaterals on both intellectual property and investment more broadly.

Developing countries and the G-77 in particular suffered a dramatic decline in clout after the collapse of the Soviet Union. They could no longer graft diplomatic victories by playing off East against West. A veto coalition of the Soviet bloc and the developing countries might at times prevail against the economic power of the West. Since 1998, since Seattle and the rout of the Multilateral Agreement on Investment, the possibility of a new kind of veto coalition is apparent. It is of developing countries and Northern NGOs. In Seattle, developing countries and Northern NGOs had very different positions, for example on labor standards. But then developing countries and the Soviet bloc never had the same interests. You don't need to agree on what to do to make a veto coalition work. You only need to agree on what to block. At this point in history one thing developing countries might be expected to agree on with a wide range of NGOs and transnational advocacy networks that exploit the political power of the Internet is that there should not be a new round of the WTO until standstill and selected rollback (on matters such as AIDS drugs) is accepted as the outcome of the Uruguay Round.

Beyond developing countries, there are some developed nations that are net importers of intellectual property rights that are beginning to have doubts about TRIPS. Even within US business there are second-generation computer software companies such as Sun Corporation that have called for more balance in the setting of copyright standards and on other intellectual property issues. Educational and health systems everywhere have become progressively more engaged with the cost implications for mass education and health of escalating copyright and patent protection. The Digital Future Coalition in the US, which counts associations representing libraries, universities, educators, software developers and computer equipment manufacturers among its members, is a concrete example of how copyright issues have brought public and private actors together in an activism of resistance against copyright as a tool of information feudalism. We have seen that other international regimes such as the human rights regime and environmental regimes such as the Convention on Biological Diversity are beginning to assert themselves against the WTO. A broad coalition of civil society in the North comprising these kinds of disparate elements, combined with unified developing country opposition, might be a formidable veto coalition against further ratcheting up of intellectual property standards. Because international politics is a two-level game[9] where states must look not only across the table to opposition from other states but also backward to the table of domestic politics and the coalition of domestic opposition arrayed against them, a developing country and North–South civil society coalition may not be as weak as it seems.

For developing countries and NGOs to be effective in demanding TRIPS standstill and rollback, or more ambitiously a new accord on the global transfer of technology and knowledge, they would have to learn from the dismal experience of TRIPS that we have documented in this book. They would have to learn to work better in coalition so that they are less vulnerable to being picked off in bilaterals on terms dictated by US multinationals. They would also have to learn to trust one another to share responsibilities for coalition technical leadership on specific issues. Developing countries cannot afford to have technical experts in Geneva on every important issue that comes up in WTO negotiations. Nor can NGOs. So it is imperative for coalitions to nominate this member as responsible for leadership on biodiversity, that one on indigenous rights, another on compulsory licensing for pharmaceuticals patents, and so on.

The specific form of TRIPS rollback most immediately needed is aggressive use of compulsory licensing of patents to ensure that poor people have access to lifesaving drugs when they are at risk of diseases like AIDS. The Declaration on the TRIPS Agreement and Public Health that NGOs and developing countries fought for and won at the Doha WTO Ministerial in 2001 paves the way for this. This must include a right to export and import from generic manufacturers once a nation has issued a compulsory license (an issue the declaration refers to the Council for TRIPS). In the aftermath of the collapse of the pharmaceutical multinationals' litigation against South Africa and the outcome at Doha, there is genuine political feasibility in this as a first form of TRIPS standstill and rollback. TRIPS also leaves open government use provisions that allow government use of patents for public noncommercial use. Legal advocacy groups need funding or pro bono law firm assistance to help developing countries to introduce strong public use laws that will be TRIPS-legal. In developed countries as well, strategic legal advocacy groups need support to develop a public use case law.

CHAPTER 14

On the Importance of the Publicness of Knowledge

PROPERTYLESS CREATIVITY

Western pharmaceutical companies frequently say that communist pharmaceutical producers invented little of value in the 20th century. This observation is basically correct. It is also correct that the superiority of the capitalist system of intellectual property rights over communist property rights is one reason for this. Yet this is not the main reason. There are few if any domains of human creativity where intellectual property rights are the main reason for inventiveness. The last few decades of the 18th century and the first few of the 19th was the greatest half-century in the history of music, giving us Mozart, Haydn, Beethoven, Mendelssohn, Schubert, Schumann, Berlioz and Chopin. It was also the era when these composers, especially Beethoven, pushed for the refinement of an Italian invention, the piano, to create the greatest instrumental innovation in the history of music. There was no copyright in central Europe during this half-century of the greatest flourishing of musical genius, nor in the next in Italy when Rossini, Donizetti, Bellini, Verdi and Puccini were responsible for the most important period in the history of opera.

The period from Mozart to Beethoven was also a great era of creativity in literature that gave us Austen, Goethe, Wordsworth, Coleridge, Byron and Hugo, among others. At the end of this period came Charles Darwin who reinvented biology after the voyage of the *Beagle* (1831–1836). We saw the foundation of the modern discipline of chemistry at the hands of Lavoisier and Dalton, the foundations laid for the industrial revolution through inventions such as James Watt's steam engine, George Stephenson's locomotive, Michael Faraday's first electric motor and indeed one of the foundations of the postindustrial (information) economy through the invention of photography by Louis Daguerre. This was one of the great eras of philosophy: Kant, Hegel, Bentham, Hume and ironically Adam Smith. The 20th century, the first in which philosophers have universally enjoyed the benefits of copyright in their works, has been one of the weakest centuries for philosophy. The greatest philosophers of the 20th century—Wittgenstein, Russell and perhaps Habermas—are simply not as important as those of the 19th, 18th and 17th centuries or arguably of the last centuries before Christ. What was most important to nurturing the great philosophers of Ancient Greece and the Enlightenment were the cultures and institutions of scholarship that flourished in those times and places.

We could make the same point about law itself. Legal innovation flourished most when there were great institutionalizers of legal debate: Justinian with the Roman empire; the Glossaters with the resystematizing of Roman law at the University of Bologna; Grotius with the systematization of international law including international commercial law in the emerging capitalism of the Dutch Republic; the Code Napoleon with its decisive abolition of property rights in serfs; and the Federalists with the republican reinvention of constitutional law in the new US. The most recurrently important institution that these institutionalizers of legal innovation promoted from Bologna to Jefferson's greatest pride—founding the University of Virginia—was the university. It is the institution of the university itself that has been the greatest fount of innovation, not the intellectual property laws systematized in its faculties of law.

In the vast sweep of the history of human creativity the impact of intellectual property rights has been negligible because for most of that history those rights have not existed and, where they have, for the most part they have been poorly designed and even more poorly enforced. It is only with TRIPS that states have begun to systematically criminalize the infringement of intellectual property. Our short historical discussion also suggests that we should be suspicious of incentive views of creativity. Seeing creativity as a supply-side problem that can be best met by meeting individual demand curves for intellectual property rights is an impoverished account, to say the least, of what motivates people to create. It is unlikely, for example, that those driven to write for a living will become more motivated by the extension of the copyright term from 50 years to 70 years after the death of the author, even if publishers seeking to protect monopolies in lucrative works invoke the authors' creative interests in their lobbying campaigns to get such extensions. People to a large extent are naturally disposed to create. Intellectual property is not irrelevant to the reward of creative work, but it is for reasons that we articulate in the next section not the most significant means that a society has for supporting and rewarding such work. In the final section of this chapter we suggest that there are strong social interests in encouraging some individuals to work in institutional settings that reward them, but allow the expression of their creative endeavors to remain a public good.

PROTECTING PRIVATE PROPERTY, PROTECTING PUBLIC UNIVERSITIES

The most fundamental reason for the preeminence of the US as the source of invention in the 20th century is not its intellectual property laws. As we have seen in this book, the US was actually one of the latest starters of the capitalist democracies in expanding the scope of intellectual property. A more important fount of 20th-century US innovation was the preeminence of its universities. Not that American universities created all that distinction; they also attracted it, especially from Europe. A second, connected, reason for the American century was therefore its early openness to multiculturalism. This also accounts for the US being the source of the greatest 20th-century innovation in music—jazz/blues/soul with its later influence on swing, rock, rap and most emergent contemporary musical forms. Notwithstanding racism, the multicultural openness to innovation of New York and Chicago was responsible for the diffusion and creation of a market for jazz and the blues.

Like Ancient Greece, the Italian Renaissance and the Scottish Enlightenment, the 20th-century US engendered a culture of innovation that touched every aspect of life. Fundamentally this was a cultural accomplishment. But the institutional supporters of this cultural momentum of ideas are also significant. We find universities and intellectual property rights to be the most important of these. Yet we want to keep them in perspective. They were not responsible for the leadership of the US in jazz (as we saw in Chapter 11), basketball or any other form of music/entertainment/sport. The institutionalized support of the American university and intellectual property systems certainly reinforces US excellence in sport and music. Michael Jordan was nurtured by the American college system; his extraordinary wealth was created more by trademarks than by match payments. This excellence and this wealth are certainly extra reasons why so many young Americans aspire to approach the benchmark Jordan has set.

Our claim is simply that the two most important institutional supports of innovation—universities and intellectual property—are only parts of the story of a culture of innovation. And that universities are the more important part of those two. In this book we have seen that two of the three most consequential technological breakthroughs of the last century—the Internet and the new molecular biology spawned by unlocking DNA—were the fruits of public investment mainly in universities, not of the commercial pursuit of patents or copyright. In Chapter 10 we saw that 70 percent of scientific papers cited in biotechnology patents originated in solely public science institutions compared with 16.5 percent from the private sector. Similarly with the conceptual breakthroughs in computer software, which laid the foundations for the Internet; these preceded the application of copyright to computer software. This, however, could not be said of the pioneering work of IBM in laying the foundations for the computer hardware revolution, which was very much motivated by patent laws. The third most consequential scientific breakthrough of the 20th century was not so positive in its effects—nuclear energy. Yet it too was a product of US public investment attracting the best minds not only from its own universities, but also from those of Germany, the UK, Australia and Canada to the Manhattan Project. Moreover, the US government in the case of the Internet, the human genome and the secrets of splitting the atom decided to put them into the intellectual commons rather than into the realm of intellectual property. In the case of atomic secrets Eisenhower did so only on condition that the other developed economies sign up for an "Atoms for Peace" accord that has performed better than expected in preventing the proliferation of nuclear weapons.

For good or ill, the three most consequential scientific transformations since World War I were products of public investment in the scientific talent of universities. They were made consequential by making knowledge of them public goods. So while pharmaceutical company public relations are right to say that the accumulated drug breakthroughs of the 20th century are a result of Western intellectual property laws, this is also a very partial truth. First, it ignores the important role of US federal funding in drug development, especially in the category of drugs that afford significant therapeutic gain. So, by way of example, of the 327 drugs and biological products approved by the Food and Drug Administration in 1991, only 5 were classified as offering significant therapeutic gain.[1] All five were developed with federal funds. Second, it neglects the fact that the most consequential improvements in health that have so increased longevity over the past century have been in the realm of public health innovations developed in university medical schools and state health departments—food regulation, quarantine, clean water and sanitation systems in large cities. Third, the comparison with the abysmal performance of communist countries in discovering therapeutic breakthroughs is made without recognizing that the Soviets could have matched US innovation in medicine had they chosen to. The health of their people was simply a lower priority than matching the US in the space race, sporting competition and the development of weapons of mass destruction. Notwithstanding their weaker economy and weaker universities, by concentrating their public investment in innovation on the things that mattered to them they were able to match and sometimes beat the US in these fields.

At least with pharmaceuticals it is true that the patent system has been important in therapeutic breakthroughs, but not in the simple causal way that pharmaceutical companies claim. Penicillin, for example, among the handful of the greatest medical breakthroughs of the 20th century, has a line of public research going back to Louis Pasteur and Jules Joubert's description of bacterial activity in 1877, Alexander Fleming's 1929 paper describing the effects of a mold on a specimen of staphylococcus and the work of Howard Florey and Ernst Chain in isolating and testing penicillin in its pure form. US pharmaceutical companies were important in the mass production of penicillin after 1941, the year in which Florey flew to the US asking the government and the pharmaceutical industry to become involved. Crucial to this mass production were the compulsory licenses the US government issued in order to make sure the industry could meet its needs for the invasion of Normandy. We also saw in Chapter 10 that the changes in the patent system that occurred in relation to biotechnology patenting were not causes of the bioindustrial revolution, but rather an outcome.

One of the good things about increasing our investment in great universities is that most of the money does not go to making scientists richer. Rather it mainly goes into employing more scientists, doing more experiments, imparting more knowledge to the next generation of students as well as contributing to the existing stock of public knowledge for others to use. Contrast R&D tax breaks for industry. Most is wasted on the financial machinations of appropriators of innovations. In Australia in recent years R&D has been the greatest vehicle for promoters of aggressive tax shelter arrangements. Corporate Australia seems to have infinite creativity in defining cleaning the office floor as "R&D on detergents," and a singular lack of creativity in actually inventing the new. R&D tax fiddles, using intellectual property to shift profits into tax havens, are standard today in most developed economies. Government R&D support for the private sector should be transparent on the expenditure side of budgets, not another hidden tax expenditure. One reason is that the benefits that flow from support for corporate R&D should have to compete with claims for R&D support from universities.

Our deep suspicion is that once the benefits from the huge transfers (and scams) through R&D tax breaks are measured, it might be obvious that there is a need to shift resources from the private sector to universities. Not that there isn't mediocrity in universities and a lot of wonderful scholarship that has nothing to do with economic innovation. Yet the main reason we suspect extra public investment in basic university science and education will return more to an economy than higher R&D tax deductions is rather simple. It is that universities are deeply, profoundly committed to building knowledge, almost to the exclusion of other priorities. In contrast business is much more committed to making money than to building knowledge. And unfortunately in modern conditions it is often easier for firms to make money by hiring a tax lawyer to create an appearance that they have a huge R&D investment than it is to actually have one; if you do actually have one, we have shown it will often pay better to lock up the knowledge than to share it with bigger minds than your own.

Intellectual property lawyers and tax lawyers may, by taking advantage of the law's rule complexity, help a company to large profits, but how socially productive this is, is another question. There is no social benefit, for example, in patent lawyers sneaking through a patent on what amounts to the same chemical invention, thereby making society pay for that invention twice over. Profits to be made through the manipulation of intellectual property rules are an example of a broader phenomenon economists call "rent seeking."[2] Rent seeking through intellectual property rules brings with it high costs because included in those costs are the social costs that flow from not allowing knowledge to be freely available (for example, the use of that knowledge in other innovation).

So far we have seen that creativity has been motivated in the absence of intellectual property rights and that in fact it can flourish with public investment in public institutions, returning to a society knowledge goods as public goods. In the final section of this chapter we suggest that the importance of keeping knowledge as a public good has increased rather than decreased, making it all the more important to resist the project of information feudalism in the ways we described in Chapter 13.

GLOBAL PUBLICS, PUBLIC GOODS AND KNOWLEDGE

One of Adam Smith's conclusions in *The Wealth of Nations* was that the cost of some institutions and public works of benefit to society would have to be met "by the general contribution of the whole society."[3] The failure to tax individuals in order to provide public works such as roads and institutions such as education would mean that either they would not be provided or they would be undersupplied. Society would be worse off as a result. Taxation was necessary because not enough individuals could be counted on to volunteer payment for public works and institutions. Since Smith there has been an ocean of theorizing on how to meet the costs of providing a sufficient supply of goods that have widespread benefits, but that individuals are unable or unwilling to pay for.

Public goods are defined in terms of two characteristics: nonrivalry and nonexcludability. Knowledge provides an example of the characteristic of being nonrivalrous in consumption. My use of the knowledge of the method of mouth-to-mouth resuscitation to save a life does not "consume" the knowledge; it remains available for others to use. The provision of defense, a standard example of a public good, illustrates the quality of nonexcludability. Once an army is created to protect a territory it is not feasible to exclude any one individual from the benefit of its protection. It is difficult to supply defense to the person willing to pay for it while at the same time not supplying to the person unwilling to pay for it. Where nonpayers cannot be excluded from the benefits of a good the market is not likely to supply the good in question or may undersupply it. This leaves the provision of public goods to governments or to the voluntary acts of individuals. Individuals do occasionally band together to hire mercenaries or to provide schools. But, overall, economists take the view that relying on voluntary action to fund public goods is likely to lead to a dramatic undersupply of such goods since not enough individuals will volunteer contributions to fund goods such as the construction of roads and investment in basic research. This line of argument leads to the conclusion that governments have to supply public goods using taxes to fund the cost. Even here there are constraints that lead to an undersupply, one of the most important being the election politics of tax.

Knowledge is an example of an impure public good because although it is nonrivalrous in consumption it does not always possess the quality of being nonexcludable. In fact the project of information feudalism we have described in these pages is to turn knowledge into a matter of private supply by being able to exclude nonpayers by means of intellectual property rights or technological locks. From the point of view of individual profit making, knowledge is the ideal object of propertization since it is nonrivalrous in supply. The same knowledge can be endlessly recycled to many generations of consumers, each new generation having to pay for its use. The incentives for individuals to seek profit through a redefinition of the intellectual property rules that form the basis of the knowledge economy are great. But as we pointed out in the last section individual profit seeking does not always line up with efficiency and social welfare. Competition, we have suggested, suffers when intellectual property rights are overextended. We would not want an idea like the home delivery of pizza to be the subject of monopoly protection because these kinds of basic business ideas need to be accessible to all in order for competition to take place. We want a number of fast-food businesses to be given the opportunity to beat a path to our door, rather than one having the exclusive right to do so and charge accordingly. Competition at base depends on businesses being able to imitate and learn from each other. Yet when the patent system expands to cover business methods corporations are given both the incentive and the means to lock up basic business ideas and practices. The risk of information feudalism is that it will lead us into a postcompetitive order.

Another and perhaps more fundamental objection to information feudalism is the threat it poses to the supply of knowledge as a public good at a time when people around the world are becoming more and more dependent on knowledge goods as public goods. When one state carries out research into an infectious disease and stops its spread to other states it provides a benefit to the populations of other states as well as its own. The greater movement of people and animals around the globe means that diseases also travel more. Climate change and environmental change are likely to release viruses into new areas. The disease burden over the coming decades may well shift and turn in unpredictable ways, creating relations of dependence among states. The problem is that many states in the world, especially the least developed, do not have the capacity to fund research into disease or pay for its treatment. They are reliant on knowledge about disease and treatments as an international public good. There are other examples of dependency on international public goods. Raising agricultural productivity matters to food security, especially in poor countries, but these countries are not in a position to fund the research needed to develop new plant varieties. All countries benefit from research into global warming and many benefit from research into the problem of desertification.

The provision of national public goods usually relies on a government possessing the power of taxation. In the case of international public goods there is no world sovereign that possesses the power to tax globally in order to finance international public goods, nor is there likely to be in the foreseeable future. Supranational institutions like the IMF, World Bank and United Nations, which provide international public goods, rely on financial contributions from their members. They do not have the power of taxation.

Basically, the creation of international public goods has relied on voluntary initiatives by single rich states or nonstate actors such as charitable foundations, voluntary cooperation by groups of wealthier states or voluntary complex alliances of state and nonstate actors. So, for example, research on increasing plant yields in developing countries has been carried out by the 16 centers that make up the Consultative Group on International Agricultural Research, a group of centers that is funded by a variety of actors including the Food and Agriculture Organization, the World Bank, the Rockefeller and Ford Foundations, a number of individual states and the EU. Other examples of actors organizing to provide international public goods include the New Medicines for Malaria Venture, in which the World Health Organization, the World Bank, the Rockefeller Foundation and the International Federation of Pharmaceutical Manufacturers Associations are active, and the complex partnership of private, public and civil society actors that has operated in West Africa for the last 25 years to control river blindness disease.

There has been a growing consensus in development circles that more international public goods need to be supplied as part of development strategy.[4] In the absence of world government, increasing the provision of international public goods will be influenced, we believe, by the extent to which inspirational individuals or groups of individuals, who see an international collective need, step in to play a leadership role to help organize other actors to provide the funds to meet that collective need. The funding initiatives in relation to the AIDS crisis that are now being talked about in the United Nations, by the international pharmaceutical industry and US and EU officials, have their genesis in the work of a handful of individuals from the NGO sector like James Love. These individuals have since the early 1990s been campaigning on the issue of better access to medicines by poor people and have been steadfast critics of the globalization of patent rules through TRIPS. In *Global Business Regulation* we argued that individuals who were wired into influential networks and had regulatory models waiting in the wings could, especially under conditions of crisis and mass public concern, globalize those models. Those individuals who had thought about marine safety regulation before the sinking of the *Titanic* were in a much better position to influence the international development of that regulation after the *Titanic* sank. Similarly, an important factor in increasing the supply of international public goods will be the extent to which pioneering individuals step forward to create global networks of voluntarism.

We are not suggesting that such networks will result in an ideal supply of international public goods. Global voluntary action is a slender thread by which to hang support for international public goods. In the case of the access to medicines campaign it has taken millions of deaths from AIDS in Africa and a decade of work by activists to stir the pharmaceutical industry and US and EU officialdom into positive action. It takes time and energy to build networks that are capable of providing an international public good and time and energy to make sure the network stays in place for the long haul, rather than just the duration of the photo opportunities. Figuring out how to optimize the supply of international public goods in the absence of world government will occupy economists and others in debate for some time to come. We simply wish to point out that under conditions of information feudalism the supply of knowledge goods as public goods will probably suffer.

One important reason for the likely undersupply of public knowledge goods has to do with the impact of intellectual property rights on universities. Universities to date have been places where the rewards to individuals for the creation of knowledge have flowed from its diffusion rather than from keeping it a secret or placing a price on it. The diffusion of knowledge is a precondition to rewards of peer recognition and reputation. It is through the many individual acts of communication of their research at conferences, classes, in conversation, through journals, on the Internet and so on that researchers build the publicness of knowledge, a publicness that travels across many sectors of society and across borders. Through unrestricted communication knowledge goods come to life in a society as public goods. The project of information feudalism is to change these patterns of communication.

There is some evidence that this is happening. Universities, especially in the US, have steadily increased their patent portfolios to the point where they routinely patent less significant innovations.[5] In health technologies they have become significant patent players, accounting for 15 percent of all patents. One obvious effect of this is that an important societal source of public goods is drying up. At an individual level researchers become less motivated to explore areas of research where there is not some patent pay-off. This is troubling because university researchers will end up making the same kinds of profit calculations about basic research that companies do. Like companies they may decide not to pursue a problem the solution to which does not promise some commercial payoff. While we want some communities of researchers to be making predictions about the commercial relevance of their research we do not want *all* researchers operating in this way. The social and commercial benefit of much research is simply not predictable. Encouraging institutions that build knowledge on the basis of its inherent value, through curiosity rather than commercialism, is in fact a highly societally adaptive response because in that way the beneficial but unpredictable is found. When philosophers of logic like Russell and Whitehead spent time studying formal systems of logic, no one much thought they were laying down the foundations of computing languages. These days, of course, philosophers know to relabel their work as artificial reasoning or artificial intelligence in order to get corporate funding, as well as not to talk to researchers in other institutions about their work if they happen to hook on to an algorithm that looks like it might have the Midas touch about it.

Another reason why information feudalism will make the voluntaristic provision of international public goods harder has to do with the difficulty of making intellectual property owners part with their rights once they have acquired those rights. Under information feudalism intellectual property comes to be seen and protected as part of the natural order of things. Once intellectual property is seen in a more customary way, governments and other actors wishing to make use of knowledge assets for public good purposes will have a much harder time gaining access to those assets. Intellectual property owners may be reluctant to become part of a voluntary network to provide an international public good if it means giving up some of their intellectual property. Pharmaceutical companies are much happier with initiatives involving voluntary drug donations than with ones that threaten their intellectual property holdings. In the case of complex knowledge goods such as those to be found in biotechnology there may be so many intellectual property owners required to join the network that the network never comes to pass because of the negotiating costs of putting it together.

Information feudalism is a regime of property rights that is not economically efficient, and does not get the balance right between rewarding innovation and diffusing it. Like feudalism, it rewards guilds instead of inventive individual citizens. It makes democratic citizens trespassers on knowledge that should be the common heritage of humankind, their educational birthright. Ironically, information feudalism, by dismantling the publicness of knowledge, will eventually rob the knowledge economy of much of its productivity.

Notes

1 INTRODUCTION

1 See US Patent 6,368,227, issued 9 April 2002.
2 See Duncan Campbell, "Drug runs to Mexico offer a lifeline for US sick," *Guardian Weekly*, May 9–15, 2002, p3.
3 For details of the rise of prescription drug prices and its effects on the retired, see the AARP (formerly the American Association of Retired Persons) website at http://www.aarp.org/press/2002.
4 See Press Release, 17 November 1998, "Myriad Genetics Awarded Broad US Patent On BRCA2 Gene," at http://www.myriad.com.
5 George Orwell, "Marrakech" in George Orwell, *Collected Essays*, Mercury Books, London, 1961, p24.
6 http://www.unaids.org.
7 See *Report on the Global HIV/AIDS Epidemic*, June 2000, "Waking up to Devastation," available on the UNAIDS website.
8 For a description of anti-retroviral therapy, see "The Opportunities and Challenges of Introducing Anti-retroviral Therapy (ART) in Resource-Poor Settings," a consensus statement by organizations delivering AIDS projects for the Canadian International Development Agency, Ottawa, November 2001.
9 According to World Bank data, in 1998 46.3 percent of the population in sub-Saharan Africa were living on less than US$1.00 a day. See *World Development Report, 2000/2001: Attacking Poverty*, OUP, NY, 2001, p23. Globally 1.2 billion people live on less than US$1.00 a day and 2.8 billion live on less than $2.00 a day. See *Human Development Report 2001: Making New Technologies Work For Human Development*, United Nations Development Programme, OUP, NY, Oxford, 2001, p9.
10 This has been true in the past because of, among other things, cartelism in the pharmaceutical industry. See John Braithwaite, *Corporate Crime in the Pharmaceutical Industry*, Routledge, London, 1984, chapter 5. See also Gary Gereffi, *The Pharmaceutical Industry and Dependency in the Third World*, Princeton University Press, Princeton, New Jersey, 1983. For a survey of a sample of 16 drugs in 36 countries that shows the price of some proprietary drugs to be higher in the countries of Africa and Latin America than in OECD countries, see K. Bala and Kiran Sagoo "Patents and Prices," *HAI News*, No. 112, April/May 2000, p1–9. Even if the nominal price of a proprietary drug is cheaper in a developing country than it is in an OECD country, the crucial question is what percentage of a person's income does the price represent? GlaxoSmithKline is offering its anti-retroviral drugs AZT/3TC for US$2.00 a day, but if you live on a dollar a day it is twice your daily income.

11 4.2 million according to the UNAIDS website.

12 See Oxfam Background Briefing, "South Africa vs. the Drug Giants: A Challenge to Affordable Medicines," available from http://www.oxfam.org.uk/cutthecost.

13 The details of this international effort are described in "US Government Efforts to Negotiate the Repeal, Termination or Withdrawal of Article 15(c) of the South African Medicines and Related Substances Act Of 1965," United States Department of State, Washington, DC, 20520, 5 February 1999.

14 See Article 27.1.

15 See, for example, James P. Love, "The Orphan Drug Act and Government Sponsored Monopolies for Marketing Pharmaceutical Drugs," comments submitted to the Subcommittee on Antitrust, Monopolies, and Business Rights of the Committee on the Judiciary, US Senate, January 1992, Taxpayers Assets Project, Working Paper No. 6; James P. Love, "The Other Drug War: How Industry Exploits Pharm Subsidies," *The American Prospect*, 1993, No. 14, p121; Ralph Nader and James P. Love, "Federally Funded Pharmaceutical Inventions," testimony before the Special Committee on the Aging of the United States Senate, Taxpayers Assets Project, Working Paper No. 7, 24 February 1993.

16 For an account, see Ruth Mayne, "The Global NGO Campaign on Patents and Access to Medicines: An Oxfam Perspective" in Peter Drahos and Ruth Mayne (eds.), *Global Intellectual Property Rights: Knowledge Access and Development*, Macmillan, UK, 2002, chapter 15.

17 See *Fatal Imbalance: The Crisis in Research and Development for Drugs for Neglected Diseases*, Médecins Sans Frontières, Access to Essential Medicines Campaign and the Drugs for Neglected Diseases Working Group, September 2001, p10.

18 Roughly 60 percent of drugs would not have been discovered or would have been significantly delayed without public sector funding. See R. A. Maxwell and S. B. Eckhardt, *Drug Discovery: A Casebook and Analysis*, Humana Press, Clifton, NJ, 1990.

19 See, for example, the criticisms made of the large pharmaceutical industry's figures and assumptions in *Fatal Imbalance: The Crisis in Research and Development for Drugs for Neglected Diseases*, Médecins Sans Frontières, Access to Essential Medicines Campaign and the Drugs for Neglected Diseases Working Group, September 2001, p17.

20 See, for example, Communication from the Commission to the Council and the European Parliament: Programme for Action: Accelerated Action on HIV/AIDS, Malaria and Tuberculosis in the Context of Poverty Reduction (COM [2001] 95).

21 For a report of the meeting, see Barton Gellman, "A Turning Point That Left Millions Behind," *Washington Post* staff writer, Thursday, 28 December 2000; pA01, http://www.washingtonpost.com.

22 See Keith E. Maskus, "Intellectual Property Rights and Economic Development," *Case Western Reserve Journal of International Law*, vol. 32, 2000, p471; *Global Economic Prospects and the Developing Countries*, World Bank, Washington, DC, 2002, p133.

23 Office of Regulation Review, *An Economic Analysis of Copyright Reform*, Commonwealth of Australia, 1995, p39.

24 Nicholas Gruen, Ian Bruce and Gerard Prior, "Extending Patent Life: Is it in Australia's Economic Interests?," Industry Commission, Commonwealth of Australia, 1996.

25 See Surendra J. Patel, "Intellectual Property Rights in the Uruguay Round: A Disaster for the South?," *Economic and Political Weekly*, May 6, 1989, pp978, 980.

26 Douglass C. North, *Institutions, Institutional Change And Economic Performance*, Cambridge University Press, Cambridge, 1990.

27 R. Cooter and T. Ulen, *Law and Economics*, Addison-Wesley, Reading, Massachusetts, 1997.

28 M. Olson, *The Logic of Collective Action*, Harvard University Press, Cambridge, 1965.

29 See "Industry that Stalks the US Corridors of Power," *The Guardian*, Tuesday, 13 February 2001, p3.

30 P. Drahos, *A Philosophy of Intellectual Property*, Dartmouth, Aldershot, 1996.

31 Plato, *The Republic*, Penguin, 1974, p77.

32 See James Boyle, "A Politics of Intellectual Property: Environmentalism for the Net?" *Duke Law Journal*, vol. 47, 1997, p87.

2 PIRACY

1 From an English ballad published in 1609 and reproduced in part in Alfred P. Rubin, *The Law of Piracy*, Naval War College Press, Newport, RI, 1988, pp15–16.

2 See Philip Gosse, *The History of Piracy*, Longmans, Green and Co., London, 1932, p115.

3 This story is nicely told by Gosse, op. cit., pp110–111.

4 See *Sydney Morning Herald*, Monday, 23 May 1994, p25.

5 Philip Gosse, op. cit., p177.

6 Alfred P. Rubin, *The Law of Piracy*, Naval War College Press, Newport, RI, 1988.

7 Marcus Rediker, *Between the Devil and the Deep Blue Sea*, Cambridge, Cambridge University Press, 1989, p283.

8 Plutarch cited in Alfred P. Rubin, op. cit., p6.

9 Alfred P. Rubin, op. cit., p7.

10 "Microsoft plants secret users' code," *The Independent*, Monday, 8 March 1999, p2.

11 Response of Microsoft to the EC's Green Paper on Counterfeiting and Piracy in the Single Market, p7.

12 Anthea Worsdall and Andrew Clark, *Anti-Counterfeiting: A Practical Guide*, Jordans, Bristol, 1998, p1.

13 The story of the invention of printing is well told in G. H. Putnam, *Books and Their Makers During the Middle Ages*, 2nd ed, G. P. Putnam's Sons, New York, 1898, vol. 1, part II, chapter 2.

14 Cyprian Blagden, *The Stationers' Company: A History, 1403–1959*, George Allen & Unwin Ltd., London, 1960, p70.

15 Cyril Bathurst Judge, *Elizabethan Book-Pirates*, Harvard University Press, Cambridge, MA, 1934, p38.

16 The text of their defense is reproduced in Cyril Bathurst Judge, op. cit., pp86–87.

17 For an account of the book police, see Daniel Roche, "Censorship and the Publishing Industry," in Robert Darnton and Daniel Roche (eds.), *Revolution in Print: The Press in France 1775–1800*, University of California Press, Berkeley, CA, 1989, p3.

18 Raymond Birn, "Malesherbes and the Call for a Free Press," in Robert Darnton and Daniel Roche, op. cit., pp50, 51.

19 Ibid.

20 Carla Hesse, "Economic Upheavals in Publishing," in Robert Darnton and Daniel Roche, op. cit., pp69, 90.

21 Ibid.

22 William Briggs, *The Law of International Copyright*, Stevens & Haynes, London, 1906, p37.
23 M. Kampelman, "The United States and International Copyright," *American Journal of International Law*, 1947, vol. 41, pp406, 415.
24 William Briggs, op. cit., p40.
25 Cited in William Briggs, op. cit., p101.
26 William Briggs, op. cit., p93.
27 This description of the Austrian law appeared in an article in the *Scientific American*. Austrian authorities were referred to it by the American minister in Vienna. See Edith Tilton Penrose, *The Economics of the International Patent System*, Johns Hopkins Press, Baltimore, MD, 1951, p45.
28 Cited in Harold G. Fox, *Monopolies and Patents*, University of Toronto Press, Toronto, 1947, p71.
29 Harold G. Fox, op. cit., p70.
30 Harold G. Fox, op. cit., p127.
31 Edith Tilton Penrose, op. cit., pp16–17.
32 John Braithwaite, *Corporate Crime in the Pharmaceutical Industry*, Routledge, London, 1984, chapter 5.
33 See K. Bala and Kiran Sagoo, "Patents and Prices," *HAI News*, no. 112, April/May 2000, p1.
34 H. G. Henn, "The Quest for International Copyright Protection," *Cornell Law Quarterly*, 1953, vol. 39, pp43, 65.

3 THE KNOWLEDGE GAME

1 Peter Drucker, *Post-Capitalist Society*, Harper Business, New York, 1993, p8.
2 David A. Hounshell and John Kenly Smith, Jr., *Science and Corporate Strategy: DuPont R&D, 1902–1980*, Cambridge University Press, Cambridge, 1988, p11.
3 David Mercer, *IBM: How the World's Most Successful Corporation Is Managed*, Kogan Page, London, 1987, pp24–26.
4 The term comes from Ikujiro Nonaka and Hirotaka Takeuchi, *The Knowledge-Creating Company*, OUP, New York, Oxford, 1995.
5 David A. Hounshell and John Kenly Smith, Jr., op. cit., p2.
6 Edison, cited in David F. Noble, *America by Design*, Alfred A. Knopf, New York, 1979, p8.
7 David A. Hounshell and John Kenly Smith, Jr., op. cit., p366.
8 David F. Noble, op. cit., pp112–113.
9 Alfred D. Chandler, Jr., *The Visible Hand: The Managerial Revolution in American Business*, Belknap Press of Harvard University Press, Cambridge, MA, 1977, p375.
10 David F. Noble, op. cit., p116.
11 Alfred D. Chandler, Jr., *Strategy and Structure: Chapters in the History of the Industrial Enterprise*, The MIT Press, Cambridge, MA, 1962, p375.
12 Alfred D. Chandler, Jr., op. cit., 1962, p24.
13 David F. Noble, op. cit., p9.
14 Henry Ford in David F. Noble, op. cit., p113.
15 See the address by R. B. Ransford, president of the Chartered Institute of Patent Agents, "The Profession of Patent Agency," in *The Chartered Institute of Patent Agents: Transactions*, vol. XXXVIII, Session 1919–20, pp15, 20.

16 Edwin J. Prindle, "The marvellous performance of the American patent system," *Journal of the Patent Office Society*, 1927–28, vol. 10, pp255, 258.

17 Comments, *Journal of the Patent Office Society*, 1922, vol. 4, pp361, 362.

18 Prindle, in David F. Noble, op. cit., p89.

19 Dr. Hermann Isay, *Die Patentgemeinschaft im Dienst des Kartellgedankens* (1923) quoted in Ervin Hexner, *International Cartels*, Sir Isaac Pitman & Sons, London, 1946, p72.

20 Norman Waddleton, "The British Patent Agent in the last 100 years," Presidential Address to the Chartered Institute of Patent Agents, 17 December 1980, p7.

21 David A. Hounshell and John Kenly Smith, Jr., op. cit., p302.

22 David A. Hounshell and John Kenly Smith, Jr., op. cit., p370.

23 This story is nicely told in Paul Carroll, *Big Blues; The Unmaking of IBM*, Weidenfeld & Nicolson, London, 1994, pp343–345.

24 The director of DuPont's Chemical Department, Elmer Bolton, cited in David A. Hounshell and John Kenly Smith, Jr., op. cit., p177.

25 George W. Stocking and Myron W. Watkins, *Cartels in Action*, Twentieth Century Fund, New York, 1947, p467.

26 Abraham S. Greenberg, "The Lesson of the German-Owned US Chemical Patents," *Journal of the Patent Office Society*, 1926–27, vol. 9, pp19, 20.

27 Felix Frankfurter, "The Business of the Supreme Court: A Study in the Federal Judicial System," *Journal of the Patent Office Society*, 1926–27, vol. 9, pp8, 10.

28 See a letter written to the *New York Times*, 2 February 1930, by Joseph J. O'Brien, reprinted in *Journal of the Patent Office Society*, 1930, vol. 12, pp225–230.

29 Alfred D. Chandler, Jr., op. cit., 1977, p317.

30 A copy of the agreement is to be found in William S. Stevens (ed.), *Industrial Combinations and Trusts*, Macmillan Company, New York, 1913, pp4–7.

31 William S. Stevens (ed.), op. cit., p2.

32 For a 19th-century text that discusses what was then recent case law in the US see Thomas Carl Spelling, *A Treatise on Trusts and Monopolies*, Little, Brown, and Company, Boston, 1893, chapter V.

33 A copy of the trust agreement is to be found in William S. Stevens (ed.), op. cit., pp14–17.

34 A point that Louis Brandeis made in the Hearings before the Committee on Interstate Commerce on the Control of Corporations, Persons and Firms engaged in Interstate Commerce, 62nd Congress, 2nd Session. The relevant passage is contained in William S. Stevens (ed.), op. cit., p579.

35 Joseph E. Davies, Commissioner of Corporations, *Trust Laws and Unfair Competition*, report of Bureau of Corporations, Department of Commerce, Government Printing Office, Washington, DC, 1916, p9.

36 Judge Edward B. Whitney cited in Joseph E. Davies, op. cit., p9.

37 Northern Securities Co. vs. US 193 US 197 (1904).

38 See Alfred D. Chandler, Jr., op. cit., 1962.

39 Jerrold G. Van Cise, *A Practical Guide to the Antitrust Laws*, Practicing Law Institute, US, 1949, p20.

40 See, for instance, US v. United Shoe Mach. Co. 247 US 32, (1918); US v. Gen. Elec. Co. 272 US 476, (1926); Sidney Henry v. A. B. Dick Company 224 US 1, (1912).

41 Paul Carroll, op. cit., p111.

42 David A. Hounshell and John Kenly Smith, Jr., op. cit., pp495–497.

43 Alfred D. Chandler, Jr., op. cit., 1962, p377.

44 Alfred D. Chandler, Jr., op. cit., 1977, p480.

45 George W. Stocking and Myron W. Watkins, op. cit., p448.

46 George W. Stocking and Myron W. Watkins, op. cit., p4.

47 George W. Stocking and Myron W. Watkins, op. cit., p329.

48 L. Jacobs cited in William F. Hellmuth, Jr., "The Motion Picture Industry," in Walter Adams (ed.), *The Structure of American Industry*, 3rd ed, Macmillan Company, New York, 1961, pp393, 399.

49 Straus & Straus v. American Publishers' Association 231 US 222, (1913).

50 US v. Paramount Pictures, Inc. 334 US 131, (1948).

51 See US v. Addison-Wesley Publishing Co., 1976–2 Trade Cas. (CCH) 61,225.

52 David A. Hounshell and John Kenly Smith, Jr., op. cit., p193.

53 Evidence cited in US v. Chemical Foundation 294 Fed. 300, 309 (D.C.Del.).

54 A. C. Seward, *Science and the Nation*, 1917, cited in Abraham S. Greenberg, op. cit., pp19, 22.

55 Abraham S. Greenberg, op. cit., pp19, 23.

56 See US v. Chemical Foundation Inc., 272 US 1, (1926).

57 Abraham S. Greenberg, op. cit., pp19, 23.

58 President of the US in his message of 20 May 1919 to Congress, quoted in US v. Chemical Foundation 294 Fed. 300, 310 (D.C.Del.).

59 Paul Carroll, op. cit., p5.

60 Christopher Tugendhat, *The Multinationals*, Pelican, 1973, p153.

61 See John H. Dunning and Robert D. Pearce, *The World's Largest Industrial Enterprises*, Gower, Aldershot, UK, 1981, p36.

62 David A. Hounshell and John Kenly Smith, Jr., op. cit., p510.

63 See David A. Hounshell and John Kenly Smith, Jr., op. cit., p346.

64 See Paul Carroll, op. cit., pp32–33, 89.

65 R. Ballance, J. Pogany and H. Forstner, *The World's Pharmaceutical Industries: An International Perspective on Innovation, Competition and Policy*, Edward Elgar, Aldershot; Brookfield VT, USA, 1992.

4 STEALING FROM THE MIND

1 Royal Dutch Shell and Unilever for each of those years except 1978 when National Iranian Oil replaced Unilever. See John H. Dunning and Robert D. Pearce, *The World's Largest Industrial Enterprises*, Gower, Aldershot, UK, 1981, p148.

2 See F. T. Blackaby (ed.), *De-industrialization*, Heinemann, London, 1979.

3 See Ajit Singh, "The Long-term Structural Disequilibrium of the UK Economy: Employment, Trade, and Import Controls," in Gunnar Sjostedt and Bengt Sundelius (eds.), *Free Trade—Managed Trade?*, Westview Press, Boulder, CO, 1986, p51.

4 R. J. Barnet and John Cavanagh, *Global Dreams*, Simon and Schuster, New York, 1994, pp46–47.

5 See W. Max Corden, "The Revival of Protectionism in Developed Countries," in D. Salvatore (ed.), *The New Protectionist Threat to World Welfare*, North-Holland, New York, 1987, pp45, 61–64.

6 A good account of the company's early history is to be found on the Pfizer website, www.pfizer.com.

7 See Michael A. Santoro, "Pfizer: Protecting Intellectual Property in a Global Marketplace," Harvard Business School, Cambridge, MA, 1992, p2.

8 See the Pfizer website, www.pfizer.com/150/1951.htm.

9 See Michael A. Santoro, op. cit., 1992, p6.
10 See Michael A. Santoro, op. cit., 1992, p7.
11 See Michael A. Santoro, op. cit., 1992, pp2, 4.
12 See Dr. David J. Hill, "Letters to the Editor," *The Independent*, 17 December 1998, p10.
13 See the speech by Pratt at www.pfizer.com.
14 See Michael A. Santoro, op. cit., 1992, p8.
15 Ibid.
16 The recommendations of ACTN are contained in some unpublished papers: "Summary of the Recommendations of the Advisory Committee on Trade Negotiations' Task Force on Intellectual Property," undated, 11 pages; "Summary of the Phase II: Recommendations of the Task Force on Intellectual Property to the Advisory Committee for Trade Negotiations," March 1986, 8 pages.

5 THE ILLUSION OF SOVEREIGNTY

1 Richard Webb, "Wage Policy and Income Distribution in Developing Countries," in C. R. Frank, Jr. and Richard C. Webb (eds.), *Income Distribution and Growth in the Less-Developed Countries*, The Brookings Institution, Washington, DC, 1977, p215.
2 G. Myrdal, *Asian Drama: An Inquiry into the Poverty of Nations*, vol. III, Penguin, Harmondsworth, 1968, p1647.
3 G. Myrdal, op. cit., 1968, p1641.
4 G. Myrdal, *The Challenge of World Poverty*, Penguin, Middlesex, England, 1970, p176.
5 G. Myrdal, op. cit., 1968, p1693.
6 G. Myrdal, op. cit., 1968, p1698.
7 S. Ricketson, *The Berne Convention for the Protection of Literary and Artistic Works: 1886–1986*, Centre for Commercial Law Studies, London, 1987, p791.
8 S. Ricketson, op. cit., p792.
9 Bureaux internationaux réunis pour la protection de la propriété intellectuelle (WIPO's predecessor organization).
10 See Alan H. Lazar, "Developing Countries and Authors' Rights in International Copyright," in *Copyright Law Symposium*, vol. 19, Columbia University Press, New York, 1971, pp1, 17–18.
11 S. Ricketson, op. cit., pp799, 803.
12 Alan H. Lazar, op. cit., p14.
13 S. Ricketson, op. cit., p593.
14 C. F. Johnson, "The Origins of the Stockholm Protocol," *Bulletin of the Copyright Society of the USA*, 1970–71, vol. 18, pp91, 142–143, 180.
15 A. Tournier, the director-general of Société des Auteurs, Compositeurs et Editeurs de Musique, cited in Alan H. Lazar, op. cit., p4.
16 Letter from the vice chairman of the British Copyright Council, *The Times*, 13 April 1967, cited in C. F. Johnson, op. cit., p180.
17 See Article 28(1)(b)(I) of Stockholm Act of the Berne Convention. See also D. M. Schrader, "Analysis of the Protocol Regarding Developing Countries," *Bulletin of the Copyright Society of the USA*, 1969–70, vol. 17, pp160, 232.
18 J. T. Simone, Jr., "Protection of American Copyrights on Books in Taiwan," *Bulletin of the Copyright Society of the USA*, 1987–88, vol. 35, pp115, 120, fn15.

19 See W. T. S. Gould, *People and Education in the Third World*, Longman Scientific & Technical, Harlow, UK, 1993, pp50–59.

20 A report of the debates at the seminar is to be found in "East Asian Seminar on Copyright," *Copyright*, 1967, vol. 3, pp42–48. The following states sent designated participants: Afghanistan, Cambodia, Ceylon, India, Indonesia, Iran, Japan, Korea, Laos, Malaysia, Nepal, Philippines, Singapore, Thailand.

21 Mr. Dadameah, "East Asian Seminar on Copyright," *Copyright*, 1967, vol. 3, p43.

22 Secretary Kirpal's inaugural address is available at *Copyright*, 1967, vol. 3, pp50–51.

23 Alan H. Lazar, op. cit., p26.

24 House of Commons, *Parliamentary Debates*, 19 March 1907, cited in Edith Penrose, *The Economics of the International Patent System*, Johns Hopkins Press, Baltimore, MD, 1951, p140, fn9.

25 See S. M. Thomas and N. Simmonds, *The Industrial Use of Genome Resources in Europe*, European Commission, Science Research and Development, Luxembourg, 1999, p7.

26 Edith Penrose, op. cit., p112.

27 Ove Granstrand, *The Economics and Management of Intellectual Property: Towards Intellectual Capitalism*, Edward Elgar, Cheltenham, UK, 1999, p92.

28 Z. Mirza, "WTO, Pharmaceuticals and Health: Impacts and Strategies," in *International Roundtable on Responses to Globalization: Rethinking Equity in Health, Geneva, 12–14 July 1999*, p21.

29 Z. Mirza, "WTO/TRIPS, Pharmaceuticals and Health: Impacts and Strategies," *Development*, 1999, vol. 42(4), pp92, 93.

30 Ervin Hexner, *International Cartels*, Isaac Pitman and Sons, London, 1946, pp308–339.

31 S. Vedaraman, "The New Indian Patents Law," *International Review of Industrial Property and Copyright Law*, 1972, vol. 3, pp39, 43.

32 S. Vedaraman, op. cit., p46.

33 From 1963 to 1968 the membership of the convention increased from 51 to 79. See G. H. C. Bodenhausen, *Guide to the Application of the Paris Convention for the Protection of Industrial Property*, BIRPI, Geneva, 1968, p7.

34 Dealt with in Article 5A of the Paris Convention. See D. M. Mills, "Patents and the Exploitation of Technology Transferred to Developing Countries (in Particular, Those of Africa)," *Industrial Property*, 1985, vol. 24, pp120, 122.

35 "The Indispensable Trade Weapon: 301/Special 301," Jack Valenti, president and chief executive officer, Motion Picture Association of America, before the Senate Finance Committee, Washington, DC, 6 March 1992.

36 See Article 4 of the GATT 1947.

37 See T. D. Andersen, *Geopolitics of the Caribbean*, Praeger Publishers, New York, 1984, pp148–151.

38 See Section 212(b)(5).

39 See Section 212(b)(2)(B)(ii).

40 See HR Rep. No. 98–325, 98th Cong., 1st Sess. 55 (27 July 1983).

41 See the reported remarks of Emery Simon, director of intellectual property in the Office of the USTR, *BNA's Patent, Trademark & Copyright Journal*, vol. 32, 22 May 1986, p80.

6 THE BILATERALS

1 See Senator Max Baucus, "A New Trade Strategy: The Case for Bilateral Agreements," *Cornell International Law Journal*, 1989, vol. 22, p1, fn4.

2 Senator Max Baucus, op. cit., p1.

3 P. Hoffer, "Upheaval in the United Nations System: United States' Withdrawal from UNESCO," *Brooklyn Journal of International Law*, 1986, vol. 12, pp161, 162, fn6.

4 Title V of the Trade Act 1974.

5 See *BNA's Patent, Trademark & Copyright Journal*, 9 February 1984, vol. 27, p358.

6 Susan K. Sell, "Intellectual Property Protection and Antitrust in the Developing World: Crisis, Coercion, and Choice," *International Organization*, 1995, vol. 49, pp315, 322.

7 This is not entirely accurate. Some Caribbean states had inherited copyright law from the UK.

8 See Report of Committee on Trade and Development (L/5913) in *Basic Instruments and Selected Documents, General Agreement on Tariffs and Trade*, 32nd Supplement (1984–1985), 21, 26.

9 Like the EC, the US had little interest in influencing the poorest countries: "With Bangladesh, you have nothing to win and nothing to lose. They have no capacity to copy with top quality. So you disregard them in the debate" (1993 EC interview).

10 See Jacques J. Gorlin, "A Trade-based Approach for the International Copyright Protection for Computer Software," unpublished, 1 September 1985.

11 See *BNA's Patent, Trademark & Copyright Journal*, 11 February 1988, vol. 35, p282.

12 "Special 301" was an amendment made to Section 182 of the Trade Act of 1974 by the Omnibus Trade and Competitiveness Act of 1988. Codified as 19 USC Sec. 2242. There were further amendments under the Uruguay Round Agreements Act of 1994.

13 The following information is taken from an undated information sheet provided by the IIPA.

14 Statement of Eric H. Smith, executive director and general counsel, IIPA, Hearing before the Subcommittee on Intellectual Property and Judicial Administration of the House Committee on the Judiciary, on Right of Distribution (Including Rental and Importation in connection with examination of Questions Concerning a Possible Protocol to the Berne Convention and Questions Concerning a Possible Instrument on the Protection of Rights of Performers and Producers of Phonograms), 29 April 1993, p2.

15 See 19 USC 2412.

16 IIPA Press Release, 12 February 1993.

17 The Fact Sheet is reproduced in *BNA's Patent, Trademark & Copyright Journal*, 1 June 1989, vol. 38, pp131–134.

18 A point made by the Italian government in its "Report on Videographic Piracy" unpublished, 1992, p2.

19 See IPPA 1993, "Special 301 Recommendations and Estimated Trade Losses Due to Piracy," submitted to the United States Trade Representative on 12 February 1993.

20 Jacques J. Gorlin, op. cit., p10.

21 Stephen E. Siwek and Harold Furchtgott-Roth, Economists Incorporated, produced *Copyright Industries in the US Economy*, November 1990, *Copyright*

Industries in the US Economy: 1977–1990, September 1992 and *Copyright Industries in the US Economy: 1993 Perspective,* October 1993 for the IIPA.

22 Stephen E. Siwek and Harold W. Furchtgott-Roth, Economists Incorporated, *The US Software Industry: Economic Contribution in the US and World Markets,* prepared for the Business Software Alliance, Spring, 1993, p40.

23 Stephen E. Siwek and Harold W. Furchtgott-Roth, op. cit., p41.

24 Letter of 22 July 1992 from Carla A. Hills to Mr. Frank G. Wells, president and chief operating officer of the Walt Disney Company.

25 "The Indispensable Trade Weapon: 301/Special 301" Jack Valenti, president and chief executive officer, Motion Picture Association of America, before the Senate Finance Committee, Washington, DC, 6 March 1992, pp9–10.

26 Details of these cases are available from the table of initiated Section 301 cases on the USTR's website at www.ustr.gov.

27 See chapter 4 of Summary of Federal Register Submissions, Second Report to Congress on the Operation of the Caribbean Basin Economic Recovery Act, 1992–1996, available at www.ustr.gov/reports.

28 See *BNA's Patent, Trademark and Copyright Journal,* 3 May 1990, vol. 40, pp9, 10.

29 The EC adopted the same philosophy: "Hungary is in an ante chamber—a waiting room while they are proving themselves to Europe. They are moving. IP is important for attracting foreign direct investment. Albania—IP is a luxury for them; they'll get to it later. This does not mean we can't reach strong agreements on IP with them. We do. We just give them a long transition period to get around to putting it in place" (1993 EC).

30 "Technological Progress and American Rights: Trade Policy and Intellectual Property Protection," Testimony of Ambassador Richard W. Fisher, Deputy US Trade Representative, Subcommittee on International Economic Policy and Trade House Committee on International Relations, Washington, DC, 13 October 1999, p3.

31 Thailand, USTR's *2000 Special 301 Report.*

32 J. Braithwaite and P. Drahos, *Global Business Regulation,* Cambridge University Press, Cambridge, 2000, p180.

33 Susan K. Sell, op. cit., p325.

34 Yeutter's talk is reported in *BNA's Patent, Trademark & Copyright Journal,* 30 October 1986, vol. 32, p736.

35 In 1995 the US trade surplus with Korea was US$1.2 billion, a shift from a US$1.6 billion deficit in 1994. Source 1996 National Trade Estimate.

36 19 USC 2242(b)(1)(C).

37 See, for example, R. E. Hudec, "Dispute Settlement," in J. J. Schott (ed.), *Completing the Uruguay Round,* Institute for International Economics, Washington, DC, 1990, pp180, 198. On the action against Brazil the trade expert John H. Jackson observed that the "United States action is clearly a violation of the GATT." See "Remarks of Professor John J. Jackson" in Symposium: Trade-Related Aspects of Intellectual Property in *Vanderbilt Journal of Transnational Law,* 1989, vol. 22, pp343, 346.

38 One of the Four Heavenly Kings of Hacking. See Sang Ye (Geremie R. Barmé, trans.), "Computer Insect," *Wired* July 1996, pp82, 84.

39 USTR's *2000 Special 301 Report,* p11.

40 See Special 301 USTR "Fact Sheet" for 1996.

7 AGENDAS AND AGENDA-SETTERS: THE MULTILATERAL GAME

1 Arpad Bogsch, *Brief History of the First 25 Years of the World Intellectual Property Organization*, World Intellectual Property Organization, Geneva, 1992.
2 In 1965 the contracting parties allowed the head of the GATT secretariat to be known by the title of director-general.
3 Generally the protection of indications of source or appellations of origin remains in international terms comparatively undeveloped despite being recognized in Article 10 of the Paris Convention for the Protection of Industrial Property and being the subject of a special union within the Paris Union (the countries that are members of the Paris Convention) — the Madrid Arrangement for the Registration of False or Deceptive Indications of Source. The Lisbon Agreement for the Protection of Appellations of Origin and their International Registration of 31 October 1958, as revised, has a small membership and is not mentioned in TRIPS. For a discussion of the reluctance of countries to protect this form of intellectual property too strongly see Stephen P. Ladas, *Patents, Trademarks, and Related Rights*, vol. 3, Harvard University Press, Cambridge, MA, 1975, chapter 43.
4 See also Articles XII(3)(c) and XVIII(10).
5 Pointed out by Alice Zalik, in "Remarks of Alice T. Zalik," Symposium: Trade-Related Aspects Of Intellectual Property, *Vanderbilt Journal of Transnational Law*, 1989, vol. 22, p330.
6 See Ulrich Joos and Rainer Moufang, "Report on the Second Ringberg-Symposium," in Friedrich-Karl Beier and Gerhard Schricker (eds.), *GATT or WIPO?: New Ways in the Protection of Intellectual Property*, Max Planck Institute for Foreign and International Patent, Copyright, and Competition Law, Munich, and VCH Publishers, Weinheim, 1989, pp3, 30.
7 L/5424: BISD 29S/19.
8 Daniel Gervais, *The TRIPS Agreement: Drafting History and Analysis*, Sweet and Maxwell, London, 1998, p8, fn25.
9 Daniel Gervais, op. cit., p8.
10 See Michael Blakeney, *Legal Aspects of the Transfer of Technology to Developing Countries*, ESC Publishing Limited, Oxford, 1989, pp98–104.
11 Hans Peter Kunz-Hallstein, "The United States Proposal for a GATT Agreement on Intellectual Property and the Paris Convention for the Protection of Industrial Property," *Vanderbilt Journal of Transnational Law*, 1989, vol. 22, p265.
12 Jacques Gorlin, "A Trade-Based Approach for the International Copyright Protection for Computer Software," unpublished, 1 September 1985, p22.
13 See WIPO, "General Information," Geneva, 1990, p71.
14 See J. Braithwaite and P. Drahos, *Global Business Regulation*, Cambridge University Press, Cambridge, 2000, chapter 24.
15 Hamish Sandison, "The Berne Convention and the Universal Copyright Convention: The American Experience," *Columbia-VLA Journal of Law & Arts*, 1986, vol. 11, pp89, 97.
16 See Ndéné Ndiaye, "The Berne Convention and Developing Countries," *Columbia-VLA Journal Of Law & Arts*, 1986, vol. 11, pp47, 53–54.
17 Arpad Bogsch was elected director-general of WIPO in 1973 and reelected in 1979, 1985 and 1991.

18 See Private Sector Advisory Committee System, USTR, 1994 Annual Report, www.ustr.gov/reports.
19 See Charter of the Advisory Committee for Trade Policy and Negotiations.
20 Taken from "Summary of the Recommendations of the Advisory Committee on Trade Negotiations' Task Force on Intellectual Property," undated.
21 Taken from "Recommendations of the Task Force on Intellectual Property to the Advisory Committee for Trade Negotiations," Summary of Phase II, March 1986.
22 Jacques Gorlin, op. cit., p47, fn 47.
23 See BNA's Patent, Trademark & Copyright Journal, 13 February 1986, vol. 31, p285.
24 See Edmund Pratt, "Intellectual Property Rights and International Trade," speech to US Council for International Business, available at www.pfizer.com/pfizerinc/policy/forum.
25 IPC, "Accomplishments and Current Activities of the Intellectual Property Committee," 14 June 1988.
26 F. Warshofsky, Patent Wars, John Wiley, Chichester, 1994.
27 Document MIN.DEC of 20 September 1986, reprinted in Terence P. Stewart (ed.), The GATT Uruguay Round: A Negotiating History (1986–1992), vol. 3, Kluwer Law and Taxation Publishers, Deventer, Boston, pp1–10.
28 Daniel Gervais, op. cit., p11.

8 PERSUASION AND PRINCIPLES

1 Talk by Emery Simon at the Second Ringberg Symposium, 13–16 July 1988, summarized in Ulrich Joos and Rainer Moufang, "Report on the Second Ringberg-Symposium," in Friedrich-Karl Beier and Gerhard Schricker (eds.), GATT or WIPO?: New Ways in the Protection of Intellectual Property, Max Planck Institute for Foreign and International Patent, Copyright, and Competition Law, Munich, and VCH Publishers, Weinheim, New York, 1989, pp3, 25.
2 See Council Regulation 2641/84.
3 See the observation that "GATT negotiators must guard against the diminution of intellectual property protection," in Basic Framework of GATT Provisions on Intellectual Property: Statement of Views of the European, Japanese and United States Business Communities, The Intellectual Property Committee (USA), Keidanren (Japan), UNICE (Europe), 1988, p24.
4 Speech by Edmund T. Pratt to US Council for International Business, "Intellectual Property Rights and International Trade," available at www.pfizer.com/pfizerinc/policy/forum.
5 IPC Press Release, Tuesday 14 June 1988.
6 Friedrich Kretschmer, head of the Legal and Insurance Department, BDI (Federation of German Industry), "The Present Position of the US, Japanese and European Industry," in Friedrich-Karl Beier and Gerhard Schricker, op. cit., pp95, 96.
7 Basic Framework of GATT Provisions on Intellectual Property: Statement of Views of the European, Japanese and United States Business Communities, The Intellectual Property Committee (USA), Keidanren (Japan), UNICE (Europe), 1988, p32.
8 "Existence, scope and form of generally internationally accepted and applied standards/norms for the protection of intellectual property," World Intellectual Property Organization, WO/INF/29 September 1988, issued as GATT document number MTN.GNG/NG11/W/24/Rev. 1.

9 For a discussion of US bilateralism on copyright and computer software, see Thomas Dreier, "National Treatment, Reciprocity and Retorsion—The Case of Computer Programs and Integrated Circuits," in Friedrich-Karl Beier and Gerhard Schricker, op. cit., pp65–74.

10 For example, the report points out that there is a "general trend towards the elimination of formalities as a condition of copyright protection," an important exception being the US where the copyright notice is a "condition of enjoyment and exercise of copyright." See "Existence, scope and form of generally internationally accepted and applied standards/norms for the protection of intellectual property," World Intellectual Property Organization, WO/INF/29 September 1988, Part II: Copyright, Section 2, para (iii).

11 "Suggestion by the United States for Achieving the Negotiating Objective," GATT-Doc.MTN.GNG/NG11/W/14 (20 October 1987) and "Suggestion by the United States for Achieving the Negotiating Objective—Revision," GATT-Doc.MTN. GNG/NG11/W/14Rev. 1 (17 October 1988).

12 This is true in Section III of the communication by the US of 13 October 1988. This section describes the standards for protection of intellectual property rights and in doing so draws on the fundamental principles articulated by the Basic Framework.

13 David P. Angel, *Restructuring for Innovation: The Remaking of the US Semiconductor Industry*, The Guilford Press, New York, 1994, p1.

14 David P. Angel, op. cit., pp39–40.

15 Article 9 of TRIPS excludes moral rights as set out in Article 6[bis] of the Berne Convention for the Protection of Literary and Artistic Works from being part of the rights and obligations created by TRIPS.

16 Article 14 of TRIPS recognizes minimal rights of protection for performers.

17 Friedrich Kretschmer, op. cit., p95.

18 Ibid.

19 The GATT Antidumping Code of 1979 was the subject of negotiation in the Uruguay Round.

20 See USTR Fact Sheet for "Special 301" on Intellectual Property in *BNA's Patent, Trademark & Copyright Journal*, 1 June 1989, vol. 38, p131.

21 European negotiators knew it was just a matter of time. Included in the 17 countries that were placed on the Special 301 watch list in 1989 were Greece, Italy, Spain and Yugoslavia. Canada and Japan, both Quad partners, were also listed. In 1993 a USTR Fact Sheet (30 April 1993) reported that the European Community was retained on the priority watch list because it "restricts market access for US audiovisual exports and engages in other objectionable practices" concerning US intellectual property.

22 Article 27(1) of TRIPS requires that patents be available "without discrimination as to place of invention." The US implemented the required change to Section 104 in the 1994 Uruguay Round Agreements Act, which allows the establishment of a date of invention by reference to knowledge in a WTO member country.

23 Amendments to Section 337 in the 1988 Trade Act made it easier for US plaintiffs to succeed in preventing the importation of infringing articles into the US. A GATT panel did decide that Section 337 violated the GATT.

24 UNICE Position Paper, "GATT and Intellectual Property," 12 May 1987, p2.

25 The best evidence of this is the communication to the GATT by the European Communities, entitled "Guidelines proposed by the European Community for the negotiations on trade-related aspects of intellectual property rights," 19

November 1987, GATT-Doc. MTN.GNG/NG11/W/16. The document referring to the Punta del Este declaration suggests that new rules and disciplines need to be drawn up for intellectual property and that these "should apply to all IPRs." Much like the IPC, the European negotiators now saw in the Punta del Este declaration a strong mandate to develop a trade-based intellectual property regime that went well beyond the problem of counterfeiting and piracy.

26 Intellectual Property Committee paper entitled "Accomplishments and Current Activities of the Intellectual Property Committee," 14 June 1988, p4.

27 The Friends Group included the US, European Community, Japan, Canada, Switzerland, Sweden and Australia.

28 The meeting produced a document outlining areas of agreement and difference among the respective delegations. See "Notes on Informal Meeting on Intellectual Property Standards, 7–11 March 1988," in Friedrich-Karl Beier and Gerhard Schricker, op. cit., pp335–352.

29 *Basic Framework of GATT Provisions on Intellectual Property: Statement of Views of the European, Japanese and United States Business Communities*, The Intellectual Property Committee (USA), Keidanren (Japan), UNICE (Europe), 1988, p8.

30 Barbara Ringer, "The Role of the United States in International Copyright—Past, Present, and Future," *Georgetown Law Journal*, 1968, vol. 56, pp1050, 1051.

31 Article 5(2) of the Berne Convention.

32 For a discussion, see Hamish Sandison, "The Berne Convention and the Universal Copyright Convention: The American Experience," *Columbia-VLA Journal of Law & Arts*, 1986, vol. 11, pp89, 104–119.

33 Jacques Gorlin, "A Trade-Based Approach for the International Copyright Protection for Computer Software," unpublished, 1 September 1985, p59.

34 Ringer in Jacques Gorlin, op. cit., p59, fn54.

35 Statement of Mr. Kenneth W. Dam, vice president, IBM Corporation, cited in "Existence, scope and form of generally internationally accepted and applied standards/norms for the protection of intellectual property," World Intellectual Property Organization, WO/INF/29 September 1988, issued as GATT document number MTN.GNG/NG11/W/24/Rev, Part II, para (3)(i).

36 Jacques Gorlin, op. cit., p61.

37 See Annette V. Tucker, "The Validity of the Manufacturing Clause of the United States Copyright Code as Challenged by Trade Partners and Copyright Owners," *Vanderbilt Journal of Transnational Law*, 1985, vol. 18, pp577, 580.

38 For a more detailed history of the lobbying, see J. Hayden Boyd, "Deregulating Book Imports," *Regulation*, 1991, vol. 14, p64.

39 The Report of the Panel was adopted on 15–16 May 1984.

40 J. Hayden Boyd, op. cit..

41 There are some technical qualifications to this, having to do with the application of the section to works imported or distributed in the US between 1 January 1978 and 1 July 1986. See Goldstein, *Copyright*, 2nd ed, 1999 Supplement, 3.16.

9 AT THE NEGOTIATING TABLE

1 A. Jane Bradley, "Intellectual Property Rights, Investment, and Trade in Services in the Uruguay Round: Laying the Foundations," *Stanford Journal of International Law*, 1987, vol. 23, pp57, 81, fn 72.

2   See *Decisions of 28 January 1987* (GATT/1405 5 February 1987), reprinted in Terence P. Stewart (ed.), *The GATT Uruguay Round: A Negotiating History (1986–1992)*, volume III, Kluwer Law and Taxation Publishers, Deventer, Boston, 1993, pp11–25.

3   See para 2 of Annex 2A of *Decisions of 28 January 1987*.

4   See Annex 2 of *Decisions of 28 January 1987*.

5   A list of the working documents within the TRIPS negotiating group is to be found in the bibliography in J. C. Ross and J. A. Wasserman, "Trade-Related Aspects of Intellectual Property Rights," in Terence P. Stewart (ed.), *The GATT Uruguay Round: A Negotiating History (1986–1992)*, volume II, Kluwer Law and Taxation Publishers, Deventer, Boston, 1993, pp2241, 2320–2329.

6   This is based on a count of the working documents to be found in J. C. Ross and J. A. Wasserman, op. cit., pp2320–2329.

7   See USTR Fact Sheet for "Special 301" on Intellectual Property, in *BNA's Patent, Trademark & Copyright Journal*, 1 June 1989, vol. 38, p131.

8   See "Mid-Term Meeting," in Terence P. Stewart (ed.), op. cit., pp44–45.

9   For a detailed account of the role of the GATT secretariat, see Chakravarthi Raghavan, "India Yields in Uruguay Round," *Mainstream*, 6 May 1989, p15.

10 See Chakravarthi Raghavan, op. cit., pp22.

11 Jayashree Watal, *Intellectual Property Rights: In the WTO and Developing Countries*, OUP, New Delhi, 2001, p27.

12 Mr. S. P. Shukla, Indian ambassador to the GATT at that time quoted in *Agriculture in Dunkel's Draft of GATT—A Critical Analysis*, Third World Network, New Delhi, 1993, p6.

13 See, for example, Daniel Gervais, *The TRIPS Agreement: Drafting History and Analysis*, Sweet and Maxwell, London, 1998, p15; Jacques J. Gorlin, *An Analysis of the Pharmaceutical-Related Provisions of the WTO TRIPS (Intellectual Property Agreement)*, Intellectual Property Institute, 1999, p2; J. C. Ross and J. A. Wasserman, op. cit., p2273.

14 See 19 USC 2242(b)(1)(C).

15 *The Tokyo Round of Multilateral Trade Negotiations: Report by the Director-General of GATT*, Geneva, April 1979, p16.

16 *The Tokyo Round of Multilateral Trade Negotiations: Report by the Director-General of GATT*, Geneva, April 1979, p14.

17 Jacques J. Gorlin, op. cit., p4.

18 The information was obtained in an interview at the GATT in 1993 and another in the WTO in 2001.

19 Emory Simon, "Remarks of Mr. Emory Simon," in Symposium: Trade-Related Aspects of Intellectual Property, *Vanderbilt Journal of Transnational Law*, 1989, vol. 22, p367.

20 A good example of this is the book by Gorlin in which, drawing on the views of the European Community negotiator for TRIPS, Peter Carl, he characterizes Article 8 of TRIPS, which appears to be a gain for developing countries, as "non-operational and hortatory." See Jacques J. Gorlin, op. cit., p17. For the views of one of the key Indian negotiators who was responsible for TRIPS from May 1989 to March 1991 see Jayashree Watal, "The TRIPS Agreement and Developing Countries: Strong, Weak or Balanced Protection?" *The Journal of World Intellectual Property*, 1998, vol. 1, p281.

21 Daniel Gervais, op. cit., p18.

22 Some developing country submissions suggested that WIPO could have a much larger role in dispute settlement, something that US industry especially was keen to avoid. A submission by Chile, for example, in 1990 argued that GATT and WIPO ought to have a complementary relationship in the area of dispute settlement. See *FOCUS* (GATT Newsletter), March 1990, vol. 69, p5.

23 Anell himself pays tribute to the "invaluable support" that the staff of WIPO gave to him and the GATT secretariat during the negotiations. See the Foreword by Anell in Daniel Gervais, op. cit., pvii.

24 The text of the chairman's report, "Fundamental changes in positions are necessary," is available in *FOCUS* (GATT Newsletter) November 1990, vol. 76, pp2–3.

25 Noted by Dunkel in his stock-taking report of the negotiations in November 1991. See J. C. Ross and J. A. Wasserman, op. cit., p2280.

26 The Brussels Draft version of Article 27 of TRIPS is reproduced in Daniel Gervais, op. cit., pp145–146.

27 See Jacques J. Gorlin, op. cit., p6.

28 See *Basic Framework of GATT Provisions on Intellectual Property: Statement of Views of the European, Japanese and United States Business Communities*, The Intellectual Property Committee (USA), Keidanren (Japan), UNICE (Europe), 1988, pp34–40.

29 Diamond v. Chakrabarty 206 U.S.P.Q. 193 (1980).

30 See Articles 53(a) and (b) of the European Patent Convention.

31 For a description of Canada's opposition on this issue, see Jacques J. Gorlin, op. cit., p25.

32 The scheme is described by Eric Smith of the International Intellectual Property Alliance in his testimony before the Subcommittee on Trade of the Committee on Ways and Means, United States House of Representatives, 23 January 1992, p4.

33 Eric Smith of the International Intellectual Property Alliance in his testimony before the Subcommittee on Trade of the Committee on Ways and Means, United States House of Representatives, 23 January 1992, Appendix B.

34 Eric Smith of the International Intellectual Property Alliance in his testimony before the Subcommittee on Trade of the Committee on Ways & Means, United States House of Representatives, 23 January 1992, p6.

35 The US position can be seen from the 23 July 1990 draft of TRIPS in Daniel Gervais, op. cit., p163.

36 MTN.TNC/W/FA (20 December 1991) available in Terence P. Stewart (ed.), op. cit., p457.

37 J. C. Ross and J. A. Wasserman, op. cit., p2284.

38 *FOCUS* (GATT Newsletter) November 1993, vol. 103, p7.

39 See *Inside US Trade*, 10 January 1992, vol. 10(2), p2.

40 See *Inside US Trade*, 10 January 1992, vol. 10(2), p3.

41 Testimony of Jacques J. Gorlin, consulting economist to the Intellectual Property Committee, before the Subcommittee on Economic Policy, Trade and Environment of the Committee on Foreign Affairs, United States House of Representatives, 8 March 1994, p3.

42 Statement by Mr. Arthur Dunkel to TNC on 20 December, reproduced in *FOCUS* (GATT Newsletter) January/February 1992, vol. 87, p2.

43 See *Inside US Trade*, 26 November 1993, vol. 11(47), p20.

44 Article 31(c) of TRIPS imposes the condition that in the case of a nonauthorized use of a patent relating to semiconductor technology that use "shall only be for

public non-commercial use or to remedy a practice determined after judicial or administrative process to be anti-competitive." These words do not appear in the Brussels draft of TRIPS. Article 37(2), which deals with nonvoluntary licensing of a layout design, also sets very tight constraints on the use of compulsory licenses.

45 See Japan-Measures Concerning Sound Recordings, complaint by the US (WT/DS28), 9 February 1996. The case settled on 24 January 1997.

10 BIOGOPOLIES

1 For a survey, see Ervin Hexner, *International Cartels*, Sir Isaac Pitman & Sons, London, 1946.

2 Ibid.

3 For an excellent account, see Peter Temin, "Technology, regulation, and market structure," *The Bell Journal of Economics*, 1979, vol. 10, p429.

4 Peter Temin, op. cit., p435.

5 The law begins to develop early in this field. See Kuehmsted v. Farbenfabriken of Elberfeld, 179 F. 701 (7th Cir. 1910), dealing with purified acetyl salicylic acid (aspirin).

6 Peter Temin, op. cit., p442.

7 Obtaining protection for both chemical products and processes was vital for US companies since it would increase the range of options they had at their disposal for protecting knowledge. Many countries did not recognize patents for pharmaceutical products, meaning that in those countries US companies had to rely on process protection. If a US company wanted strong protection in that country for its product, it would have to patent as many processes as it could in order to protect the product. In the US the company could rely on product protection and keep the process secret or disclose only one process (not the cheapest one). TRIPS, by requiring states to recognize both product and process protection, provides multinationals with more options for how they will protect their products. They may well choose to rely more on product protection than on process protection. One effect of the patent part of TRIPS may well be that it will lower the number of processes that end up in the public domain via the patent system.

8 Editor's Page, "Is the Patent Monopoly Waning?," *Journal of the Patent Office Society*, 1931, vol. 13, pp363, 364.

9 Isenstead v. Watson Comr. Pats., 115 USPQ 408, 410 (DC DistCol 1957).

10 Gary Gereffi, *The Pharmaceutical Industry and Dependency in the Third World*, Princeton University Press, Princeton, NJ, 1983, p244.

11 Licensing can limit the profitability of the patentee. For example, streptomycin was patented, but licensed widely with the result that its price fell from US$160 (10 grams) in 1946 to 36 cents in 1960. See Gary Gereffi, op. cit., p107, fn10. The lesson for the drug companies was that the real profits lay in not licensing the product. Compulsory licensing is anathema to pharmaceutical multinationals.

12 Figures from the US PTO, reproduced in US Congress, Office of Technology Assessment, *New Developments in Biotechnology: Patenting Life — Special Report*, US Government Printing Office, Washington, DC, 1989, pp63–64.

13 See The Crucible II Group, *Seeding Solutions*, vol. 1, International Development Research Centre (Ottawa), International Plant Genetic Resources Institute (Rome), Dag Hammarskjöld Foundation (Uppsala), 2000, p31.

14 This application led to the resignation of James Watson from the Human Genome Organization. The application was ultimately withdrawn. See Philip Grubb, *Patents for Chemicals, Pharmaceuticals and Biotechnology: Fundamentals of Global Law, Practice and Strategy*, Oxford University Press, Oxford, 1999, p249.

15 US Patent no. 4,237,224.

16 See Rebecca S. Eisenberg, "Genes, Patents, and Product Development," *Science*, 14 August 1992, vol. 257, pp903, 907.

17 Merck & Co, Inc. v. Olin Mathieson Chemical Corp. 116 USPQ 484 (CA 4 1958).

18 Brenner v. Manson 148 USPQ 689, 695 (US SupCt 1966).

19 Ibid.

20 Ibid.

21 For a survey of the important liberalizing decisions, see Annex C of F. K. Beier, R. S. Crespi and J. Straus, *Biotechnology and Patent Protection*, OECD, Paris, 1985.

22 Noel Byrne, *Commentary on the Substantive Law of the 1991 UPOV Convention for the Protection of Plant Varieties*, Centre for Commercial Law Studies, London University (undated), p8.

23 For the history, see J. Kloppenburg, *First the Seed: The Political Economy of Plant Biotechnology 1492–2000*, Cambridge University Press, Cambridge, 1988.

24 In Ex Parte Hibberd, 227 USPQ 443 (1985) the Board of Patent Appeals and Interferences of the PTO ruled that plants could be protected under a utility patent. In JEM Ag Supply, Inc. v. Pioneer Hi-bred Int'l, Inc., 534 US 124 (2001), the US Supreme Court decided that utility patents could be granted for seeds and seed-grown plants.

25 US Congress, Office of Technology Assessment, op. cit., p79.

26 See "Industry that stalks the US corridors of power," *The Guardian*, Tuesday, 13 February 2001, p3.

27 See, for example, Lord Diplock's comments on the expired patents in Beecham Group Ltd. v. Bristol Laboratories Ltd. and Bristol-Myers Co. [1977] FSR 217.

28 In the case of the Prozac patents the US Court of Appeals for the Federal Circuit held invalid a patent claim claiming the active ingredient in Prozac because an earlier expired patent had already claimed it. See Eli Lilly and Co. v. Barr Laboratories Inc., 251 F. 3d 955 (2001).

29 A. Silverman, "Intellectual Property Law and the Venture Capital Process," *High Technology Law Journal*, 1990, vol. 5, no. 1, p157, fn 62.

30 See Tom Arnold, "Using ADR Instead of Litigation," in Barry Grossman and Gary Hoffman (eds.), *Patent Litigation Strategies Handbook*, Bureau of National Affairs, Washington DC, 2000, pp25, 26; Philippe G. Ducour, *Patenting the Recombinant Products of Biotechnology and Other Molecules*, Kluwer Law International, London, 1998, p3.

31 E. H. Lang and B. K. Thomas, "Disposition of Patent Cases by Courts During the Period 1939 to 1949," *Journal of the Patent Office Society*, 1950, vol. 32, p803.

32 Robert L. Harmon, *Patents and the Federal Circuit*, The Bureau of National Affairs, Inc., Washington, DC, 1988, p382.

33 Robert L. Harmon, *Patents and the Federal Circuit*, 4th ed, The Bureau of National Affairs, Inc., Washington, DC, 1998, p980.

34 See Barry Grossman and Gary Hoffman (eds.), *Patent Litigation Strategies Handbook*, Bureau of National Affairs, Washington, DC, 2000, pxiii.

35 See Senator Birch Bayh, "Address Before the Patent Law Association of Chicago," *Journal of the Patent Office Society*, 1979, vol. 61, pp679, 686.

36 The Bayh-Dole Act is codified as Chapter 38 of Title 35 (Patents) of the USC.
37 US Congress, Office of Technology Assessment, op. cit., p43.
38 See Douglas D. Parker, David Zilberman and Federico Castillo, "Offices of Technology Transfer: Privatizing University Innovations for Agriculture," *Choices*, First Quarter 1998, pp19, 24.
39 The Bayh-Dole Act was extended to larger businesses subject to some qualifications by Presidential Memorandum in 1983. The thrust of US federal patent policy during the 1980s was to encourage the patenting of federally funded inventions by the private sector, partnerships between federal research institutions and the private sector, and the transfer of government-developed technology to the private sector.
40 G. S. McMillan, F. Narin and D. L. Deeds, "An Analysis of the Critical Role of Public Science in Innovation: The Case of Biotechnology," *Research Policy*, 2000, vol. 29, pp1, 2.
41 S. M. Thomas, A. R. W. Davies, N. J. Birtwistle, S. M. Crowther and J. F. Burke, "Ownership of the Human Genome," *Nature*, 4 April 1996, vol. 380, p387.
42 G. S. McMillan, F. Narin and D. L. Deeds, op. cit., pp1–8.
43 A copy of the complaint is available in *Biotechnology Law Report*, 2000, vol. 19(3), p357.
44 Nuffield Council on Bioethics, *Genetically Modified Crops: The Ethical and Social Issues*, 1999, para 3.36.
45 See para 85.
46 Gary Gereffi, op. cit., pp196–197.
47 OECD, *Biotechnology: Economic and Wider Impacts*, OECD, Paris, 1989.

11 INFOGOPOLIES

1 *Basic Framework of GATT Provisions on Intellectual Property: Statement of Views of the European, Japanese and United States Business Communities*, The Intellectual Property Committee (USA), Keidanren (Japan), UNICE (Europe), 1988, p64.
2 J. Band and M. Katoh, *Interfaces on Trial: Intellectual Property and Interoperability in the Global Software Industry*, Westview Press, Boulder, CO, 1995, p18.
3 Allen Wagner, "Debunking IBM's Agenda for Software Media Patents," *Managing Intellectual Property*, December 1998/January 1999, vol. 85, p13.
4 See R. O. Nimtz, "Development of the Law of Computer Software Protection," *Journal of the Patent Office Society*, 1979, vol. 61, pp3, 8.
5 J. Band and M. Katoh, op. cit., p25.
6 See Tohru Nakajima, "Legal Protection of Computer Programs in Japan: The Conflict between Economic and Artistic Goals," *Columbia Journal of Transnational Law*, 1988–89, vol. 27, p143.
7 *Patent World*, March 2001, p6.
8 For a broader discussion of these issues, see Lawrence Lessig, *Code and Other Laws of Cyberspace*, Basic Books, New York, 1999.
9 For an account, see R. Cassady, Jr., "Monopoly in Motion Picture Production and Distribution: 1908–1915," *Southern California Law Review*, 1959, vol. 32, p325.
10 Jeanne Thomas Allen, "The Decay of the Motion Picture Patents Company," in Tino Balio (ed.), *The American Film Industry*, The University of Wisconsin Press, Madison, WI, 1976, pp119, 123.

11 Thomas H. Guback, "Hollywood's International Market," in Tino Balio (ed.), op. cit., pp387, 390.
12 In the US the lobbying was successful. Congress passed the Sonny Bono Copyright Term Extension Act of 1998. Under the act, works by authors like Faulkner, Fitzgerald and Hemingway will not enter the public domain for at least another 20 years.
13 The information about who owns what was obtained from *Columbia Journalism Review*, www.cjr.org.
14 Robert Burnett, *The Global Jukebox: The International Music Industry*, Routledge, London, 1996, p25.
15 David Puttnam, *The Undeclared War*, Harper Collins, London, 1997, p345.
16 James Von Schilling, "Records and the Recording Industry," in M. Thomas Inge (ed.), *Concise Histories of American Popular Culture*, Greenwood Press, Westport, CT, 1982, p313.
17 Michael Chanan, *Repeated Takes: A Short History of Recording and its Effects on Music*, Verso, London, 1995, p87.
18 For a summary, see Keith Negus, *Music Genres and Corporate Cultures*, Routledge, London, 1999, pp37–45.
19 An exception being UK copyright, which recognized copyright in sound recordings in 1911.
20 See Eugen Ulmer, "The Rome Convention for the Protection of Performers, Producers of Phonograms and Broadcasting Organizations," *Bulletin of the Copyright Society of the USA*, 1962–63, vol. 10, pp90, 94.
21 On industry's views see Averill C. Pararow, "Viewpoint of the Phonograph Record and Music Industries," *Bulletin of the Copyright Society of the USA*, 1963–64, vol. 11, pp25, 26.
22 Stephen Stewart quoted in Dave Laing, "Copyright and the International Music Industry," in Simon Firth (ed.), *Music and Copyright*, Edinburgh University Press, Edinburgh, 1993, pp22, 31.
23 James Von Schilling, op. cit., p318.
24 Michael Chanan, op. cit., p84.
25 Dave Laing, op. cit., p37.
26 See http://www.riaa.com.
27 See, for example, *Inquiry into the Prices of Sound Recordings*, Prices Surveillance Authority (Australia), Melbourne, 1990; *The Supply of Recorded Music*, Monopolies and Mergers Commission, HMSO, London, 1994.
28 Robert Burnett, op. cit., p62.
29 Keith Negus, op. cit., p58.
30 Jaron Lanier, "Piracy Is Your Friend," *New York Times*, 9 May 1999, available at www.maui.net.

12 DEMOCRATIC PROPERTY RIGHTS

1 A. D. Chandler, Jr., *Scale and Scope: The Dynamics of Industrial Capitalism*, Belknap Press, Cambridge, MA, 1990.
2 Oxfam, *Cut the Cost: Fatal Side Effects: Medicine Patents Under the Microscope*, Oxfam, Oxford, 2000.
3 D. C. North, *Institutions, Institutional Change and Economic Performance*, Cambridge University Press, Cambridge, 1990.

4 J. Braithwaite and P. Drahos, *Global Business Regulation*, Cambridge University Press, Cambridge, 2000.

5 M. Olson, *The Logic of Collective Action*, Harvard University Press, Cambridge, MA, 1965.

6 See P. Drahos, "BITs and BIPs: Bilateralism in Intellectual Property," *The Journal of World Intellectual Property*, 2001, vol. 4, pp791, 807–808.

7 See I. Ayres and J. Braithwaite, *Responsive Regulation: Transforming the Deregulation Debate*, Oxford University Press, New York, 1992, chapter 2.

13 RESISTING THE NEW INEQUALITY

1 Oxfam, *Cut the Cost: Patent Injustice: How World Trade Rules Threaten the Health of Poor People*, Oxfam, Oxford, 2000, p36.

2 D. Somaya, "Obtaining and Protecting Patents in the United States, Europe and Japan," in R. A. Kagan and L. Axelrad (eds.), *Regulatory Encounters: Multilateral Corporations and American Adversarial Legalism*, University of California Press, Berkeley, CA, 2000, p275.

3 D. Soskice, "Divergent Production Regimes: Coordinated and Uncoordinated Market Economies in the 1980s and 1990s," in H. Kitschelt, P. Lange, G. Marks and J. D. Stephens (eds.), *Continuity and Change in Contemporary Capitalism*, Cambridge University Press, Cambridge, 1999, p101.

4 P. Grabosky and J. Braithwaite, *Of Manners Gentle*, Oxford University Press, Melbourne, 1986, p185

5 See J. Braithwaite and P. Drahos, *Global Business Regulation*, Cambridge University Press, Cambridge, 2000, pp74–75.

6 See I. Ayres and J. Braithwaite, *Responsive Regulation: Transforming the Deregulation Debate*, Oxford University Press, New York, 1992, chapter 3.

7 For a discussion of dependency licenses and how the balance between patents and competition rules might be struck, see John H. Barton, "Patents and Antitrust: A Rethinking in Light of Patent Breadth and Sequential Innovation," *Antitrust Law Journal*, 1997, vol. 65, p449.

8 Paragraph 4 of the declaration states that the "TRIPS Agreement does not and should not prevent Members from taking measures to protect public health." Paragraph 5(b) states that "[E]ach Member has the right to grant compulsory licences and the freedom to determine the grounds upon which such licences are granted."

9 R. D. Putnam, "Diplomacy and Domestic Politics: The Logic of Two-Level Games," *International Organization*, 1988, vol. 42, p425.

14 ON THE IMPORTANCE OF THE PUBLICNESS OF KNOWLEDGE

1 For a comprehensive study of the role of federal funding, see Ralph Nader and James P. Love, "Federally Funded Pharmaceutical Inventions," Taxpayers Assets Project, Working Paper No. 7, 24 February 1993.

2 "Rent" refers to a "payment that is not needed to elicit productive labor or the productive services of some other input": W. J. Baumol, S. Blackman and E. Wolff, *Productivity and American Leadership*, MIT Press, Cambridge MA, 1991, p274.

3 See Adam Smith, *An Inquiry into the Nature and Causes of the Wealth of Nations*, book IV.ix.52 (R. H. Campbell and A. S. Skinner (eds.), Clarendon Press, Oxford, 1976).

4 See Marco Ferroni, "Reforming Foreign Aid: The Role of International Public Goods," OED Working Paper Series, no. 4, spring 2000, The World Bank, Washington, DC.

5 D. Hicks, T. Breitzman, D. Olivastro and K. Hamilton, "The Changing Composition of Innovative Activity in the US—A Portrait Based on Patent Analysis," *Research Policy*, 2001, vol. 30, pp681, 689.

Index

Monsanto 38, 41, 58, 118, 164–5, 188, 201
Morgan, Henry 22–3
Morgan, J. P. 41–2, 54
motion picture industry 54, 125, 132, 144, 169, 174–80, 185–6; and 301 process 82, 94; Big Five 174, 179; and Caribbean Basin states 82–3, 100; distribution system 175, 179; and Dunkel draft 148; and IIPA 91
MPA 81–2, 86, 91–4, 97, 99, 147, 175–8
MPEA 102, 104, 175
MPPC 54, 174
multilateralism 73, 102, 104, 108–20, 191, 194, 196
MPPDA 175
multinational companies 167–8, 205
Murdoch, Rupert 201
music 15, 92, 145, 169, 179, 180–6, 192, 210; see also sound recording industry

Napster 15, 185–6, 198
National Aniline Chemical 151
National Association of Manufacturers 131
National Foreign Trade Council 69
National Music Publishers Association 91
National Research Council, US 44
national treatment, principle of 28, 145
NEC 96
Neimeth, Bob 69, 73
New Medicines for Malaria Venture 217
New York Patent Law Association 44
New Zealand 193
News Corporation 179–80
NGOs 16–17, 204–7, 208–9, 217; health issues 7, 161; indigenous people's issues 199–200
NIH 156

No Electronic Theft Act, US 185
nondomination 14, 190–2, 206–7
North, Douglass 13, 189
Novartis 165
Novell 91
nuclear energy 212–13
Nuffield Council 167

Olivetti 119, 172
Olson, Mancur 14
Omnibus Trade and Competitiveness Act, US 132
Opel, John 73, 115, 117–18, 195
Orwell, George 5
Oxfam 7, 16, 199

Pacific Pharmaceuticals 193
paper industry 75; Conference on Pulp and Paper Development 75
parallel importation 6, 36–7, 191
Paramount Pictures 174, 178, 179
Paris Book Guild 31–2
Paris Convention 36, 71, 79, 81, 111, 121, 195, 201
Paris Union 80
Parke Davis 41, 152–3
Pasteur, Louis 159, 213
Patent Cooperation Treaty 111
patent law 44, 143–4, 150, 160, 161–2
Patent Law Association of Chicago 163
patent offices 20, 161, 201–7
patent professionals 43–8
patent system 36, 59, 80, 119, 156, 187; and biotechnology 155–6; chemical industry 153–4
patentability 124, 157, 205
patents 34, 51, 142, 151, 160, 187, 188; and pharmaceuticals 6, 8; utility requirement 158, 203
penicillin 65–6, 152, 155, 213
Perkin-Elmer Corporation 164
Pfizer, Charles 65
Pfizer Corporation 17
Pfizer International 65–71, 73, 90,